Social Anthropology
and Law

A.S.A. MONOGRAPH 14

Social Anthropology and Law

Edited by

IAN HAMNETT

University of Bristol

1977

ACADEMIC PRESS

London · New York · San Francisco

A Subsidiary of Harcourt Brace Jovanovich, Publishers

ACADEMIC PRESS INC. (LONDON) LTD.
24/28 Oval Road,
London NW1

United States Edition published by
ACADEMIC PRESS INC.
111 Fifth Avenue,
New York, New York 10003

This volume derives mainly from material presented at a conference on social anthropology
and law sponsored by the Association of Social Anthropologists of the Commonwealth
held at the University of Keele, 27-30 March 1974

Library of Congress Catalog Card Number: 77-71304
ISBN: 0-12-322350-4

Printed in Great Britain by
THE SCOLAR PRESS LTD
59/61 East Parade   Ilkley   Yorkshire

PREFACE

It is the practice of the Association of Social Anthropologists, each year, to depute one or more of its members to convene
a future conference on an agreed topic. I was invited to convene
a conference on Social Anthropology and Law, which was held (at
Professor R. Frankenberg's kind suggestion) at the University of
Keele, Staffordshire, in March 1974.

Lawyers and social anthropologists have always had much in
common, both historically and substantively, and it was felt
timely to provide a forum where they could take part in a systematic exchange of ideas. It would have been a megalomaniac pro-
ject, of course, to have ranged over the whole fields of law and
anthropology, or even over the narrower area of overlap that can
be called the anthropology of law. I invoked the aid of the late
Professor Max Gluckman, who was characteristically generous with
his advice and his time, and together we devised a way of circum-
scribing a manageable yet significant topic for discussion. It
was agreed that the main theme of the conference should concern
the relative weight to be attached to "norms" or "rules" on the
one hand and to "power" or "interests" on the other in processes
of dispute settlement – the theoretical relationship, in other
words, between the two dimensions of "social order" and "social
interaction". A subsidiary conference theme looked at the
anthropology of the legal profession itself.

A leading principle of the conference was that contributors
and participants should include both lawyers and social anthropologists. Not only were we successful in recruiting members of
each of these disciplines (and a political scientist as well),
but we secured the participation of several contributors with a

formal training in both.

Altogether some seventeen papers were delivered - arguably to
many for a three-day conference. The present volume contains
revised versions of a coherent and self-contained selection from
these papers, together with a short editorial introduction, all
concerned with the central conference theme of "interests" and
"rights".

The introduction includes detailed acknowledgment of our debt
to many friends and participants. In this place, however, I
should like to place on record our very sincere gratitude for th
generous subvention awarded to us by those long-standing friends
of the A.S.A., the Wenner-Gren Foundation for Anthropological
Research. The financial stringency under which they suffered
at the time makes us especially appreciative of their kindness.

August 1976   Ian Hamnet

ACKNOWLEDGEMENTS

This volume is dedicated to the memory of Max Gluckman, for reasons which no legal or anthropological reader will need to have spelled out. I have a special reason, however, as convener of the Keele Conference, to put on record my personal debt to him, for his advice and moral support in my attempts to recruit a strong team of contributors, and to give to the conference theme a definition narrow enough to focus the papers and discussion, and yet broad enough to permit a wide-ranging debate on the anthropology of law. Whatever success I have had in so constructing the conference framework is largely due to Max Gluckman. The deficiencies, of course, are mine alone. It was a case, if ever there was one, of Hamlet without the Prince that despite both his efforts and ours the conference had to take place at a time when an earlier commitment in the United States prevented him from being with us. He generously supplied us, nevertheless, with specially reproduced copies of his Wilson Memorial Lecture before its journal publication (Gluckman, 1973b). As we are all so sadly aware, he died on 13 April 1975, a year after the conference but many months before this volume went to press.

It is sad to have to record another death among those whom we had hoped to be with us. Lloyd A. Fallers, in fact, was forbidden by his doctors to attend the conference more or less as he was preparing to fly to England with his wife to present the paper included in the present volume. As we know, he died not long after, still a comparatively young man. I am deeply indebted to his widow, Mrs Margaret Fallers, both for her permission to publish his valuable article and also for her help in preparing the original draft for final publication.

viii

The financial pressures of publishing at this time have
limited the length of this volume and obliged me to exclude many
of the contributed papers. Professor A.N. Allott's health at
the time prevented his delivering a paper, but we were grateful
for his contributions to discussion and for his help in taking
the chair. The late Dr Nan Wilson's unpublished thesis was
briefly presented by me as convenor (Wilson, 1965). My own
introductory paper has been subsequently absorbed into a separate monograph (Hamnett, 1975).

I am grateful to Mr John Farrar, of the Faculty of Law,
University of Bristol, for help in locating some references
beyond my powers to trace; to Mr F.D.D. Winston, of the School
of Oriental and African Studies, London, for advice on the
transliteration of Diola; and to Dr J.S. La Fontaine (Chairman),
Mr J.W. Tyler (Hon. Treasurer), and the Committee of the Association of Social Anthropologists, for endless practical help
and support in bringing this volume to the point of publication.

REFERENCES

Gluckman, M. (1973). 'Cross-examination and the substantive law
in African traditional courts'. *Juridical Review* 1973,
pp. 221-53.

Hamnett, I. (1975). *Chieftainship and Legitimacy: an Anthropological Study of Executive Law in Lesotho*. Routledge and
Kegan Paul, London.

Wilson, N. (1965). The Sociology of a Profession: the Faculty
of Advocates. Ph.D. thesis, University of Edinburgh.

In memory of

MAX GLUCKMAN

1911–1975

Founder Member of

the

Association of Social Anthropologists

CONTENTS

INTRODUCTION

Ian   Hamnett

"Our lawyers... with justice... tell us, that the law is the
perfection of reason." — Thus Blackstone, that folk-hero of
the eighteenth-century common law, who qualifies this dictum only
in unimportant ways. "Not", he concedes, "that the particular
reason of every rule of law can at this distance of time be
always precisely assigned; but it is sufficient that there be
nothing in the rule flatly contradictory to reason"; and where it
happens that one judge's actual decision is indeed "most evidently contrary to reason", he shows us how "the subsequent
judges do not pretend to make a new law, but to vindicate the old
one from misrepresentation... It is declared, not that such a
sentence was bad law, but that it was not law..." (Blackstone
1783:68-71).

These delightful passages, in their innocence and complacency,
must surely captivate the social anthropologist, who will seize
on them as the epitome of a folk culture that is crucially
unaware of the relativities which make nonsense of its unguarded
self-assurance. Jurisprudents, however, and indeed thoughtful
lawyers of any kind, are too near the matter to take so friendly
a view. The falsity of Blackstone's account is a cause of
impatient irritation for them, since they have often to live and
work with its consequences.

It is too readily assumed that Blackstone's view of the law
has been so totally discredited as no longer to be taken seriously. Far from it. A startling recent example occurred in
1955, when a judge issued an order orally at the conclusion of

a civil action and a few days later confirmed it in
writing (1). In the interval between the oral and the written
order, the House of Lords made a decision in another case (2),
stating the law in such terms as to render the judge's orally
pronounced order in the first action inappropriate. The question
arose whether the judge, on learning the House of Lord's decision
in the other case, should have modified his order before committing it to writing (as he was certainly entitled to do). This
question was itself taken to appeal, where Lord Justice Jenkins
stated:

"As to the argument to the effect that the orders orally pronounced by the judge were the proper orders at the time of their
pronouncement and should therefore be allowed to stand, this
seems to us to be based on the erroneous supposition that
Chapman v. *Chapman*.... altered the law, whereas in truth that
decision merely declared the law as it always was, and showed it
to have been theretofore misapprehended in the courts below.
"The law having been declared by the House of Lords in
Chapman v. *Chapman* before Roxburgh J.'s orders were perfected,
in terms which clearly indicated that those orders ought not to
have been made, and this having come to the judge's knowledge,
it was in our opinion right that he should recall the orders
orally pronounced by him, notwithstanding the fact that at the
time when they were pronounced they appeared to be correct
according to the authorities as they then stood" (3).

---

(1) *In re* Harrison's share under a settlement. Harrison *v.*
    Harrison [1955] Ch. 260. I am grateful to Dr Thomas Crump
    for alerting me to this case.

(2) Chapman *v.* Chapman [1954] A.C. 429.

(3) *Per* Jenkins L.J. at p. 283. The House of Lords has since
    stated that it will not be bound by its own past decisions:
    Practice Statement [1966] 1 W.L.R. 1234. However, their
    Lordships have made so little use of their self-conferred
    freedom that this modification of the *stare decisis* prin-
    ciple has hardly disturbed traditional attitudes.

When Sawer describes what we may call this "declaratory theory" of law (4) as involving "the myth of decision-inevitability", he is using the word "myth" in a non-technical sense that is more than half pejorative (Sawer 1965:105). But the social anthropologist is free, and often eager, to snatch at the notion of "myth" in contexts like this and give it a more specialised meaning. Blackstone and the many others before and after him who have written about the common law and the nature of judicial decision in these terms will be seen as the proper object of anthropological analysis: as the architects of an indigenous model which will be at once preserved, destroyed and surpassed in the analytical *Aufhebung* performed upon it by the anthropologist. At this higher level of discourse, all is understood and (as it were) pardoned.

Thus dicta like those of Blackstone confirm the social anthropologist in his own different yet quite as complacent self-assurance. They make it easy for him to patronise "lawyer's law" as ethno-law, on a par with the ethno-botanies, ethno-zoologies, ethno-medicines etc., that are studied in pre-scientific cultures by post-scientific ethnographers. And in fact the student who exchanges a career as a lawyer for one as a social anthropologist may well find the change of discipline liberating and exhilarating. Social anthropology will seem to him a successful and necessary enterprise in debunking the myth of formal perfection that a legal system claims to embody — opening out a closed, self-validating structure, demystifying its reifications and questioning an institution that never puts any but rhetorical questions to itself. The "social science" approach offers in return (so it may seem) a securer basis for law, by founding it on a larger reality: society itself. To demystify, then, is not after all (it is argued) to debunk, however much the anthropologist's former legal brethren may resent the condescension which they detect in his "reduction" of their skilled professionalism to an underlying social base.

But if this sense of liberation is the converted lawyer's first response, he will soon feel himself disturbed by some features of his new discipline in its approach to the law and legal issues. After the initial intoxication of learning to talk grandly about "social control" has begun to fade, he will start to reassess his new intellectual world with a now

(4) This declaratory theory is more fully considered, and its implications for the anthropology of law brought out, in Hamnett 1975, esp. pp. 102 ff.

disillusioned sobriety. "Social control" itself may often look
like a way of evading some ugly problems, and be itself a mystification. The problem, the reality, which social anthropology
in some of its moods seems to evade or obscure is nothing less
than the *specificity of law*. The specifically *legal* mode of
social action emerges as a scandal to any kind of sociological
reductionism. It has therefore to be not merely demystified by
anthropologists but debunked by them. The specificity of law
then emerges as no more than the ideological charter of a particular professional group, and thus as subject to, rather than
constitutive of, the anthropologist's analysis.

Confronted by these doubts, the zealous convert's first
puzzlement may therefore be to wonder if the anthropologists may
not be right after all. Perhaps his doubts are just the *damnosa
hereditas* of his own lawyerly past. Perhaps his lingering
consciousness of "the law" is simply evidence that he has not
yet been effectively initiated. Until he learns to use the language of "social control" with fluency and conviction, he will
never be able to live down his ideological past, or to look an
anthropologist in the eyes and talk to him as a colleague rather
than as an informant.

But if these uncertainties only reflect the notorious
embarrassments of the tiro and his dread of committing any
faux pas to uncover his callowness, nevertheless there are more
serious difficulties too. As a student of law, he grew tired
of those jurisprudential deserts traversed by all undergraduates
at one time or another, when elaborate but sterile discussions
are mounted on the definition of law, the nature of law, law and
morality, law and custom, law and "other social rules"...
Perhaps not quite all of these arguments were about semantics but
most of them ended up as little else. The convert is therefore
relieved and delighted to find (for example) Lucy Mair regretting
the "floods of ink" wasted on this barren topic (Mair 1962:19;
and see Gulliver 1969a:12 f.). Accordingly, when he moves
towards an insistence on the "specificity of law" he may fear
that he is edging back on to that old metaphysical terrain, where
all the signs read *impasse*... Perhaps, after all, it is safest
and best to think of "law" as a merely spurious category, or at
most as just a special case of social control, whose specialty
is constituted only by the illusions of its practitioners and
will not survive analysis.

But the lawyer has other good reasons, admittedly drawn from
his own discipline, for opposing the dissolution of law into the

general category of social control. The word "control" itself
gives the discussion a curious emphasis, recalling as it does
the criminal, as against the civil, law. There is no way in
which the layman's stereotype of the law differs more sharply
from that of the professional than in the relative emphasis
given to these two aspects of law. When he thinks of the law
and lawyers, the layman usually talks in terms of "prosecution",
"jury", "verdict", "sentence", "guilty", "acquittal", and so
forth. He thinks of the advocate as succeeding or otherwise in
"getting his client off." These terms all refer either exclusively or primarily to criminal procedure. Advocates themselves
(unless they have a large criminal practice) think rather in
terms of a civil law stereotype, using the language of "plaintiff", "pursuer", "liability", "damages", "decision", etc.
A special study would have to be devoted to exploring all the
reasons for this difference in emphasis. Obviously some of the
reasons (for instance, the fact that civil work tends to be much
more lucrative) have no theoretical relevance here. But one
distinctive difference between the two kinds or aspects of law
is that whereas the criminal law tends to be in evidence principally in the breach, the civil law — the law of contract,
delict (5), property, marriage, succession, etc. — is arguably
most effective precisely when it is least attended to: when it
simply forms the defining context of mutual actions and expectations. Of course, it is often in cases of dispute that the
civil law comes to be more narrowly defined and specified; and
conversely, the criminal law is immeasurably more often observed
than breached. But whereas a criminal prosecution necessarily
implies some element of wrongdoing, many civil actions occur
where there is no suggestion that any of the parties have done
"wrong" at all. In civil matters, litigation occurs in only a
very small proportion even of disputes, and these in their turn
are almost infinitesimally few in comparison with the huge
number of interactions where the law serves merely as a consensual and implicit context of transactional discourse. Indeed,
what the law in all its branches principally offers to social
actors is the crucial advantage of knowing more or less where
they and their partners stand. Notions of "control" do more to
obscure than to illuminate this feature of law.

The argument can be taken further. Many provisions of law,
so far from being properly regarded as constraints, are best
seen as *facilitating* mechanisms that make possible transactions

---

(5) A more universal term than the Anglo-American "tort", which
is the nearest common-law approximation.

and relationships that would otherwise have been difficult or
even impossible to establish. The so-called "executory contrac'
is a good example. For a contract to be valid even when neithe'
party has performed is in no way a "natural" state of affairs,
but is the result of a specific and active development of the la
of obligations. This development made possible the creation of
relationships that would have lacked a secure social base without a facilitating legal provision. Of course, to say that a
contract is valid is usually to imply that it can be enforced,
and here an element of "control" is necessarily present. But
even so, one man's duty is another man's right: control is onl'
half the story. If the law accords binding force to a given
class of agreements, the effect is not only to "control" the
obligated party. It is also to confer a facility on the
creditor in the relationship. More often than not, however,
the real effect is to facilitate the creation of a mutual
relationship to the advantage of both.

In his study of "crime and custom" Malinowski (1926), as his
title indicates, was concerned with a special aspect of social
control, and it is well known that this volume reveals only a
part of his thinking about law (Schapera 1957). However, it ha
probably had a more formative effect on the anthropological
approach to law than any other single monograph from the heroic
age of British social anthropology. For a start, it is brief
and uncluttered, fluent, vivid and to all appearances true to
life. It is an excellent teaching resource and probably out-
strips all other anthropological classics as required reading
for first-year students in social science departments generally
It also did much to lay to rest a number of illusions about the
nature of "savage society" and the factors that made for the
maintenance of order within it. It remains an unrivalled cor-
rective to notions of primitive automatism with regard to "custom", and it introduced a refreshingly positivist and common-
sensical note into areas where mystification often masqueraded
as explanation. The influence and popularity of the book are n
hard to explain. To many students, even the famous reference t
"codes, courts and constables" seems to come with all the revel
ation of new truth — though it is clear that even while reject
ing so crassly institutional an approach to law, Malinowski
remains within the criminal law paradigm. He thus encourages tl
reader to approach issues of normative regulation within a control framework. What he does, and does so successfully, is to
relate such "control" to the day-to-day situational logic and
interactional context without which the normative order appears
suspended in a void of mystery-mongering abstraction. He is

concerned to show how "control" need not be exercised by or
mediated through specialised institutions of enforcement but
may (and in fact normally does) arise out of the felt reciprocities and interdependencies of concrete interaction in face-to-
face groups. The price of his success is to risk the loss, for
many of his readers, of the normative element in the social
order. The Trobriander, from being an automaton enslaved by
custom, becomes at a stroke a utilitarian positivist endowed with
a nice sense of individual costs and benefits. This second
stereotype is scarcely less implausible than the first. The vice
in explaining social order by talking about the cake of custom
was that it implied an automatic adherence to *practice*. But as I
have argued at some length elsewhere (Hammett 1975:9-23, 107-
115) customary law is not a statement of practice. It is a
normatively clothed set of abstractions from practice, "a set of
norms which the actors in a social situation abstract from practice and which they invest with binding authority" (ib., p. 14)
(6).

An alternative approach to Malinowski's can be found in
Gluckman's classic studies of the Barotse (Gluckman 1955, 1965,
1967, 1972, 1973a). He states that "Lozi have law as a set of
rules accepted by all normal members of the society as defining
right and reasonable ways in which persons ought to behave in
relation to each other and to things, including ways of obtaining
protection for one's rights" (1955:229, italics omitted). Again,
law is described as "the body of rules, the *corpus juris,* on
which judges draw to give a decision... and as *adjudication,* a
process by which cases are tried and judgments or *legal rulings*
given" (1955:226-7, original emphasis). This emphasis on rules
implies what elsewhere he makes explicit, that law in Lozi

---

(6) See also the old-fashioned but sensible discussion by
   Seagle (1937).
   An ambivalent remark by Podgorecki (1974:67) seems to
   imply that Malinowski was influenced by the "psychological"
   jurisprudence of Leon Petrazycki, the Polish legal scholar
   who also worked and taught in pre-revolutionary Russia.
   However, I have so far been unable to find positive evidence of this, though it would be surprising if Malinowski's
   concern for and interest in Polish scholarship
   (Kryzyzanowski 1959; Symmons-Symonolewicz 1959a) had not
   given him an acquaintance with Petrazycki's work. For
   Petrazycki, see for instance Langrod and Vaughan 1970, and
   for Malinowski's intellectual formation, Symmons-
   Symonolewicz 1959b.

society is a specific and irreducible social fact; it is indeed
a matter for direct observations: "empirically *law*... influences
the behaviour of both Lozi judges and public" (1955:352, original
emphasis). "Law as such will be distinguished by observers, and
distinguished by the people, from other types of social fact"
(1955:265).

L.A. Fallers has followed, if rather diffidently, Gluckman's
approach. Faller's more cautiously argued endorsement of the
specific reality of law is not to be accounted for only on the
grounds of any differences in this respect between the Barotse
and the Basoga. It is curious that in his Soga monograph (1969)
he expressed surprise that the Barotse have a word for law,
mulao. As he tells us (1969:331-2), he was at first inclined to
regard this as a Bantuisation of the English word "law" (*-lao;
mu-* is the Class 3 prefix) and needed Gluckman's personal reassurance that the stem was indigenous. I have noted elsewhere
(Hamnett 1971b:329) that the indigenous character of the stem
-lao is fully established in the literature on Southern Bantu
and occurs in cognate languages (cf. Sotho *molao*) (7). What is
significant about Faller's initial uncertainty is that it reveals
how even an author who argues for the existence of a specifically legal dimension cannot quite believe that it exists on the
ground in a "traditional" society in so concrete a form that a
word for "law" could occur in the language.

The principal goal of the Keele Conference was to explore the
differences between these two approaches to law in traditional
societies. In the preliminary invitation sent out to potential
contributors it was stated that "the specific theme on which
papers are invited can be described as the significance of norms
and rules, and the role of 'interest', in processes of adjudication, conciliation, mediation, etc.... Another way of expressing
the conference theme might be to say that it will explore the
'social order' and 'social interaction' dimensions in the anthropology of law." The papers printed here, however, do not take
sides in any factitious jousting between Durkheimians and Malin-
owskians, between the apostles of order and the evangelists of
interaction. The authors consider aspects of the anthropology of
law without polemic, raising questions (and sometimes answering
them) that further our understanding of the central issue, not by

---

(7) For a discussion of the meaning of *molao*, etc., and its
    relationship to "law", "custom", "usage", etc., in Southern
    Bantu languages, see Allott 1965:25 ff.; Comaroff and
    Roberts, *infra*; Gluckman 1966:164-5; Hamnett 1971a *passim*.

marshalling forces on one side or the other of a conflict between "order" and "interaction", between "right" and "interest",
but rather by showing how crudely any such polarisation distorts
the reality of law in society.

The most general discussion, in fact, is the article by
Gulliver on mediators. This sets out some basic conceptual
markers that help us to organise the field for much of what
follows. His paper is valuable not only for its sensitivity to
both anthropological and legal thinking, but also for the attention paid to work within the International Relations field (see
too Burton 1972:150-163) (8). Fallers, from a more particular
vantage point, sensitises us to the crucially relevant issue of
what it means to have, or to purport to have, a policy distinguished by the "rule of law". He underlines the impossibility
of seeking any straightforward institutional test with the
pleasing paradox (see note 2 to his article, *infra*) that "legislatures... adjudicate and administer, while courts and administrative agencies make law." Comaroff and Roberts, noting that
"no obvious relationship exists between the clarity with which
abstract norms are articulated, the way in which they are
employed and their importance in decision-making", seek to
identify the internal and intrinsic determinants of what we may
call the "normativeness" of a particular system of law.

Snyder's close discussion of the Bandial (Diola) "pledge" in
Senegal argues that "economic changes and their channelling by
colonial courts led to changes in transaction practice and in
specific transaction rules without any change in legal concepts."
The possibility of transition from "pledge" (*gailen*) to commodity
invokes the presence of capitalism and the structures of modern
society within traditional legal systems. Other aspects of this
presence are described by Moore and by Perry. Moore conceptual-
ises the relationship between traditional and modern agencies in
Tanzania in terms of "articulation", and analyses dispute settlement procedures as a kind of interface between the different

---

(8) He also demonstrates once more the distance (already apparent in Gulliver 1969a and 1969b; see also 1971) between his
present view of the role of norms in dispute settlement, and
the interpretation he appeared to favour in his earlier
Arusha monograph (Gulliver 1963). It is high time that
fellow anthropologists stopped referring to him as an
example of an exaggeratedly "interest-based" approach to
settlement processes! If he was ever such, he is so no
longer.

levels of structure. Perry uses the notion of "brokerage" to found a study of how what he calls different "law codes" in Lesotho can be brought into relationship. In both these papers, we are helped to see that, just as interests can be generalised as norms, so may norms be themselves a special case of interests

The last word, for the time being, perhaps lies with the greatest of all English observers of law in action: F.W. Maitland. In his eyes, law is seen not so much as "order" against "interaction", nor as "right" against "interest", but precisely as the point of intersection between the two. Of fourteenth century England he writes that "law was the place where life and logic met" (Maitland 1903:xxxvii); and in an earlier gloss (xix) he yet more nicely observes how, throughout most of concrete social activity, "logic yields to life, pro-testing all the while that it is only becoming more logical". A well-judged anthropology of law, while regarding such pro-tests with scepticism, will (like Maitland) treat them with respect too, and even contrive to see in lawyers at their best "the great mediators between life and logic, a reasoning, reasonable element" in society (lxxxi).

REFERENCES

Allott, A.N.   (1965).   *Law and Language* (Inaugural Lecture). School of Oriental and African Studies, London.

Blackstone, W.   (1783).   *Commentaries on the Laws of England,* 9th edition.

Burton, J.W.   (1972).   *World Society.*   Cambridge University Press, Cambridge.

Fallers, L.A.   (1969).   *Law without Precedent.*   Chicago University Press, Chicago.

Firth, R. (ed.)   (1957).   *Man and Culture.*   Routledge and Kegan Paul, London

Gluckman, M.   (1955).   *The Judicial Process among the Barotse of Northern Rhodesia.*   Manchester University Press for the Rhodes-Livingstone Institute, Manchester.

Gluckman, M.   (1965).   *The Ideas in Barotse Jurisprudence.* Yale University Press, New Haven and London.

Gluckman, M.   (1967).   Second enlarged edition of Gluckman, 1955.

Gluckman, M.   (1972).   Second edition of Gluckman 1965, with new preface.   Manchester University Press for Institute of Social Research, Zambia.

Gluckman, M.   (1973a).   Third edition of Gluckman 1955 and 1967, with new preface.

Gluckman, M.   (1973b).   'Cross-examination and the substantive law in African traditional courts', *Juridical Review* 1973, pp. 221-53.

Gulliver, P.H.   (1963).   *Social Control in an African Society.* Routledge and Kegan Paul, London.

Gulliver, P.H.   (1969a).   'Introduction' to 'Case Studies in Law in Non-Western Societies', in Nader 1969, pp. 11-23.

Gulliver, P.H.   (1969b).   'Dispute Settlement without Courts: the Ndendeuli of Southern Tanzania', in Nader 1969, pp. 24-68.

Gulliver, P.H.   (1971).   *Neighbours and Networks: the Idiom of Kinship among the Ndendeuli of Tanzania.*   University of California Press, Berkeley.

Hamnett, I.   (1971a).   'Some notes on the concept of custom in Lesotho'. *Journal of African Law* 15, 3, pp. 266-73.

Hamnett, I.   (1971b).   Review of Fallers 1969, *Africa* 41, pp. 328-9.

Hamnett, I.   (1975). *Chieftainship and Legitimacy.* Routledge and Kegan Paul, London.

Krzyzanowski, L.   (1959).   'A postscript to "Bronislaw Malinowski: an Intellectual Profile" '. *Polish Review* 4, 1-2, pp. 156-7.

Langrod, G.S. and Vaughan, M.   (1970).   'The Polish psychological theory of law', in Wagner 1970, pp. 299-362.

Mair, L.   (1962). *Primitive Government.* Penguin Books, Harmondsworth.

Maitland, F.W.   (1903).   'Introduction' to *Year Books of Edward II*, Volume 1.   Selden Society, Volume 17.   Bernard Quaritch, London.

Malinowski, B.   (1926). *Crime and Custom in Savage Society.* Kegan Paul, Trench and Trubner, London.

Nader, L. (ed.)   (1969). *Law in Culture and Society.* Aldine Press, Chicago.

Podgorecki, A.   (1974). *Law and Society.* Routledge and Kegan Paul, London.

Sawer, G.S. (1965). *Law and Society*. Clarendon Press, Oxford.

Schapera, I. (1957). 'Malinowski's theories of law', in Firth 1957, pp. 139-55.

Seagle, W. (1937). 'Primitive Law and Professor Malinowski'. *American Anthropologist* 39, pp. 275-90.

Symmons-Symonolewicz, K. (1959a). Correspondence. *Polish Review* 4, 3, p. 105.

Symmons-Symonolewicz, K. (1959b). 'Bronislaw Malinowski: Formative Influences and Theoretical Evolution'. *Polish Review* 4, 4, pp. 17-45.

Wagner, W.J. (ed.). (1970). *Polish Law throughout the Ages*. Stanford University: Hoover Institution Press.

Wilson, N. (1965). The Sociology of a Profession: the Faculty of Advocates. Ph.D. thesis, University of Edinburgh.

ON MEDIATORS

P. H. Gulliver

This paper deals with an aspect of that process of negotiations in which two individuals (or groups) seek to reach some settlement of a dispute between them. In that process each party is concerned to direct information, persuasion and influence to the other party with the aim of reaching an agreement which is mutually tolerable and acceptable to both. The process is to be contrasted with and distinguished from that in which each party presents his case and argument to a third party in order to obtain a decision in his favour – that third party having the power to decide on the issues in dispute and to give his judgement accordingly (Fuller 1963:19). In negotiations there may be, but not invariably is, a third party who, though he has no ability to give a judgement, acts in some ways as a facilitator in the process of trying to reach agreement. This is a mediator. The precise line of distinction between mediator and adjudicator is clear in general but not always so in particular contexts. Mediators can, in some extreme circumstances, virtually take control and make effective decisions, whilst adjudicators may sometimes relinquish control and seek only to improve communication and to use persuasion. In either case the change in role may be temporary, at some stage in the process, though it can be more permanent. Nevertheless, and despite this important caveat, the two roles and the processes within which they occur are analytically distinct and in most real life situations are effectively different. (1)

It must be emphasised at the outset that the focus of this paper is on third parties as mediators between two other partie who are in process of negotiating to seek settlement of some dispute between them. This has not been the invariable refer- ence of the term 'mediator' in the social sciences where it has been used, sometimes quite loosely, in numerous ways. No un- ambiguous term suggests itself for present purposes. The some- time synonym, 'intermediary', is no less broad and vague in its implications. Other analytically comparable, intermediate thir party roles — for instance, that of 'broker' (Paine 1971:21) — are not considered here, although comparison would be fruitful.

Analytically, there are two principal and interconnected aspects to be considered in an examination of the role of mediator. First, there is the nature of negotiations as essen- tially a communication and learning process between the two dis puting parties, leading to some degree of co-ordination by them The mediator acts within this process to affect and somehow to facilitate communication and to promote co-ordination. That is to say, the significance of the role of mediator is understand- able only within this general process. However, and secondly, the intervention of a mediator modifies that process by changin, the original dyad of negotiations into a triad of inter- communication, learning and decision-making. The mediator usually has interests of his own, or represents the interests o: others, which affect the process and his role in it in this triadic context, (2) as he seeks to protect or enhance them. For convenience of exposition in this paper, the first aspect is predominant in the earlier part whilst the second aspect is emphasised in the later part.

------

(1) A.S. Meyer (a professional mediator who became chairman of the New York State Mediation Board) has written: "Mediatio and arbitration have conceptually nothing in common. The o involves helping people to decide for themselves; the other involves helping people by deciding for them. However the two processes have a way of shading into each other." (Meyer 1960:164).

(2) There may be more than a single mediator, perhaps a co- ordinated team of mediators, which adds to the processual complexity.

THE NEGOTIATION PROCESS

Negotiations may be initiated when two parties in disagreement are unable and/or unwilling to settle their differences on an interpersonal basis in the ordinary continuum of social life. The matters are therefore put into public or semi-public arena and in some degree taken out of that interpersonal context. This constitutes a statement, effectively by both parties, that the matters are of perceived importance where neither is prepared to accept the claims of the other, that according to the arena chosen certain ground rules apply, and that the affair becomes in part a public one and its eventual settlement more or less a matter of at least public knowledge. Often each party recruits a team of supporters and co-participants, (3) or the nature of the dispute itself tends to produce teams which are representative of the two opposing sides. (4) Such teams are not ubiquitous but it is the inter-team context that I have especially in mind here. My own principal research experience has been in such contexts and much of the better reporting refers to them. However, the main argument in this paper does not only apply to inter-team negotiations.

At the outset each party (5) seeks as far as possible to determine for himself what are the items in dispute: some will, of course, have been raised already but a party may now wish to add others and he must expect possible additions by his opponent. The party considers what relevant information is available or can usefully be obtained and assesses its significance and implications. A range of actions is perceived relative to the items and their likely results are evaluated in terms of the information available, the party's own preferences and his understanding and expectations of his opponent. There will be established, deliberately or not, some kind of structure of preferences. This structure may be able to rank the various items in some order of

---

(3) As among the Arusha (Gulliver 1963), the Ndendeuli (1971), or Middle East villagers (Antoun 1972).

(4) For example, employers and employees in Western industrial disputes.

(5) For convenience of exposition, the term 'party' is used throughout this paper to indicate either the principal disputant or the whole team acting in support of him. Third person singular pronouns are used for the sake of simplicity.

importance. It may be possible to define minimal levels for
each — or for packages of them — below which the party thinks
he will refuse to go. It will also be possible to define expect
ations of what, above those minima, may be obtainable and is to
be sought. Further decisions have to be made about the level an
nature of initial, overt demands, offers and denials of expected
demands by the opponent. All this is unlikely to be a simple
matter of unilinear utility functions. Because most usually
several, even many, items are involved there are likely to be
problems, not immediately solvable, of incommensurability betwee
them: chalk, cheese and honour — how much of each? and how muc
less of one in order to gain more of another? Some, and perhaps
the more important, may not be measurable in more than the most
general way. In any event, a party may not be at all clear what
he wants nor what he can expect to obtain nor what may be the
result of different courses of action. There will be the need t
accept ignorance and to hold options open until more helpful
information is available: decisions must be made whether to
admit or to disguise this ignorance in the information given to
the opponent.

This kind of preparation — information gathering and assessment, preference structure, perceived action possibilities, stra
tegy decisions — may be more or less thorough (as often in West
ern industrial disputes) but it may be in part the result of
accepted cultural assumptions, intuition, speculation and wishfu
thinking. Operational strategy may be fairly clear but it may
be, and have to be, left indeterminate in some ways until the
situation clarifies. The whole can be affected where the party
comprises a team whose members are not altogether in agreement
and leadership is weak. In any case, a party is aware that
information is incomplete and that expectations may have to be
revised. Although the expectations, preferences, strengths and
weaknesses, and probable strategies of the opponent are taken
into account as far as possible, there is still something to be
learned as the opponent takes action and reveals more of his
position. And, of course, there may be new data forthcoming and
new interpretations to be considered.

As negotiations get under way, each party is concerned to
obtain what information he can from his opponent, from the state
ments, claims and denials, evidence, threats and promises put
forward and the norms and rules to which reference and appeal ar
made. The manner in which these matters are communicated also
carries information. But a party must necessarily give information to his opponent. Each party attempts to control the

information he gives out so as not to reveal what is thought best hidden, permanently or for the time being, and yet to influence the opponent's knowledge and assessment of it. Seldom is it possible — never altogether — merely to draw out the opponent whilst revealing nothing from one's own side: seldom is it a useful strategy in any case for the extent of one's demands, the strength with which they are made and the threats and promises which accompany them are all intended to influence the opponent to shift towards one's own position. There has to be an exchange of information; but one in which each party seeks to learn as true a version of its opponent's position as possible, including preferences and expectations, whilst at the same time endeavouring to give out such information as is thought likely to influence the opponent most effectively.

Particularly in the earlier phases of negotiation, messages may be wrapped in emotional and ideological rhetoric. In any case, demands (6) are not likely at first to be put at points where the party might, or definitely would, be prepared to settle rather than have no settlement at all, for such announced minima would tend to become effective maxima. Demands may be somewhere near what is hoped for (expectations) above the minima, but they may well be considerably above that if bluff is attempted or it is thought useful to leave room for conciliatory 'trading' concessions as negotiations continue. Demands on certain items may be fairly specific, though not necessarily at either minimal or expected levels, whilst on other items they are quite vague because of ignorance, indecision or perceived weakness.

As negotiations continue there is a process of interaction, exchange, learning and adjustment. A party learns more about his opponent's preferences, perceptions, expectations, strengths and weaknesses: this leads to readjustment or reinforcement of his own preferences, perceptions and action decisions. This, or some edited version of it, is communicated back to the opponent with the aim of influencing and changing his position. These responses are assessed by the opponent and further adjustments

(6) The term 'demand' is here intended to include claims, denials of claims, counter-claims and offers with reference to items in dispute.

made as required ..... and so on. (7) This exchange process may
be efficiently ordered so that each party sends messages in turn
feeding in new information and reacting to it alternately. Commonly the process is much less orderly. Messages go both ways at
the same time, attention jumps from item to item, reactions may
be irrelevant or delayed, and messages are misunderstood or not
even received at all.

In brief, each party comes to understand the situation more
clearly. Each obtains more factual data (or what are assumed to
be so) and an improved appreciation of them and of the nature and
strengths of the opponent's expectations and demands. As a
result of learning, each party readjusts his own expectations and
demands, and perhaps also his preferences. This interactive process gradually builds up, either indicating the apparent impossibility of reaching agreement as demands remain quite incompat-
ible — when negotiations fail — or bringing the two parties
closer together towards compatibility and eventual agreement. If
negotiations are successful (8) the information-learning process
leads to increasing co-ordination between the parties and ultimately to their collaboration in the achieved result. There is,
then, a shift from some degree of competition, even hostility, to
at least some degree of co-ordination, even co-operation, and
agreement.

In all this it is not assumed, nor need it be, that information and perception of it ever become anything like complete.
It is not necessary to follow the game-theorists in such un-
natural analytical assumptions: indeed, it is dangerous as well
as faulty to do so. The parties will undoubtedly never gain

---

(7) Additional evidence may also be obtained elsewhere and is
    often actively sought in order to augment and check the
    validity of messages received from the opponent and the
    party's interpretation of these. For example, there may be
    reports of the activities of the opponent, expressions of
    public opinion or data and analysis by experts.

(8) 'Successful' in this context means achieving a mutually
    agreed settlement — not necessarily a final solution nor
    one that altogether accords with society's norms or equity.
    As a minimum, settlement means the end of the dispute at
    least for the time being. It may in effect leave things
    pretty well as they were, or solve some but not all prob-
    lems, or significantly re-establish or re-organize
    relations between the two parties.

complete knowledge and perfect perception nor will they invariably think and act rationally. We can, fortunately, continue to regard the disputing negotiators as human beings rather than disembodied actors playing a game. Settlement may, in part, be achieved because one party (and often both) does not know or adequately appreciate a significant part of the whole situation, maybe because his opponent has successfully kept important data or their implications from him, perhaps because he has inadequate skill or experience, perhaps because the opponent has been able to manipulate his fears, his loyalties or his self-image, and perhaps because the parties in collusion do not take account of certain factors. It is well known, I think, that too much information, let alone complete information, positively hampers decision-making in real life; and in any case information is not absolute but always subject to cognition of it.

There is an important and illuminating difference between this kind of process and that which involves adjudication. In the latter there is form, pattern and structure in the process of dispute settlement. There is the role and authority of the adjudicator; there are institutionalized rules, procedure and roles, and a more or less clear idea of due process. The dispute and the disputants are brought within all this so that the total process leading to decision settlement is given recognizable and understood structure. People know where they are, what to do and how to do it. Under negotiations there is initially no such structuring. The disputants have problems which they seek to resolve by voluntary, mutual probings and exchange of information, leading to bargaining and decision making. This process has to be organized in some way, be given a structure, if there is not to be breakdown or stultifying stalemate but instead a reasonable chance of co-ordination leading to success. The two parties do not just come together and somehow, fortuitously, find an agreeable solution. There is initial disorder — the dispute — and an endeavour to reach order — the settlement; and that endeavour itself requires ordering. (9)

The interesting thing is that the structuring of negotiation processes seems to be similar in essentials whether they occur in the context of American industry or of an African village, whether the teams comprise professionals or ad hoc amateurs,

(9) I am not proposing a "phase model" in which the disruption of peace leads to an eventual restoration of peace (Swartz *et al*. 1966:38) with its built in assumptions about equilibrium in social systems.

whether they are concerned with a ten cents wage increase or wit family honour, whether the two parties have approximately equal power or not. Some negotiations concern highly complex issues (though these certainly do not occur only in more complex societies), some take a long time and many sessions of meetings to reach a settlement whilst others reach an end quite quickly. All these kinds of consideration, though not unimportant, seem not to affect the essential structuring of the negotiation processes.

A general model of the structure of negotiations has been outlined and discussed elsewhere (Gulliver 1973). Its main features are briefly summarised here. It is essentially a *model of overlapping phases* in which each phase opens the way to the succeeding one in a progression towards settlement. The phases are distinguished by the nature and content of the information exchanged and the concomitant learning and by the degree of co-ordination involved.

The dispute proper is precipitated by a crisis situation: the threat, implied or actual, to withhold labour or to close the factory; or the continued refusal of the son-in-law to pay bridewealth, leaving the father-in-law declaring that something must be done. One party, or perhaps both, wishes to gain the involvement of others. So the matter is taken out of its own domain and put into the wider context of a public or semi-public domain.

There follows a search for an arena acceptable to both parties. This may be easy and obvious; but one party may be recalcitrant and require pressuring, or there may be a choice of arenas. The arena defines not merely the geographical and social location of negotiations but also who is involved and wha ground rules are to be followed. Overlapping with this search, but usually continuing afterwards, is the effort to define the issues in dispute. People are not necessarily clear exactly wha it is that is in dispute; often they scarcely can be until information exchange begins. It may not be the apparently obvious nor the more emotive issues that have to be clarified an agreed to. The precipitating crisis may produce additional matters and show new implications, especially as other people become involved. In any event, there is often more than one way of defining an issue and different ways have different implications because of the rules and norms that are involved, offering different advantages and disadvantages for each party.

When the issues have been defined tolerably well for both parties — that is, they are talking about approximately the same things and in the same cultural context — but perhaps whilst this is still going on, they begin and continue to lay emphasis on their differences. Initial stands are declared and elaborated, opening bids made, ideologies aired, strengths paraded and opponent's weaknesses expounded. Often quite extreme assertions are bandied to and fro of the "fight to the last man" kind. These give expression to competition, even hostility, and emphasise the absence of co-ordination. There is an important structuring aspect, however, in that the two parties by propounding their differences are establishing the outer limits to their dispute and the various items contained in it: the area within which negotiations will operate and a settlement be sought. At the same time, information is exchanged about relative preferences and their strengths: for example, on which particular items a party will "fight to the last man" and what degree of preference and resoluteness that indicates.

Thereafter there is a shift of orientation and interaction from hostility and difference towards co-ordination and possible co-operation. In this phase the emphasis is on narrowing the differences in two ways. One is the search for a range within which a settlement of the issue is acceptable to both parties: that is, a range of solutions which for each party may be less than it would wish but is preferable to no solution at all. A viable range lies between the minimum demand tolerable to one party and the maximum offer tolerable to the other. The other way of narrowing differences is the search for items which can be resolved separately to mutual satisfaction or be tolerably ignored by both. At the end of this phase, if all is going well, there should be a resolution of a number of items and isolation and clarification of the core differences.

Bargaining follows on those remaining items which have, in the event, proved most difficult and problematic. They are not necessarily the most 'important' in an objective sense but only relatively in the specific context. Bargaining involves offer and counter-offer, concession and reciprocal concession, 'trading' between items (we give in on this if you give in on that, for instance) and reference to arbitrary solutions by chance or by "the intrinsic magnetism of particular outcomes"

(Schelling 1963:70) such as splitting the difference. (10)

Finally, if all has gone fairly well, there is ritualization of the agreed settlement achieved, according to the culture, by actions such as handshaking, oath, invocation of the supernatural, drawing up and signing a document, commensal eating and drinking, and so on.

It must be emphasised that this is a structure of overlapping phases. There is usually no specific time at which a phase begins and ends but an accumulative trend as the interaction changes from separation in opposition (and maybe, animosity) to mutuality in collusion (and may be, trust). The struc tured pattern emerges effectively out of the interactional process of information exchange and learning, leading to the possibility of co-ordination. Anthropologists are familiar already with one occurrence of this pattern in the establishment of a marriage and affinal relations where there is sometimes marked ritualization of the phases. In other types of negotiations there may or may not be emic recognition of the evolving pattern.

This kind of structuring has been previously noted by social scientists dealing with Western industrial disputes. (11) Here I am elaborating further and suggesting an application of the model cross-culturally and universally.

The pattern is not, of course, necessarily followed in simple unilinear fashion in concrete reality. For a number of

---

(10) The terms 'negotiations' and 'bargaining' have often been used as virtual synonyms, thus confusing two rather different processes. On the market place analogy, bargaining seems best regarded as a process of exchange of demands or offers for counter-demands or counter-offers with the inter of finding an agreeable point of settlement. But negotiations are much broader in scope than that, though also including it, because much information exchange and learnir has to occur before actual bargaining can begin. In actual dispute cases the ultimate bargaining is quite often, thoug not always, quite brief where the groundwork has been well done already. Cf. Ikle 1964:3-4 and Cross 1969:3-5 for contrasting views.

(11) For example, Douglas 1955 and Walton 1969:105.

contextual reasons, negotiators may return to an earlier phase or omit a phase. For example, they may work through a phase for certain items and then go back to an earlier phase to take up other items. Agreements 'in principle' may call for a re-run to achieve agreement on details. I am not suggesting an inflexible structuring of the total process but rather a heuristic model which is considered useful for description, analysis, comparison and understanding.

MEDIATORS IN THE NEGOTIATIONS PROCESS

If a mediator becomes involved in negotiations he operates within this process of communication and learning and the general pattern of overlapping phases. What he can do and how, the strategies he adopts, are affected by these and must be reasonably congruent with them. For instance, it can be useless or even harmful if he seeks to emphasise the narrowing of differences during the phase when the negotiators are expressing the extent of those differences. A mediator is a facilitator of the exchange of information, the concomitant learning and the consequent readjustment of perception, preferences and action decisions. He therefore assists the flow of information both in quantity and effectiveness. But he can also deal with problems of conflicting information and discrepant perception, and perhaps with over-abundant information that by its bulk and complexity adds to the difficulties of deciding preferences and of dealing with non-commensurable items.

A general proposition is that a mediator is most needed and most useful during the transition from one phase of negotiations to another, or during the transition back to an earlier phase. During transition the negotiators are necessarily involved in shifts of attitude, purpose and expectations, focus and the kinds of information exchanged. These shifts can be gradually achieved as a function of the learning process; but often the parties find real difficulties in adjusting their interaction and the negotiations run into deadlock. Of particular difficulty is the transition from the phase of emphasising differences and exploring the outside limits of demands to the phase of narrowing differences and emphasising agreements. That is a shift from opposition, mistrust and perhaps hostility to co-ordination, some degree of trust and even co-operation. It is the principal watershed in the whole process. However, all transitions are intrinsically problematic for the negotiators.

This general proposition is not intended to deny the obvious
fact that mediators do operate and can be effective during a
single phase. Information exchange can bog down in sterile
repetitiveness, inter-personal relations between negotiators may
interfere adversely, misunderstandings grow from faulty signals
and inadequate perception, and sometimes one or both parties
play to the gallery rather than to each other or they may become
over-involved in intra-team problems. A mediator may come into
negotiations more or less from the start and so be available
during any phase of the process: where that is so, however, it
is most likely, and usually most effective, that he varies his
role and strategy relative to possibilities and requirements.

Empirically and logically the strategies of a mediator vary
quite widely. Cultural precepts may bar or hinder certain strategies and enjoin others. Negotiators request or tolerate some
but not others. Mediators differ in accorded prestige and influence and in their skills. The socio-cultural context of the
actual dispute affects the possibilities open to the mediator.

For the purposes of exposition and clarification, mediators'
strategies can conveniently be described on a continuum representing the range of strengths of intervention. This continuum
runs something like this: from virtual passivity to 'chairman',
to 'enunciator', to 'prompter', to 'leader', to virtual arbitrator. These terms are not intended to be principally typological
but rather to be useful indices along that continuum. Actual
strategies can be displayed as more or less resembling, more or
less near to, one or another of these indices. This states
nothing about the effectiveness of strategies. In the following
brief survey some examples are given as illustration. Comprehen-
siveness is not possible and would in any case be excessively
tedious. The intention is to indicate something of the range of
strategies or mediation.

By his very presence a quite passive mediator can encourage
positive communication and interaction between the parties,
stimulating the continuation or the renewal of the exchange of

information. (12) Because he is there, the parties are often constrained to observe minimal courtesy to each other, to reduce personal invective and to listen and to respond with some rele-vance. A party may feel it necessary to explain and justify his case, directly or indirectly, to the mediator because he is there at all or perhaps because he is perceived as a "generalised other" (G.H. Mead). Thus the parties restate their arguments, perhaps rethinking them, and they find the opportunity of start-ing or re-starting to learn. This has been a quite deliberate strategy on occasion, for example by some American industrial mediators. They attend a meeting between the two parties, but sit and say nothing and seek to show no particular reaction to what is said and done. (13) I have witnessed a similar effect by an Ndendeuli mediator, although passivity there seemed to come from a disinclination to get involved or committed rather than from a deliberate strategy to encourage positive interaction be-tween the parties. Yet the effect was much the same. Deliberate or not, the strategy appears to be effective where deadlock occurs when positive information is not being exchanged and evi-dent possibilities are not being explored because of that. A major reason for that condition is interpersonal hostility with perhaps a deliberate policy of personal abuse by one party against the other. Sometimes a party seeks intentionally to frustrate negotiations by his refusal to give information and to engage in exchange.

A mediator is not always a free agent able to choose his strategy for he can be more or less forced into some line of action by the parties. Thus passivity may be partly the result of the negotiators effectively denying the mediator active part-icipation. This occurs, for instance, where the mediator has been thrust upon them and they seek to ignore him in their inten-sive preoccupation with each other, or perhaps in collusion to

---

(12) "A wise mediator once said that the mere presence of an out-sider in collective bargaining negotiations, regardless of anything he says or does, brings about a change in the behaviour of the parties at the bargaining table. This is true enough, and where the parties are hopelessly deadlocked any change in behaviour is presumably for the better" (Rehmus 1965:118).

(13) One mediator related that he silently made voluminous notes on the proceedings; another has told how he chain-smoked, slumped in his chair, with his eyes carefully kept away from the participants.

reject third party interference. Nevertheless even in such
cases the mediator's presence can still result in some change in
the parties' interaction; indeed, collusion, or the recognition
of the common interest, may provide a new starting point.

A more active participation by the mediator produces a role
something like that of chairman. That is, in addition to the
influence of his mere presence he keeps order and tends to direc
procedure. His actions are tolerated and accepted because he ca
give suggestions for order and coherence which engender co-
ordination. At a minimum this may help to prevent a threatening
breakdown of communication. As Schelling has put it: "When
there is no apparent focal point for agreement ... [a mediator]
can create one by his own power to make a dramatic suggestion.
The bystander who jumps into an intersection and begins to direc
traffic at an impromptu traffic jam is conceded the power to dis
criminate among cars by being able to offer a sufficient increas
in efficiency to benefit even the cars most discriminated
against; his directions have only the power of suggestion, but
co-ordination requires the common acceptance of some source of
suggestion." (Schelling 1963:144) An additional implication
here is that the mediator who is once accepted as co-ordinator
may continue to be accepted more readily thereafter when further
difficulties arise.

The chairman role can be extended beyond this. The mediator
may announce and reiterate points of agreement, giving emphasis
to them: for example, agreement by the parties to ignore an
item, or to define it in a certain way, or to settle an item and
remove it from further contention. More positively, the mediato
may make procedural suggestions: to settle the immediate or
overall agenda, to have separate caucus meetings for each team o
a conclave between principals, to introduce new evidence or witnesses. He may actually take over procedural organization such
as arranging the time and place of further meetings, calling for
breaks in a particular session, or curbing excessive interrupt-
ions and irrelevancies. He may suggest new or renewed concentration of focus where information and attention have become dif-
fused or where there are problems of over-abundant information.

In all this the mediator may continue to be impartial to
either side, seeking only to improve co-ordination of exchange.
But this kind of strategy offers opportunities to influence the
negotiations and to favour one party or to push towards the
quickest settlement possible more or less irrespective of merits
There are distinct possibilities for manipulation. A party may

either be unaware of what is being done in effect or he may feel
constrained (even relieved) to accept it rather than face deadlock or extended argument of indeterminate result.

A mediator goes beyond the role of keeping order and facilitating procedure — perhaps ignoring that aspect — when he acts
as enunciator of rules and norms relevant to items in negotiation. This can take the form of clarification and emphasis of
general rules and norms or the identification of particular ones
relevant to the context. The intention is to remind the parties
of what they may have temporarily forgotten or neglected but
which might provide a basis from which to move towards agreement. It reminds the parties, too, of the moral community to
which both belong; and it articulates what may have been left
unclear between the parties. For example, in an Arusha inheritance dispute a senior co-member of the disputants' lineage
stated at successive times during the negotiations: "we are all
one lineage with one ancestor," "brothers should not quarrel,"
"property should be shared equally," "unmarried men have more
need of cattle than those who have married," and "irrigated land
is more valuable than other land but not twice as valuable."

The choice of norms, the particular juncture when they are
expressed, the way this is done and the kind of emphasis given
must inevitably - often quite purposefully - affect the learning
process. It may be done impartially or at least with that
intent, or it may be deliberately partial and manipulative.
Enunciation directs and interprets the exchange of information,
influencing the perceptions, preferences and demands of the
parties and implying possible lines of agreement. The parties
are not bound to accept the norms and rules so propounded nor
to adjust their preferences and demands accordingly. Yet the
party who has been denying some rule is likely to be put at dis-
advantage when the mediator supports his opponent. In any case,
the parties may welcome the clarification of some rule which
offers a basis for further negotiation.

In some cases a mediator is culturally expected to act as
enunciator: the respected elder, the ritual expert, the lawyer.
He represents the wider community and the rules it embraces and
he is mediator because he has special prestige and knowledge.
He is not, as such, making a judgement for he still leaves it -
as he has to - to the two parties to follow up the implications
of the rules and the mode of application to the particular circumstances of their dispute. Of course, some of the items in
dispute may be scarcely susceptible to normative assessment:

the level of wages, the degree of respect owed to a person, the
division of blame between husband and wife, the significance of
allegedly extenuating circumstances. Even if the enunciated
rules are fairly specific, the parties have still to reach an
agreed settlement. A party may deny the validity of the specified rule or he may intend to ignore it. Thus enunciation of
rules and norms may be sign-posting, offering possibilities to
the parties, or it may be rather more manipulative than that as
a mediator carefully stresses certain directions and ignores
others. He may favour one of the parties in this manner, but he
does not dictate. His role is limited. At most he is concerned to assist in establishing some rules of the game within
which the parties can move towards actual settlement.

In the role of prompter a mediator makes a more positive
contribution, although his suggestions are tentative and limited. He does not seek to press his own views, at least not
overtly, nor to take control of the negotiations. Rather he
attempts to clarify information and interpretation and to encourage growing co-ordination between the parties. For example, the
mediator as prompter asks for a restatement of a party's argument, or of particular demands, and requests further information
in support of them. He may himself restate an argument so as to
bring out the principal points in order to obtain reaction. (14)
He may realise that one party just does not apprehend the meaning
or the significance of what the other party is saying and so he
attempts an interpretation. He persuades a party to make direct
response to the opponent's points, trying tactfully to stem
irrelevancies and to dissipate smoke screens. He seeks to persuade the parties to talk about the same thing at the same time,
to follow some relevant pattern of exchange. He attempts to
gain and maintain focus on what he perceives to be the principal
priorities of each party so that each can be clearer about what
these are and their implications both for himself and for his
opponent. The prompter may in this way be able to discover and
help reveal a viable range concerning one or more items within
which both parties would be prepared to settle. Such a viable
range is often obscured by bluffing demands and denials, by
inflated expectations and by the reasonable unwillingness of a
party to commit himself immediately to something which he would,
in the end, prefer rather than get nothing at all. Where the
range of items, or the range within each principal item, is wide
the mediator's tactful questioning and suggestions may produce

_____

(14) E.g. "Am I right in saying that your position is thus and
     thus?" "As I understand it you are saying this and this."

some acceptable and useful focal point around which further exchange can concentrate. Arguments can become so diffuse that concentration and perspective have been lost. The suggestion of a focal point may be particularly valuable when there are no accepted standards for assessing the range — say, of honour — and when items are incommensurable — say, chalk and cheese. (cf. Ikle 1964). The prompter may be able to suggest packages of items to be considered together and where trading seems feasible.

The strategy of the prompter is probably most effective at the beginning of that phase of negotiations when differences are being narrowed and co-ordination developed. Parties may find themselves in entrenched positions from which it is difficult to emerge and to make concessions to the opponent. They may be arguing past one another, unintendedly or not; they may be genuinely unable to see where common ground lies or how to pro-ceed at all. False fronts have been so thoroughly developed as the results of the parties' earlier tactics that they tend to become affected by their own extreme positions and bluffs to the point of losing perspective in their appreciation of their own situation and expectations. They deceive or at least influence themselves as well as each other by their own rhetoric. The prompting mediator may be able to cut through the undergrowth or to indicate to the parties how this might be done. He does it not so much, if at all, by offering his own opinion as by orienting the parties' attention and efforts so that co-ordination becomes possible. Of course, this kind of operation offers possibilities for the mediator to manipulate the trend of the negotiations with benefit to one party or the other, or to his own benefit, should he so wish.

In the role of leader, a mediator goes beyond the rather ten-tative and indirect strategy of seeking to increase, clarify and focus the exchange of information. As leader he more or less directly injects his own messages into the exchange — his own opinions, his own suggestions — and he offers evaluation of information, preferences and demands from either party. He may be able to recommend the basis for agreement on an item or on a 'package deal'. Often these are suggestions that the mediator believes a party would like to make, or at least have discussed, but which he himself fears to raise lest they seem to indicate weakness — too great a readiness to concede — or because the implications are not yet clear. A party may then be relieved that the mediator says what he himself cannot. Coming from the mediator, such a suggestion can be ignored or repudiated should

it seem threatening in view of the opponent's reaction to it.
That is to say, the party is not committed to a position by the
mediator's suggestion, as he might be were he to make it himself
but he can take advantage of it should that seem advantageous.
An American mediator has called this, "trying on for size"
(Simkin, 1971).

A leader is not, however, limited to suggesting what is
already a possibility in the mind of a party. The negotiators
may not be able to see where and how they can shift, they may
overestimate the costs of a concession, or they may be unpre-
pared to consider the implications raised. Here the mediator can
perhaps force the issue which the parties burke. Whether and
how far the parties are willing or can be persuaded to accept
the leader's suggestions are in part dependent on how far they
feel unable to move otherwise, how far they tacitly welcome his
possible way out of impasse and what influence the mediatory
carries. Where the costs of continued negotiations are high and
the disadvantages of persisting disagreement are felt to be more
or less intolerable — that is, where some settlement is on the
whole better than nothing — the mediator's leadership is likely,
sooner or later, to be strong and perhaps decisive. This is
particularly the case where the disputants are in something like
a bilateral monopoly relationship: close kin, sedentary neighbours, employer and employees, etc. The compulsion to reach a
settlement is marked in so far as the continued relationship is
important and/or unavoidable to both. If that relationship is
significantly involved with other mutual interests and relations
— such as both being members of the same group or network
sector — the felt need for settlement is correspondingly
greater. The potential of the mediator becomes high should some
impasse be reached and he may gain additional influence if he is
a co-member of that same social unit.

For example, in an Ndendeuli case a man sought the return of
his wife and child from her father's hamlet where, it was
alleged, she had begun a liaison with another man. The father-
in-law denied knowledge of and complicity in this liaison but he
demanded payment of further bridewealth by the plaintiff and a
promise of future good treatment of his daughter should she
return. The plaintiff denied his liability for bridewealth and
rejected implied allegations of past mistreatment of the woman.
In the effective phase of narrowing the differences some minor
disagreements had been disposed of but the two disputants had
become stuck in repeating their conflicting demands and seemed
in danger of returning to overt hostility. The mediator

(co-neighbour of the disputants) suggested that the son-in-law should pay additional bridewealth whilst the father-in-law should admit to harbouring the wife and not acting vigorously enough in preventing her liaison. Such an admission implied his obligation to pay compensation to the husband. The son-in-law agreed to this but the father-in-law refused the package deal. The mediator and the son-in-law virtually ignored that refusal as the mediator then concentrated on the amount of bridewealth payment which, he asserted, should be less than had been claimed. He favoured approximately what had been claimed less the amount of compensation due to the son-in-law. He headed off with little difficulty further discussion of the supposed offence of the father-in-law, leaving the parties to discuss details of a fairly small bridewealth payment and the return of the wife.

A special case occurs where the mediator acts as go-between with the parties physically separated and not in direct communication, pending a settlement. A go-between may be no more than a straight messenger but this is generally unlikely because of his obvious opportunities for control of information. He conveys messages to and fro with the ability to change their content, emphasis and implication. He can add his own interpretation or include new messages. Each party is highly dependent on him and often has little means of knowing just how far the mediator is manipulating the information flow. A go-between may be passive, a chairman or an enunciator, but he tends to become a prompter or leader, especially if negotiations are going poorly or if, for his own reasons, he wishes deliberately to affect the settlement reached. The classic anthropological examples are the Ifugao *monkalun* (15) and the go-betweens in pre-marriage negotiations in many societies. A somewhat similar situation is established when a mediator can arrange to isolate the parties temporarily for separate caucus meetings.

Leadership is usually most needed and most influential in the transitional periods (change of phase, overlapping of phases) already noted, in the phase of narrowing differences where a stalemate is a growing danger, and in the final phase of bargaining over the core items. In general these are times when the parties may meet the greatest obvious difficulties and may

---

(15) Barton 1919 and 1939; Hoebel 1954. The leadership of the *monkalun* is evident in the only detailed case given by Barton (1930:65 ff.) though it is uncertain whether that is a recording of an actual case or only Barton's fictional reconstruction.

therefore be willing to accept positive and direct suggestions.
At other times leadership is less likely to be required and it i
less tolerable to the parties as they are working their way
through a phase of interaction or as they examine together the
implications of the mediator's earlier work. At those times
mediators tend to lapse into passivity — sometimes withdrawing
altogether — or to act as chairman. Later again they might
adopt the strategy of enunciator or prompter or resume leadership, as that seems possible, tolerable and potentially effective. This is to say that not only is there a range of media-
tional strategies but in a particular case mediators may, and
often do, vary their strategies as negotiations continue. It is
to be emphasised that these different strategies are less easily
and less clearly distinguished in practice than brief analytical
exposition might indicate. To reiterate, they are profferred as
indices along a continuum, representing varying strengths of
intervention and associated tactics and manipulative potentials.

TRIADIC INTERACTION AND THE STATUS OF THE MEDIATOR

The initial model of negotiations adopted in this paper has
been a dyadic one. Something has been shown of the kinds of
strategy a third party may use in his role as facilitator, notin
that strategy may change and re-change during one set of negotia
tions. It is not only what a mediator finds useful and expedien
but also what the disputants themselves will tolerate or require
In any case, the intervention of a mediator turns the original
dyad into a triadic interaction of some kind. (16) The parties
continue to retain the ultimate decision (actually, a set of
decisions most probably) whether or not to accept and agree to
settlement. Yet clearly the mediator exercises influence in som
degree, whether he remains largely passive or virtually controls
the exchange-learning process. That is, he himself interacts
with each party and also with both together, whilst now they may
communicate to and through him. He becomes a party in the negotiations: he becomes a negotiator. More than just that, for
inevitably he brings with him certain ideas, knowledge and
assumptions, as well as certain interests and concerns, his own
and those of people whom he represents. Therefore he is not and
cannot be neutral, a mere catalyst: he affects the interaction
and at least in part he seeks a settlement that is agreeable or

---

(16) Aubert (1963) makes a comparable observation — dyad into
     triad — with reference to the intervention of an adjudi-
     cator in a dispute case.

tolerable to him in terms of his ideas and interests. He may even come into conflict with either party.

What a mediator can do, what he chooses to do and what he is permitted to do by the principal parties are much affected by who he is in the particular context and why he is there at all. His relationship to the parties and to the items in dispute and his status in the enveloping community are crucial variables in this triad.

Some of the more common and generally significant statuses of mediators are briefly described below. Concrete actuality may well be more complex and less specific than the apparent clarity of the analytical types here depicted. They are not, therefore, proposed as a watertight set of categories; they are not altogether mutually exclusive. The intention is to give emphasis to particular characteristics that seem to have a significant bearing on the mediator's participation. Casual references are made to ethnographic examples for purposes of illustration.

The status of the mediator can initially be examined according to whether he is supposedly disinterested or acknowledged to be an interested party. By 'disinterested' is meant that the mediator is not directly related to either principal party and his own interests are not directly touched by the dispute or by possible settlements of it. A disinterested status may derive from an institutionalized role in a society, such as that of the Nuer leopard-skin chief, a Pathan saint, or a professional agent of a state board of mediation in some American states. Part of the person's role implies an obligation and readiness to act as mediator as a result of social and cultural distinction from disputants, their supporters and their interests. (17) Alternatively, the disinterested status may derive from the context of the dispute and be therefore in a sense casual and transitory. Disputants may choose or be willing to accept someone of acknowledged prestige and ability who is not himself directly concerned with the issues and their potential settlement: for instance, a distinguished elder, a religious leader, an Ifugao big man of

---

(17) Bailey has shown that the minimal definition of a Pathan saint entails the characteristics of being learned in Islamic law, having mystical power and not being the tenant of a khan (Bailey 1972:32). One might say that a saint stands outside the basic power struggles and alliances of Swat society and is also above them, although this is something of a simplification.

kadangyang rank. The choice may, however, be some person who
stands outside the structure of the community — the 'stranger'
in some sense — simply because his interests are separated from
the principal groups and categories which comprise that community. This may mean that such a person has little or no extrinsic prestige and influence. A third kind of avowedly disinterested mediator is the expert who brings some kind of speci-
knowledge and training to the dispute: a lawyer, a genealogica
expert, a technical specialist.

In contrast, mediators may be quite clearly interested parti-
when their interests suggest a real concern for the issues in
dispute and the disputants themselves. There is the person who
though not personally involved in the dispute, has definite
interests that are affected by it and are involved in whatever
settlement is reached. For example, the person who holds land
adjacent to a disputed piece of land may wish to know who his
neighbour is to be, perhaps with some urgency. He may have to
co-operate with him regarding mutual access paths or a common
irrigation channel. A tenant, maybe, wishes to know to whom he
owes rent and from whom he can claim certain rights. Uncertaint
can be disadvantageous or even downright harmful, so the third
party wants a settlement in order to be able to get on with his
own activities. He may not care much what the settlement is so
long as there is one and therefore he is acceptable as a mediator. Similarly in international affairs, a country which might
be affected if its neighbours go to war over their dispute might
therefore offer to act as mediator in order to prevent hostili-
ties dangerous to it.

It can happen that a third party is not merely interested to
encourage a settlement but positively partial to one party. Despite, or even because of, his known partiality he may be acceptable as a mediator, though maybe only as a last resort when negotiations appear to be heading for breakdown, or when it proves
difficult to get them going at all. Elsewhere I have described
such a case among the Ndendeuli (Gulliver 1971:145). Antoun has
recorded a comparable case in a Jordanian Arab village (1972:
78 ff.). An interesting example comes from San Francisco where
the Labor Council and its Executive Committee — an association
of local trade unions and clearly a pro-labour body — has been
able successfully to act as a mediator of last resort when industrial negotiations are nearing breakdown and a strike is threatened. This has been institutionalized in practice and has gaine
the approval of the employers (Liebes 1958:798-9). Sometimes
anyone is better than no one at all.

In situations where the two parties are involved in some network of relations there are people who are structurally intermediate between them: that is, roughly equally linked to both.
For instance, there is the person who is kinsman to both, or
there are members of a lineage collateral with those of the
disputants, (18) or a political or economic ally of both. The
rationale here is that, being connected to both parties, such
persons have divided loyalties, obligations to both, and may be
tolerably acceptable to both. But from the mediator's point of
view his own interests are likely to be affected and he seeks to
protect them. He wishes to maintain his advantageous relations
with both, and also with others in the same network, but finds
it difficult so long as they are at serious odds. He seeks to
encourage both a speedy conclusion to the negotiations and a
settlement which will damage as little as possible his interests
with either party.

The mediator may be in some sense a representative of the
community to which both parties belong: lineage, village,
association, political or religious group. In that case he is
likely to be a person of prestige, even a leader, in that community, such as a member of the gentry or the headman in a traditional Chinese village (Cohen 1967). He may be a local politician, an administrator, the lineage head. He acts as mediator
in order to assist his fellow-members of the community, but also
in order to influence and pressure them so as to restore peace
and adequate working relations there. He may take the opportunity to impress, both on the disputants and other members, the
moral norms of the community and its common interests and needs.
Although he can be helpful to the disputants, he commonly has the
interests of the community, and perhaps his own particular interests in it, very much in mind. He may well be inclined to put
those before the interests of the two parties. For instance, a
quick settlement is often sought by such a mediator in the interests of the community or of its leading members; this can be at
the expense of one of the parties, even both, if speed takes preference over a more genuine resolution of some important dispute.
Apart from that kind of thing, the mediator may see an opportunity to gain prestige or public attention by his efforts. He may
use his temporary role to win advantage and reputation as against
his competitors for leadership in the community, as Ndendeuli
notables sometimes did, for example (Gulliver 1971:187). He may
see an opportunity to gain the indebtedness of one or both

---

(18) For example, the Lebanese *waasta* as described by Ayoub
     (1965:13).

parties as a result of his services in assisting with the
settlement of the dispute. In all this the parties do not
necessarily suffer, of course. Often, however, their interests
and preferences are in some way distorted, even disregarded,
depending on the strength of influence and manipulation of the
mediator and his interests at the time.

One way or another, then, it is highly probable that a person
can and does gain advantage from taking the role of mediator. I
suspect that the truly disinterested mediator is in fact rather
rare. He may perhaps be quite impartial towards the two parties
but he is likely to be quite partial towards his own interests,
sometimes at the expense of one or both disputants. We should
maintain a healthy cynicism here and enquire what is in it for
the man in the middle. Even the professional neutral likes to
gain a reputation for ability and success, as that is judged by
his superiors: he may get a raise in salary, promotion or more
interesting cases in the future. It seems evident that a Pathan
saint, the conventional mediator between khans in Swat society,
could gain both land and followers as a result of his successful
mediation. An Ifugao *monkalun* and probably a Nuer leopard-skin
chief could acquire wealth and followers in much the same
way. (19) Structural intermediaries, such as the kinsman of
both parties, have obvious interests to preserve and foster.

It strains credulity unnecessarily to believe that these kind
of interests and rewards do not affect the possible manipulation
that are available to mediators – whatever their strategies – in
the exchange of information and learning process in negotiations
Rather, we need to take account of this in seeking to understand

---

(19) On Swat Pathan saints, see Barth 1960 and Bailey 1972:28 ff
     Bailey has suggested that some saints may have gained such
     rewards from mediation that they themselves could have
     become like khans, possibly losing the ability to continue
     as acceptable mediators. On the Ifugao Barton wrote: "It
     is greatly to the interest of the *monkalun* to arrange a
     peaceful settlement, not only because he usually receives a
     somewhat larger fee in such cases, but because the peaceful
     settlement of cases in which he is a mediator builds up a
     reputation for him, so that he is frequentlȳ called and so
     can earn many fees." (1969:88-9) On the Nuer leopard-skin
     chief, see Evans-Pritchard 1940 and Howell 1954. The Nuer
     data are most unsatisfactory and have recently been used fc
     contradictory analyses (Greuel 1971 and Haight 1972).

the significance of mediation. There is a strong, Western, cultural stereotype of the purely impartial mediator which is neither invariably correct in our own society nor valid cross-culturally. Yet it seems to have given an idealistic, ethnocentric bias to accounts of mediation by anthropologists and others. The supposedly impartial mediator is probably seeking some degree of advantage beyond that of the disputing parties. At least this is a matter for investigation: the kinds of additional interests involved and how they affect the mediator's intervention. He may be on the side of the angels, exercising his manipulative influence for the greater good of the community or on behalf of the wronged or weaker party. He may primarily be concerned with his own interests. Either way his assessment of the situation and his choice of strategy and tactics will be affected and may significantly affect the process of negotiations.

In any case, so many mediators in so many contexts are effectively interested parties. Their suitability and acceptability for the role are often overtly founded on that recognition. Disputants may hope to gain the benefits of these mediators' facilitation of negotiations without surrendering much if anything to the perceived interests of the mediator. They may be more or less successful in this. Often they are not, however; often they are aware that they are not and cannot be so altogether. Yet it can still be worthwhile for a disputant to accept this as an additional cost of negotiations. Sometimes there may be rather little choice in the matter when it is exceedingly difficult to refuse the intervention of a mutually linked third party or of some representative of the common community. If the mediator is partial to one of the parties then that party will probably welcome his intervention.

The point is that in examining mediation we need to take full account of the mediator's interests. This means that we have to take account of three — not merely two — sets of interests, preferences, learning and action choices in a triadic structure. The manipulative opportunities offered to a mediator can be considerable, as I indicated earlier. Moreoever, each disputant is concerned to manipulate not only the knowledge, perceptions and preferences of his opponent but also those of the mediator. He too can be induced to act in ways thought advantageous to a disputant.

For example, one strategy is to accept the intervention of a mediator in the expectation of persuading him of the validity or

strength of one's own demands or of the reality of one's commitment to a stand (Schelling 1963:24 ff.) in order to gain his
influence against the opponent. Another strategy is sometimes
adopted by a party who sees the inevitability of giving way in
large part to the opponent's demands. By agreeing to mediation
he may be able to put the blame on the mediator, using him as a
scapegoat: just as a Nuer could claim that he would have used
his spear, as a good Nuer should, but that out of deference to
the leopard-skin chief he reluctantly accepted a peaceful settle
ment, though he and everyone else may have been wanting that any
way. In other words, the presence of a mediator offers a way to
save face, a way to make concessions without too obviously
appearing to show weakness. As an American mediator put it: th
parties have locked themselves into a position where "they can'
retreat and they do not themselves wish to fight." A negotiatin
team representing some larger constituency (such as union or
lineage leaders vis-à-vis their followers) may wish to demonstrate to its constituency that the mediator forced them to give
way; or alternatively that the mediator could help to get no
better terms of settlement than the team itself could. In these
kinds of circumstances the mediator is being manipulated, with o
without his consent or knowledge.

THE RATIONALE OF MEDIATION

Already the reasons for the involvement of a mediator have
been suggested in this paper. They can be conveniently summarised before going on to consider why mediators do not invariably appear in negotiations.

In many societies a mediator is regularly imposed on the disputing parties by the community, through its leaders or by other
who feel constrained to intervene, on the grounds that all disputes between members potentially or actively affect other members. Disputants thus have no right to complete self-sufficienc
even though adjudication of their conflict is not imposed. The
more highly integrated the community the greater the compulsion,
morally and materially, for the intervention. Such is the case,
for example, in Moslem villages of the Middle East or in traditional Chinese villages. The parties have little or no
choice, though they may be glad of the expected assistance.

The disputants themselves may agree to invite in a mediator
for the help he may give. A recognised deadlock may threaten th
prospects of a settlement where neither party wishes this to

happen, and for a variety of reasons. The mediator can perhaps discover a way out of the deadlock by improving communications; he can be a scapegoat or face-saver when concessions have to be made; he can be used to demonstrate that a party has indeed done all that is possible in the circumstances; each party may hope to gain the mediator as an ally.

The parties are sometimes prepared to tolerate the inervention of a third party whose interests are manifestly involved in the dispute and its settlement, where that third party takes the initiative. This is a matter of recognizing his legitimate concern and/or recognizing the importance of his relations with the parties.

In actual cases there may be some combination of these reasons. The mediator can be welcomed and used, or tolerated and ignored. He is commonly an interested party in some way and may be somehow representative of the community. Explanations of the presence of a mediator are not in general principle difficult to understand, both emically and etically, though the implications and results of his intervention are often quite complex in particular cases. It seems less easy to understand why mediators do not always appear. It is probable that in the majority of societies and in most negotiations mediators do intervene, either from the beginning or at some later point. Yet not inevitably. In the United States in 1968 mediators operated in only 15% of private sector, industrial negotiations. (20) Among the Arusha, mediators seldom if ever appear in negotiations between men of different lineages or different age-groups (Gulliver 1963). In many, though not all, societies negotiations concerning marriage arrangements or marital disputes occur regularly or sometimes without third party mediation. Certainly not all international negotiations involve mediators. There is no universal imposition of mediation by a relevant community; and although there may be persons whose interests are involved in some way, the disputing parties are sometimes able to ignore them.

One suggested explanation has been that there is always, in effect mediation: if not by some individual directly then by an

---

(20) Simkin states: "At the remaining 85% of the bargaining tables the parties negotiated without any outside assistance." (1971:52) It is probable that in some, but by no means all, of these cases informal and unrecorded mediation did occur.

implicit mediator. Barkun, for instance, has written that
implicit mediation is "shared values without a physically present mediator," and that "system-preserving values themselves
constitute an *implied third party*" (Barkun 1968:106; his
italics). This is to confuse things that analytically should be
kept separate. Obviously, virtually all pairs of disputants
share some values, probably very many. These are important in a
number of ways in negotiations: they provide some frame of reference and a basis for discussion, they symbolize the significan
connections between disputants and between them and others, they
symbolize the community to which both disputants belong together
with their rights and obligations there, they may link together
seemingly disparate items in dispute, and a good deal else. The
exist, are appealed to and are used (and also are ignored and
abused) in every case of conflict between two people, whether
that conflict runs on or it is dealt with by adjudication and
through negotiations, with or without a mediator. They are part
of the subject matter of communication and learning, along with
evidence, material and technical matters, threats and promises,
demonstrations of strengths and determination, etc. It is the
way in which values — and other subject matter — are used that
is important.

Barkun also wrote that "in the most simple societies or the
less complex outer reaches of a society, implicit mediation is
the standard procedure," (1968:146) and refers for support to th
work of Schwartz and Miller (1964). This patently ignores the
facts that mediators regularly operate in some simple societies
(whatever "simple" may be), whilst one can hardly hold that
industrial disputes occur in the "less complex outer reaches" of
contemporary Western societies! There is an implication in this
kind of argument that the absence of mediators is connected in
some causal sense with less complex social systems, and possibly
too that disputes themselves are less complicated and less
requiring of actual mediators in such systems. It may therefore
be worthwhile emphasising that highly complicated disputes in
Western countries are negotiated and settled without a mediator,
even though national political and economic interests may be
touched. It may be that with the assistance of mediators such
negotiations might have been more effectively or expeditiously
conducted, though we cannot merely assume this. The parties in
such cases have been quite unwilling to accept mediation, to
cede any freedom of action; and for whatever reason the community has not enforced it on them. They have doubtless been
influenced by expression of public opinion which have become
part of the content of their inter-communication. Yet they have

continued in the primary concern to influence and persuade each other and to reach together a mutually acceptable settlement.

A case for the implicit mediator could perhaps be made with reference to public opinion and to expressions of fact and opinion by political and other leaders, the news media, etc. Yet this kind of influence, like common values, is nearly always present to some extent whilst negotiations continue, whether or not an actual mediator is present. Such outside opinion is pro- bably best regarded as part of the information that becomes available to the negotiators. How that additional information is perceived by a party and used in an attempt to affect his oppo- nent is worked out in the course of the negotiations. Some par- ticular exponent of allegedly public opinion does sometimes gradually become a mediator, even though is he not actually pre- sent at negotiations sessions. For instance, a politician might meet with each party separately to examine his position and the available information. That third party may make positive sug- gestions either privately or in public statements and thus become an actively involved, participating mediator.

The sophistry of implicit mediation does not provide any adequate explanation for the absence of a real mediator. It avoids the question instead of coming to grips with it. Rather we need to ask three questions. Do the disputants want third party intervention because of its perceived advantages to them? Are they willing to recognize and entertain the legitimate interests of a third party in their dispute and its settlement? In any case, does the relevant community, through its leaders or otherwise, insist that the disputants are not entirely free agents because their behaviour and their decisions affect that community in some way? If the answers to all three questions are 'no', then a mediator is most unlikely to appear. This seems to be the case in the instances cited, although the reasons behind the answers and the sociological implications vary from society to society.

CONCLUSION

"One might reasonably assume," wrote one social scientist in 1965, "in the light of the extensive literature and the consider- able amount of practical development of the collective bargaining process that has occurred, that studies of the dynamics of the mediation process would be most plentiful. In actual fact, the exact opposite is true. Mediation is perhaps the least studied subject in the field of industrial relations" (Rehmus 1965:118).

Although since the time that was written there have been new contributions to the subject, mediation still remains an inadequately understood process and by no means only in the single field of industrial relations. (21) Especially in anthropology the subject has been grossly neglected, along with the whole process of negotiations. These remain lacunae in both ethnography and theory: perhaps because of their seeming simplicity, perhaps because of the emphasis on law, courts and adjudication by anthropologists who have been concerned with dispute settlement. The most cursory references to mediators — who they are, how they come to the role, what they do — are the norm so that we do not have adequate data. Yet the process of negotiations and the role of mediator are well nigh universal in all kinds of societies from the most simple to the most complex. Despite their ubiquity they have been casually passed over by anthropologists with such useless aphorisms as "informal procedures", "private conciliation", "the judicial process in one of its prenascent forms" and so on. Analysis has been minimal if indeed there has been any at all. This neglect is apparent in the well known general works in the field of the anthropology of law. Apart from his excellent synthesis and reinterpretation of the data on the role of the Ifugao go-between, Hoebel (1954) has only passing references to mediators and no systematic discussion. As Moore has pointed out (1969:275), "negotiation and bargaining seem to have no place in Bohannan's scheme," nor, one might add, mediators. (Bohannan 1967: Introduction). There is no index entry for 'mediator' or a synonym in Pospisil 1971. The latter author insists, for example, that Ndendeuli mediators exercise authority and make decisions binding on disputants, thus ignoring the real distinctions between negotiations and adjudication, between mediators and judges.

In Western societies there has been a good deal of resistance to the possibility of analysing and understanding the nature of mediation. Its practitioners in particular seem to have wanted

---

(21) Some of the more recent contributions are contained in Douglas 1962, Eckhoff 1967, Fuller 1971, Simkin 1971, Walton 1969, Young 1967 and 1972. It is noteworthy that the most comprehensive study of industrial negotiations to appear in recent years (Walton and McKersie 1965) contains no treatment of mediation. Similarly, Ikle's refresh study (1964) of international negotiations has rather scant references to the topic.

to sustain an intuitive mystique about it. As one American professional has put it: the mediator "has no science of navigation, no fund inherited from the experience of others. He is a solitary artist recognizing, at most, a few guiding stars and depending mainly on his personal power of divination." (Meyer 1960:160) Describing Swedish practice, Schmidt has written: "Each mediator has his own technique and his own methods of conducting negotiations, restricted only by his particular temperament and the circumstances involved." (1952:52)

At the same time, quite strong cultural stereotypes and subjective assumptions have been proferred as fact and analysis. One psychologist saw the non-directive, impartial, catalyst role as being crucial to third party intervention (Muench 1963), apparently assuming that as "catalyst" the mediator is, and should be, neutral and disinterested. Another writer has emphasised, for instance, that third parties have, or should have, "the objective of changing the relationship between the parties from a destructively competitive win-lose orientation to a co-operative collaborative problem solving orientation," (22) though this is but one possible aim of mediators in actual disputes. There has been a good deal of protestation that mediators are or should be neutral. One researcher has noted that during her work in the field she got very strong reactions from mediators when she suggested that neutrality was a myth. Yet, as she pointed out, mediators do inevitably feed "determinants into the flow of bargaining interaction which influence and shape the outcome." (Douglas 1955:550) She concluded that the assertions of neutrality were not so much a description of the mediator's role but rather that they "stem from a common need to purge the mediator of liability for the course of treatment, regardless of whether the patient gets well or succumbs." (loc. cit.) They also relate to problems of uncertainty of role and the absence of clear public approval of their work in American society. There has also been a good deal of discussion whether the mediator's role in industrial disputes should be to encourage a just settlement, or one in accord with socio-economic conditions, or merely one that gets the dispute over as quickly as possible.

These are, of course, culture-bound arguments and polemics; but anthropologists, with their intrinsic cross-cultural concern, have not offered anything much better. They have scarcely looked for, let alone disclosed, the socio-cultural range, determinants and implications of the triadic communication and interaction.

---

(22) Fisher 1972:81, referring to Blake *et al.* 1964.

The ghost of the neutral (or impartial, or disinterested) mediator tends to haunt the scene. Alternatively, or sometimes
simultaneously, the mediator is loosely depicted as more or less
dictating solutions to the disputing parties, as being some kind
of poorly institutionalized adjudicator operating at a low level
of social organization and as somehow taking an extra-
processual role before the adjudication mechanism begins.
Careful description and first level analysis of mediation, of
cases of mediators acting within the negotiations process, are
extremely rare.

In this paper I have sought to focus on this whole area of
social interaction and to suggest some of the preliminary theoretical considerations that might lead to a more genuine appreciation of role, process and decision making that are involved. To
that limited end I have concentrated on two basic concerns which
can orient research and analysis more realistically and which
indicate the variety of phenomena involved. These are, first,
the variety of strategies that mediators use within the general
pattern of negotiations as a social process sui generis; and
second, the inevitable change from dyad to triad as a mediator
intervenes. With these in mind it is possible to deal with the
complex of more or less inter-connected factors which together
affect the role of mediator and the process of mediation.
Briefly they are as follows.

The state of negotiations, including the degree of
acknowledged difficulty in the communication-learning-
adjustment process, and the problems of particular phases
and phase transitions.

The relations between the parties, formal and actual,
before the particular dispute began and as they have
developed during the negotiations, including the rules and
norms applicable, common interests and values, co-
involvement with others and the distribution of negotiating
power between them.

The readiness of the parties to accept mediation,
including their perception of difficulties, their willingness
to cede some degree of autonomy, their willingness to acknow-
ledge the interests of others, and whether one or both parties
tolerate and/or seek mediation or a particular mediator.
This is related to:-

The perceived costs of continued negotiations or potential

failure for each party without the intervention (new or intensified) of a mediator, including the reasons for and degree of the desire and/or perceived necessity to reach a settlement, and the relative costs to each party.

The nature of the items in dispute, including the specificity of the rules and norms applicable, the variety of items and problems of incommensurability, the possibilities of package deals and trading in items, the inherent nature of the conflict (zero sum, positive sum), and the significance of items to other people's interests.

The status and interests of a mediator relative to items in dispute (manifest and latent), relative to each party and to the enveloping community, and including any culturally defined status and role of mediator, the perceived advantages to be gained by the mediator and his probable costs.

The nature of the enveloping community, including the degree of inter-dependence among members (including the parties themselves), and the presence or absence of leaders and notables expected and/or willing to intervene.

The possible alternatives to mediation, including voluntary or compulsory arbitration, adjudication, and renewal and/or development of dyadic relations between the parties, perhaps in a new arena.

REFERENCES

Antoun, R. (1972). *Arab village*. Indiana University Press, Bloomington.

Aubert, V. (1963). Research in the sociology of law. *American Behavioral Scientist*, **18**, 16-20.

Ayoub, V.F. (1965). Conflict resolution and social reorganization in a Lebanese village. *Human Organization*, **24**, 11-17.

Bailey, F.G. (1972). Conceptual systems in the study of politics. *In* Antoun, R. & I. Harick (eds.): *Rural politics and social change in the Middle East.* Indiana University Press, Bloomington.

Barkun, M. (1968). *Law without sanctions.* Yale University Press, New Haven.

Barth, F. (1960). *Political leadership among the Swat Pathans.* Athlone Press, London.

Barton, R.F. (1919). *Ifugao law.* University of California Publications in American Archaeology and Ethnology, 15, 1-186

Barton, R.F. (1930). *The halfway sun.* Brewer & Warren, New York.

Barton, R.F. (1969). *Ifugao law* (new edition). California University Press, Berkeley.

Blake, R.R., H.A. Shepard and J.S. Mouton (1964). *Managing intergroup conflict in industry.* Gulf, Houston.

Bohannan, P. (1967). *Law and warfare: studies in the anthropology of conflict.* Natural History Press, New York.

Cohen, J.A. (1967). Chinese mediation on the eve of modernization. *In* Buxbaum, D.C. (ed.): *Traditional and modern legal institutions in Asia and Africa.* Brill, Leiden.

Cross, J.G. (1969). *The economics of bargaining*. Basic Books, New York.

Douglas, A. (1955). What can research tell us about mediation? *Labor Law Journal*, 6, 545-52.

Douglas, A. (1962). *Industrial peacemaking*. Columbia University Press, New York.

Eckhoff, T. (1967). The mediator, the judge and the administrator in conflict resolution; *Acta Sociologica*, 10, 148-72.

Evans-Pritchard, E.E. (1940). *The Nuer*. The Clarendon Press, Oxford.

Fisher, R.J. (1963). Third party consultation. *Journal of Conflict Resolution*, 6, 67-94.

Fuller, L.L. (1963). Collective bargaining and the arbitrator. *Wisconsin Law Review*, 1963, 3-46.

Fuller, L.L. (1971). Mediation — its forms and functions. *Southern California Law Review*, 44, 305-39.

Greuel, P.J. (1971). The leopard-skin chief: an examination of political power among the Nuer. *American Anthropologist*, 73, 1115-20.

Gulliver, P.H. (1963). *Social control in an African society*. Routledge & Kegan Paul, London.

Gulliver, P.H.   (1971).   *Neighbours and networks*.   California
University Press, Berkeley.

Gulliver, P.H.   (1973).   Negotiations as a mode of dispute
settlement: towards a general model.   *Law & Society Review*,
7, 667-91.

Hoebel, E.A.   (1954).   *The law of primitive man*.   Harvard
University Press, Cambridge.

Haight, B.   (1972).   A note on the leopard-skin chief.   *American
Anthropologist*, 74 1313-18.

Howell, P.P.   (1954).   *A manual of Nuer law*.   Oxford University
Press, London.

Ikle, F.   (1964).   *How nations negotiate*.   Harper & Row, New
York.

Liebes, R.   (1958).   Contributions of mediation to the development of mature collective bargaining.   *Labor Law Journal*,
9. 797-800.

Meyer, A.S.   (1960).   Functions of the mediator in collective
bargaining.   *Industrial and Labor Relations Review*, 13, 159-6.

Moore, S.F.   (1969).   Law and anthropology.   *In* Siegel, B.J.
(ed.):   *Biennial review of anthropology*.   Stanford University
Press, Stanford, California.

Muench, G.A.A. (1963). A clinical psychologist's treatment of labor-management disputes. *Journal of Humanistic Psychology*, 3, 92-7.

Paine, R. (1971). A theory of patronage and brokerage. *In* Paine, R. (ed.) *Patronage and brokerage in the East Arctic.* Memorial University, Newfoundland, Institute of Social and Economic Research.

Pospisil, L. (1971). *Anthropology of law.* Harper & Row, New York.

Rehmus, C.M. (1965). The mediation of industrial conflict. *Journal of Conflict Resolution*, 9, 118-26.

Schelling, T. (1963). *The strategy of conflict.* Oxford University Press, New York.

Schmidt, C.C. (1952). Mediation in Sweden. *In* Jackson, E.: *Meeting of minds, a way to peace through mediation.* McGraw Hill, New York.

Schwarz, R.D. and J.C. Miller (1964). Legal evolution and societal complexity. *American Journal of Sociology*, 70, 159-69.

Simkin, W.E. (1971). *Mediation and the dynamics of collective bargaining.* Bureau of National Affairs, Washington, D.C.

Swarz, M.J., V.W. Turner and A. Tuden. (1966). *Political anthropology.* Aldine, Chicago.

Walton, R.E.   (1969).   *Interpersonal peacemaking: confrontation and third party consultation.*   Addison-Wesley, Reading, Mass.

Walton, R.E. and R.B. McKersie.   (1965).   *A behavioral theory of labor negotiations.*   McGraw Hill, New York.

Young, O.   (1967).   *The intermediaries: third parties in international crises.*   Princeton University Press, Princeton, N.J.

Young, O.   (1972).   Intermediaries: additional thoughts on third parties.   *Journal of Conflict Resolution,* 16, 51-65.

ADMINISTRATION AND THE SUPREMACY OF LAW

IN COLONIAL BUSOGA

L. A. Fallerɜ

The general theme of this symposium — "Social Anthropology
and Law" — invites at least two different interpretations:
shall we mean by it a social anthropological perspective on law
as a sociocultural phenomenon or do we envisage a dialogue between two disciplines: social anthropology and jurisprudence?
Inevitably, I should think, both will be involved (certainly
they will be in this paper), as they usually are in such discussion, and for good reason: While we wish to bring social anthropological methods of research and analysis to bear upon "legal
institutions", we usually find ourselves, in this process,
making use, implicitly or explicitly, of ideas about the nature
of law drawn from Western jurisprudence. Some social anthropologists have regarded this tendency with suspicion as a source
of ethnocentrism and a bookish distraction from direct observation — from the craft of fieldwork that is social anthropology's
peculiar glory. But we delude ourselves, I suggest, if we think
we can leap out of history and achieve a culturally neutral
perspective. What we *can* do is to recognize that every social
anthropological enterprise is inherently comparative — an encounter between the familiar and the exotic — between that which
we take for granted in our own intellectual equipment, drawn from
our upbringing and education in our own society — plus, of
course, our previous research experience — and that which we
seek to understand in another society, with respect to which we
know we must take as little as possible for granted. While we
cannot avoid this encounter, we can make it explicit and bring
it under intellectual discipline, as we regularly do, I think,
while seeking to understand, say, a kinship system which is
exotic to us.

In the case of law (and not only there) the situation is complicated by the fact that the Western tradition, unlike some others, has made a great deal of the idea, and practice, of law. We have erected not only complex institutions for its applicatic but also specialized systems of training in the subject and a voluminous and venerable body of intellectual reflection upon it — the literature of jurisprudence. To make matters still more complex, legal historians and comparative lawyers — persons trained in the practice of common law or civil law but possessing a wide-ranging curiosity, often stimulated by their countries' colonial or imperial encounters with non-Western peoples, have contributed powerfully to the development of comparative sociology. A long line of legal scholars, from Savigny to Llewellyn, have brought the perspective of jurisprudence to bear upon non-Western or early Western societies (1). There is, therefore, a good deal of legal thinking not only in our own general sociocultural milieu but also in our stock of more specialized social anthropological ideas. Maine, in his famous statement about the direction of development in "progres‹ sive societies" bequeathed to us a distinction based upon that between the law of tort and that of contract, and such conceptions as rights *in personam* and *in rem* and of corporations "sole" and "aggregate" have been adopted into our vocabulary (Maine 1861). More broadly, the term "jural", in the sense of consensual norms backed by sanctions, has for some among us become a central concept (one is tempted to say *the* central concept) in comparative sociological analysis.

But while our social anthropology is thus predisposed toward a concern with matters "legal", it has not always been clear about what this concern entails. The "social anthropology of law" is a very mixed bag. In particular, much of it is concerned with "social control" — a much broader notion than that of "law" as traditionally used by lawyers and legal scholars. I, myself, prefer to work with a narrower conception of law as the legal or legalistic *mode* of social control — a conception

(1) Editor's note: F.C. von Savigny (1779-1861) is regarded as the leading figure in the nineteenth-century German school of "historical jurisprudence" (Savigny 1831, 1867). For a discussion see Friedmann 1967:209 ff. The principal writin₰ of the American "realist", Kurt N. Llewellyn (1893-1962), are contained in Llewellyn 1962. Social anthropologists wil recognise him as co-author, with E.A. Hoebel, of *The Cheyenr Way* (Llewellyn and Hoebel 1941).

closer to that of jurisprudence. While not universally applicable, because law in this sense is not found in all societies,
it is, I think, of sufficient generality to pose a range of
important and interesting comparative problems.

What, then, is the specifically legal mode of social control?
From those who may be familiar with my earlier study of the
"customary" law of land tenure and marriage in the customary
courts of colonial Busoga (Uganda), I ask indulgence for briefly
recapitulating its argument here (Fallers 1969). No doubt
because of its density and lack of clarity, the book has not been
widely-read or well-understood, but I nevertheless want to use
some of the ideas contained in it as a point of departure for
discussing, again in terms of data from Busoga, a problem which
I touched upon only lightly in the book: the problem of administration and the supremacy of law. This problem is generally
thought of as a modern one in common law countries — a result
of the recent expansion of state activity and regulation — but
in a somewhat different form it existed earlier — prior to the
constitutional developments of the seventeenth century — in the
shape of a tension between "royal prerogative" and "the common
law of the realm". To put the matter concretely: could the
King's officers be held accountable in the common courts for the
legality of acts carried out in the course of their duties?
Today, of course, royal prerogative has been replaced by parlia-
mentary supremacy in Britain and by the theory of a tripartite
division and balance of powers in the United States and, while
constitutional differences give the problem somewhat different
institutional expressions in the two countries, it has in both
cases come, with democratization, to be seen as one of a tension
between "private rights" and "public interest". It has, further,
with the increasing differentiation of government, become
increasingly difficult to identify administration and adjudication respectively with particular branches of government.
"Administrative agencies" "adjudicate" while "courts" engage in
a good deal of "administration" (2). The point to be noted here
is the familiar sociological one that "adjudication", "legislation" and "administration" are best regarded as analytical categories, not concrete ones.

But to return to my recapitulation: the notion of the "rule"
(or "supremacy") of law presupposes a conception of the legal,

---

(2) Legislatures, to round off the statement, adjudicate and
    administer, while courts and administrative agencies make
    law.

and in my earlier work I made use of that developed by H.L.A.
Hart (Hart 1961:77-96). For Hart, law is pre-eminently a matter
of *rules* — rules which forbid certain acts and render others
obligatory. He further distinguishes between primary and secondary rules, the union of which is, for him, the hallmark of
law. Primary legal rules are those distinguished from the wider
universe of moral norms by their union with secondary rules of
recognition, adjudication and change. These secondary rules
first distinguish those norms which will be treated legally;
second, provide for means by which it may be determined whether
a rule has been violated in particular cases; and third, provide
for means by which rules may be changed. In my study I argued
that in the Soga courts all these kinds of rules were made use
of, though in a generally implicit or tacit manner. Though rule
were seldom explicitly stated as such, close analysis of the
arguments of litigants and the decisions of judges revealed a
coherent body of rules. Although arguments and decisions were
fully and carefully recorded in writing by court clerks, precedents were never explicitly drawn upon and such statutory laws
as the courts were empowered to administer were almost never
explicitly referred to.

I also found helpful Edward H. Levi's notion of "categorizing
concepts" as tools for legal reasoning (Levi, 1948). Common law
lawyers and judges, he suggests, make use of such concepts in
ordering their thought and discourse about rules; such concepts
("murder", "negligence", malfeasance", etc), by narrowing and
structuring the matters in dispute, frame causes of action, and
their "satellite concepts" enable lawyers and judges to argue in
an orderly way about whether or not a given set of facts falls
within the reach of a particular categorizing concept (3). I
found that Basoga judges and litigants reasoned in a similar way
although again their reasoning was generally quite implicit,
except at one point in the legal process: The Soga courts, like
common law ones, operated with a finite set of causes of action
which were made explicit in the acceptance of cases for trial.
To be placed on the docket, a cause had to be framed in terms of
one of the recognized categories, however implausible the plaintiff's case might turn out to be, and the court clerks recorded

---

(3) I somewhat modified Levi's terminology to suit my material:
    I used "concepts of wrong" and "concepts of applicability"
    and "credibility".

cases in terms of these categories (4).

Soga law was, however, less "legalistic" than Anglo-American
law in a number of respects: courts were permissive with respect
to the acceptance of both causes for adjudication and grounds for
appeal: while a cause had to be framed in terms of one of the
accepted categories, if a litigant insisted, he could get his
cause onto the docket and argue it, even though the "facts"
upon which he depended might be quite implausibly related to the
category. And grounds of appeal were simply not scrutinized; the
trial court record would be forwarded on request to the appellate court, where it would be read out in full and the appellant
invited to proceed essentially *de novo*, unless he chose to rest
on his testimony in the trial court. Finally, although case
records were used to establish previous court findings, which
were treated as authoritative, there was no systematic reporting
and communication of appellate decisions, so that there could be
no general *stare decisis* rule (5). All these mitigations of

---

(4) Editor's note: For the "causes of action" of English common
    law, see the classic study by F.W. Maitland (Maitland 1909).
    The principle of acknowledging certain limited categories
    into which cases for decision are classified and inserted is
    even more clearly seen in the earlier period of the formulary
    system in ancient Rome (Jolowicz 1939:205-242). The purpose
    of such forms was not primarily to thwart litigants or deny
    them a remedy so much as to determine the assumptions and
    implied terms that the law imported into particular kinds of
    agreement and legal relationships. The "type contracts" of
    Roman law, for example, did not seek to exclude agreements
    from enforceability but rather aimed to determine whether a
    given agreement was to be construed as a contract of sale,
    a contract of hire, etc. This would determine the mutual
    rights and obligations of the parties. (See Buckland and
    McNair 1952:265-270).
       In other words, in Levi's terms (Levi 1948), the object
    of all such "forms" and "types" is not to exclude disputes
    from judicial decision but instead to specify which "categor-
    ising concept" applies to the matter in hand. The category
    into which it falls may have a bearing on the view that the
    court takes of the rights and wrongs of the matter as well as
    on the remedy supplied.

(5) In this sense, the Soga legal system was, in Hart's terms,
    "defective".

legalism were related to the popular nature of the courts: the
bench consisted of appointed chiefs and elected laymen, none of
whom possessed formal legal training, and lawyers were not
admitted; although judges knew more law than ordinary folk and
although a certain amount of legal advice was given informally
by the more sophisticated to the more naive, each litigant was
assumed to be fit to argue his own case. And indeed, rhetorical
skill was widespread; Basoga generally enjoyed and admired the
litigious process, in which litigants argued with the bench and
with each other. Soga courts were popular in this sense as well
— popular places in which to loiter while enjoying the contest.
Finally, they were the most popular means of dealing with human
conflict. Where some other peoples might resort to magic or
violence, Basoga, it seemed to me, preferred the law.

To complete my recapitulation: The study included a
Weberian sociocultural analysis of the Soga legal institution.
I argued that this institution could be more legalistic than
those of most African societies because the judges possessed
greater authority. The chairman of each bench and one-half of
its members were bureaucrat-chiefs, salaried civil servants of
the Busoga African Local Government, whose authority rested
upon appointment from above more than upon consent from below.
(An outline of the court system is shown in Appendix A). They
formed, it seemed to me, a structurally-differentiated group
with a sub-culture of its own, which included a sense of cohesion and vocation and a generally greater knowledge of the law.
These qualities, I suggested, were related to the greater
legalism of the Soga legal sub-culture — the *corpus juris* —
and its application.

I reasoned that the moral over-simplification involved in the
legalistic mode of social control creates a tension between law
and general morality. Most situations of inter-personal conflict, looked at holistically, are complex. By the time they
reach court, all parties have done things that are, in everyday
terms, immoral, but the categorizing concepts that make up a
legalistic sub-culture — that frame causes of action and requir
decisions in terms of inclusion or exclusion ("guilty" or "not
guilty"; "liable" or "not liable") — must, in order to achieve
their rule-like quality, deal with only a narrow segment of the
full moral reality of a situation. Of course the plaintiff in
one case might be the defendant in another litigation between
the same parties, but the two causes must be kept separate. A's
allowing his cattle to trample B's crops is not excused by B's
having previously defaulted on a debt to A; rather, these are,

in legalistic terms, two distinct events, founding two separate
causes of action.

In short, the Soga legal institution, like other relatively
legalistic ones, places greater stress upon "applying the law"
than upon "settling the trouble" and this, I argued in my study,
requires a relatively authoritative bench to overcome the everyday moral desire to see simultaneous justice done to all parties
involved in a dispute (6).

But to return, now, to my principal concern in this paper,
the problem of administration and the rule of law: Administration and adjudication, as I have noted, while analytically dis-
tinguishable, are often not concretely differentiated: that is,
they may not be institutionalized in distinct social structures.
In colonial Busoga they were in part fused in the hierarchy of
civil servant-chiefs. These chiefs were not only judges but also
administrators, the lower rungs in the hierarchy extending upward
through the district and provincial commissioners to the Governor
of the Protectorate; and, like their British superiors, they
possessed the authority, under colonial legislation, not only to
decide, along with elected members of the bench, on the appli-
cability of law to particular sets of facts as found, but also, in
their administrative capacities, to issue orders having the force
of law, disobedience to which constituted the offence of
butawulira ("failure to listen"). This discretionary authority
was, to be sure, subject to statutory restraint, but it remained
far broader than anything to be found, at least under peacetime
conditions, in present-day common law jurisdictions (See
Appendix B). Thus the chiefs, *both* as judges and as administrators, possessed great authority.

But the fact that two institutional structures — in this case
the judicial and the administrative — were manned by the same
persons does not mean that there was no differentiation between
them. Persons are perfectly capable of playing different rules
in different structures; Basoga themselves recognized a distinction between the commanding demeanor appropriate to "giving
orders" (*kulagira*) and the much more inquiring attitude proper
to the adjudication of cases in court (*kusala emisango*).
Actually, the chief worked with at least a partially different

---

(6) Editor's note: The question of why some legal systems stress
    "applying the law" and others "settling the trouble" is dis-
    cussed in Kuper 1971. This paper includes specific consider-
    ation of *Law without Precedent*.

set of people in the two spheres. As a judge, he was *primus
inter pares*, chairman of a bench half of whose other members we₁
elected; while as administrator he worked with his superiors an₁
subordinates in the administrative chain of command. This partial differentiation of personnel aside, however, the *conceptua₁*
differentiation in Soga culture was clear and it underlies the
phenomenon with which I shall be principally concerned in the
remainder of this paper: *the degree to which administrative
acts were subject to judicial review in the ordinary courts.*
If chiefs acted as both judges and administrators, they not
infrequently had occasion, *as judges*, to consider the legality
of each others' acts as administrators.

Since I have been pursuing a comparison between Soga institutions and ideas and our own, I perhaps ought to insert here a
word concerning the manner in which this problem presents itsel₁
in Anglo-American legal thought. I have already mentioned that
during the middle, or Whig, period — between the constitutiona₁
settlement of 1688 and the late nineteenth century — the dominant tendency was in the direction of judicial supremacy over
administrative organs. The King's Bench was seen as the guaran-
tor of liberty, under the common law, against royal usurpation,
and this view was reinforced by suspicion of developments on the
continent, where "administrative law" received separate institu-
tionalization in "administrative courts". To greatly over-
simplify, on the continent the expanding bureaucracies characte₁
istic of modern life were brought under the "rule of law" throug
the development of separate administrative jurisdictions, while
in common law countries they have remained much more under the
scrutiny of the ordinary courts through "judicial review" of
their acts, although as the administrative structures have becom
more complex they have tended to acquire final jurisdiction over
increasingly broader areas on a piecemeal basis (Dicey, 1948;
Dickenson, 1927; [Shapiro, 1965,] Smith, 1927).

Understandably, then, the governmental arrangements established by the British in their colonial territories did not provide for separate administrative jurisdiction, as did the
French (7); nor, on the other hand, did they leave the powerful
colonial bureaucracy, with its broad order-issuing authority, to
police itself. Rather, British over-rule, at any rate in its
Uganda manifestation, established or supported (I shall consider
below the evidence for the existence of convergent views and

---

(7) Naval Intelligence Division, Geographical Handbook Series.
French West Africa, Vol. 1, 1943, pp. 261-270.

practices in pre-colonial Busoga) judicial review of administrative acts by the ordinary courts. The Soga "customary" courts in the colonial period regularly adjudicated cases in which chiefs or headmen were charged with malfeasance or dereliction of duty by their superiors or members of the public; they also heard cases arising out of alleged disobedience to lawful orders issued by chiefs, especially to their subordinate chiefs and headmen. Administrative disciplinary action might well follow upon conviction — transfer or dismissal, for example — but first the guilt of the accused had to be established by adjudication in the common courts.

A few cases will provide some idea of the manner in which the courts handled such matters.

A simple, and rather petty, example of dereliction of duty is found in *Court v. Erukana Kiriba* (41/1951/Sub-county Ssaabawaali, Kigulu). Kiriba, the deputy subcounty chief, is accused of "...paying Asumani Waibi (who had been employed by the African Local Government to repair a public road) for a day on which he did not finish his work, in contravention of the subcounty chief's orders".

Kiriba begins with a brace defence:

I shall contest this case, and I know that I will win, because since the chief ordered me not to pay (such workers), I cancelled it (Asumani's pay for that day) in the muster roll. I didn't cancel it on his ticket because another worker had it. Whenever the subcounty chief orders me to do something, I do it. Especially in matters concerning workers. I told the man myself that, under the chief's orders, I would not pay him for a day when he did not finish.

The court, however, finds this reply to the charge unsatisfactory:

Q: Haven't you seen that worker since 27 February, so that you could cancel that day on his ticket?

A: I saw him, but he didn't have his ticket until March 1, when I took it from him.

Q: Why did you enter him on the muster roll for March if he hadn't finished his work in February? .. If he hadn't brought his ticket to have that day cancelled?

A: I didn't understand that it would be wrong.

Q: Don't you remember that you were given an order not to employ any porter who fails to bring his ticket to you to get it signed?

A: I was given that order and I ordered them to bring their tickets but the workers refused to bring them. My master (the subcounty chief) has seen me scolding them about it.

Q: If you knew that Asumani was one of the people who disobeyed your orders, why did you agree to employ him again?

A: I wasn't careful about that.

Q: If their monthly pay had been brought while you were away, how would the clerk in charge of paying them know the right thing to do? The muster roll would not agree with the ticket.

A: He wouldn't have known.

Q: Now do you agree that you made a mistake in not cancelling that ticket?

A: I agree that I made a mistake ...

The Court quickly arrives at a decision:

> The accused, E. Kiriba, has lost the case. Although at first he did not believe it would go against him, he now agrees that he was mistaken in not being careful. He has been fined 3/-, or seven days imprisonment if he fails to pay He has thirty days in which to appeal.

From *Court v. E. Kiriba* we learn little more about judicial review of administrative acts than that it exists. The alleged offence here is so obvious, so trivial and so plainly the result of shiftlessness rather than evil intent that the proceedings consist of little more than a swift extraction of an admission of fault and a stern lecture by the bench. Such petty cases, however, make up the bulk of the litigation of this sort and they serve their purpose, which is to maintain discipline within the African Local Government service.

A more complex case and one which reveals a good deal more

about the interaction between judicial and administrative action
is *Wilibafosi Mukuma and six others v. Safani Muyanga* (10/1950/
Bulamogi County). This is a much more serious case, in which
seven residents of the parish of which S. Muyanga is chief
allege that after collecting their annual poll tax he failed to
issue tax receipts to them — proof of their having paid. The
total amounts to 207/-, a substantial sum. The subcounty court,
under the chairmanship of the subcounty chief, holds an initial
hearing. But the latter, instead of allowing the subcounty
court to adjudicate the case, instead forwards the record of the
hearing to the county court, with a covering letter in which he
asserts, *inter alia*, that he himself "has already investigated
the case" and believes the accused to have "stolen" the 207/-.
Before considering the hearing at the subcounty court, however,
it is necessary to add a word about the lower levels of the
governmental hierarchy.

As Appendix A indicates, the parish chief is the connecting
link between the subcounty chief and the village and sub-village
headmen. Administratively, he is the lowest rung on the African
Local Government ladder. He draws a small salary and serves on
civil service terms, being subject to administrative transfer and
dismissal. However, he chairs no court of record. The lowest
such court is that of the subcounty chief. The village and sub-
village headmen, who hold office by hereditary succession and
are remunerated by fees from land allotments, are not civil servants but nevertheless assist the parish chief in his administrative duties, including tax collection. Parish chiefs and village
and subvillage headmen chair tribunals with informal memberships
which attempt to settle disputes before they reach the official
courts of record which begin at the subcounty level. The upshot
of these arrangements (their history is explained in *Law Without
Precedent*) is that the parish chief is dependent for assistance
in carrying out his duties upon locally-rooted men -- he himself
may well come from some distance away — who know far more about
the parish and over whom he has little control. In the present
case, the accused parish chief, S. Muyanga, is clearly both over-
burdened with work and poorly served by his headmen, a kinship-
interrelated group who seem united against the "outsider".

At the initial hearing at the subcounty court, only one of the
seven accusers claims to have given his tax money directly to the
parish chief; the remaining six claim to have paid theirs to village or subvillage headmen. The headmen all claim to have paid
the money over, in turn, to the parish chief. When the latter is
questioned, in turn, about each man's tax, he disagrees with some

of the dates on which he is alleged to have been given money,
but he acknowledges the sums involved and says that he still has
all the money in his possession. It is at this point that the
subcounty chief, satisfied that there has been peculation,
breaks off the hearing and sends the case to the county court.

He has, perhaps, acted rather hastily, since only two weeks
appear to have elapsed between earliest alleged tax payment and
the hearing, but of course one man's haste may be another's
deliberation. And in any event, alleged misappropriation of
tax funds was taken very seriously by the African Local Government authorities and was readily referred to the county courts.

At the county court, then, the record of the subcounty court
hearing is read out and the accused parish chief, S. Muyanga,
is invited to add to his pleading:

Q: Do you accept what has been read as what you said at the
subcounty court?

A: It is what I said.

Q: Have you anything more to add?

A: Yes, I want to add this: The reason I delayed taking
those people's money to the subcounty headquarters to get
their tax receipts was because I was going around telling
people to uproot their dried cotton plants. (The plants
must be uprooted and burned each year to prevent the spread
of blight). I was with the subcounty chief's messenger.
I had a letter from the subcounty chief saying that he
would be in my parish March 20-21 to make sure there were
no remaining cotton plants. I didn't have time to collect
all the tax at once. I just did it as I was making my
rounds (looking for cotton plants).

In other words, the unfortunate man was being run to death by
his superior, and getting a pittance for it in the way of
salary: they then had the gall to lay a charge against him
for being a few days late.

The bench sympathizes:

Q: Did the subcounty chief come to you with the names of
those complainants or did you raise the matter with him?

A: At first Wilibafosi Mukama and Mikulosi Kige took their complaint to the subcounty chief and then when he came to my parish he had five more names.

Q: Did you accept the names of those five people? (i.e. did you accept responsibility for their having paid?).

A: I accepted them and I have their money now.

Q: Do you have evidence for the dates on which they paid?

A: I have my register in which I entered the dates and I showed it to the subcounty chief .... I also brought the register to the tax clerk to have him examine it.

One of the headmen is called to testify, and under questioning by the parish chief admits that he had not turned over his people's taxes as soon as he had claimed at the initial hearing.

The court has heard enough:

> The accused, S. Muyanga, parish chief of Mutuba II, is acquitted of the charge of stealing tax money. He accepts that he was given tax money for those men and when the sub-county chief visited the parish he found that he (the parish chief) had the money .... The parish chief delayed in taking the money to the subcounty headquarters because he was busy with cotton plants. For these reasons, the county court believes that the parish chief didn't intend to take the money for himself....

With this decision, the judicial phase of the case ends. But the county chief, who has chaired the bench, now initiates administrative action. The accused has been ill-used by his superior, and so the county chief writes to the district commissioner:

> The case of a parish chief accused of stealing tax money has been heard today, April 13, 1950 in the county court. S. Muyanga is free .... he delayed turning in the money because he was busy with cotton plants. The subcounty chief didn't bother to consult the parish chief about the complaints against him, but when he visited the parish to see about cotton plants and tax matters, and when he asked about the money, amounting to 207/-, the parish chief acknowledged having the money. He has handed it over and has received

receipts for his people.... The parish chief is acquitted
in part because the subcounty chief wasn't careful (was
hasty). The accused may return to his parish, but should
there be a vacant parish he should be transferred, as he
is no longer on good terms with the subcounty chief. The
same subcounty chief has been responsible for the dismissal
of another parish chief without sufficient reason.

Whether or not the county chief's recommendation was followed
I do not know, since I left the area shortly afterward, but my
guess is that it was. He was an experienced senior chief of
princely lineage who combined a fine sense for bureaucratic
politics with an ability to orchestrate his administrative with
his judicial role. The subcounty chief, on the other hand, was
a petty tyrant who, by too-hastily invoking his administrative
role, denied his wretched underling due process at the initial
hearing. Of course, had he allowed the case to be adjudicated
in his own court, and had he persuaded the rest of his bench to
convict, the parish chief might still have sought relief on
appeal to the county court. To S. Muyanga, the parish chief,
due process in the appeal court was vital; beset by a cabal of
headmen on the one hand and by an unsympathetic superior on the
other, he desperately needed a forum in which to argue that he
had not delayed unduly in turning in the tax money. Adjudication
at the appeal court, of course, could only provide partial
relief. It could free him of the charge of peculation, but it
could not relieve his untenable position in the parish. That
could only be accomplished by administrative action — his
transfer.

We may consider, finally, a case of alleged mistreatment of a
woman prisoner by a deputy county chief (32/1950/bulamogi
County). The situation is this: The woman, Sesiriya Kasana,
had run away from her husband, Piyo Magala, five years earlier
but now had been caught living with another man, Mukama Gaduma.
When the village chief and constable, acting on Piyo's information, came, however, Gaduma had escaped. Sesiriya had then been
taken into custody and held for two weeks in the county remand
prison until Mukama could be found and tried for adultery.
Sesiriya had been charged with no offence because in Soga law
women are not held legally responsible for adultery, though they
are held morally responsible. She had been held, so to speak,
as an "exhibit" — an object of theft. When it proved impossible
to locate Mukama Gaduma, her lover, the sub-county court had
turned her over to her husband, Piyo.

Sesiriya, however, is a spirited woman and so, instead of going along submissively with her husband, whom she loathes, she charges the deputy chief, the official in charge of the prison, with mistreating her during her confinement:

> He refused to give me my box of clothes, in spite of the fact that I had been brought in naked. He also refused to take me before the sub county chief so that I could demand my clothes.

Sesiriya is engaging in a bit of hyperbole here; under questioning she admits that she had a bark-cloth and underwear while in prison, but says that these were insufficient to protect her from the cold.

The Deputy county chief defends his conduct:

> I believe I shall win the case. Those clothes had been entered in the Remand Register. I was not entitled to give her the clothes until the case had been decided in the subcounty court. When she was arrested she denied that she was the owner of the clothes — so I refused to give them to her until I was able to turn over both the woman and the clothes to the court — At the end of the case both the woman and her clothes were handed over to her husband, Piyo.

Q: Did she ask for the clothes before or after they had been entered in the Remand Register?

A: She asked for them after they had been entered.

Q: Is it the law that if a prisoner has her clothes elsewhere and has nothing to put on she can not be given the clothes?

A: It is the law. Once entered in the Remand Register, they are not returned until the case is decided.

Q: Were those clothes under suspicion (as stolen property)?

A: I didn't know. I only knew they were brought in by her husband, Piyo, when she was arrested.

He adds that Sesirya did not even ask for her clothes until the day before the case was decided in sub-county court.

This she vigorously denies and adds, in order to indicate
that the clothes in question had not been supplied by her husband, that she had been away from him for five years and had
"by that time obtained my own clothes".

Finally, the husband, Piyo Magala, is called. He testifies
that the sub-county court has "given him his wife, together
with a box containing 23 garments — three male and nineteen
female". This tells heavily against Sesiriya, since the "male
garments" can only be those of her lover. So the court, chairec
by a county chief who is a traditionalist in these matters, finc
her complaint to lack merit:

> —— She lacks evidence to show that she was suffering
> from the cold —— The Deputy County Chief took her, together
> with the box of clothes, to the sub-county court (which)
> handed them over to her husband —— Therefore, the accused
> is not guilty.

One may well sympathize with the woman, Sesiriya. She had
undoubtedly suffered humiliation, if not cold, since a piece
of bark cloth is not considered respectable clothing in
present-day Busoga. The deputy county chief might well have
tempered the rules with a bit of kindness, but Soga morality
is not kind to adulteresses and so he is upheld in his application of the letter of the rules regarding prisoners and their
property. By Soga standards she has enjoyed full judicial
review of her case against a rather senior civil servant.

To what degree was this pattern of relations between administration and adjudication, as I observed it in the early nineteen
fifties, a product of sixty years of British colonial super-
vision and to what degree was it indigenous? In *Law Without
Precedent*, I made no real effort to reconstruct precolonial Soga
law, preferring instead to deal with Soga law as I could observe
it in action at the time of my fieldwork. It seemed, and still
seems to me, impossible, with the data available, to separate ou
with any precision the various strands which history has woven
into Soga "customary law", and in any case contemporary material
were vastly more abundant and their analysis more rewarding.
Still, the question is an intriguing one and I shall hazard a
guess, based upon the evidence I have been able to turn up.

My guess is that the "supremacy of law", as Basoga practiced
it in the nineteen-fifties, represented a convergence of common
law tradition, imported by British administrators, with

indigenous Soga legal tradition. Elderly informants, describing to me the procedures of the tribunals held at all levels in pre-colonial Busoga, said that a chief's administrative acts might be challenged before his superior. Furthermore, a chief was even held personally responsible for the legality of his tribunal's judicial acts. For neighbouring Buganda, whose governmental institutions those of the Soga states closely resembled, we have the following account (referring to precolonial practice):

> But if the unsuccessful party to the action was not satisfied with the decision, he would not pay the debt or court charges, but instead would go to the next higher chief having authority over the chief who had decided against him and complain as follows: "Such and such a chief has badly decided my case and I complain against him (Kagwa 1905:238).

The trial judge thus became the defendant on appeal!

On the British side, the situation was made clear by a provincial commissioner's complaint in 1919:

> The knowledge that came to the natives through the issue of circular No. 1 of 1919 of the High Court that there were more limitations to the powers of district commissioners than the natives had imagined has had a serious effect on the native mind and, as he has seen that the district commissioners have been unwilling to carry out administrative punishments for offenses that do not come within the letter of the law, a decidedly retrograde tendency in administration has resulted (8).

Whatever their other differences, the British and the Basoga appear to have shared a Whig view of "the supremacy of law".

---

(8) *Report of the Provincial Commissioner, Eastern Province, for the Year Ended 31 March 1919.* Central Offices, Jinja.

APPENDIX A

	JUDICIAL SYSTEM		ADMINISTRATIVE SYSTEM
National Court System	High Court		Governor
	District Commissioner as Magistrate (appeal)	Magistrate's Court (first instance)	Provincial Commissioner District Commissioner
Soga Court System	District Court		Kyebazinga (President)
	County Courts		County Chiefs
	Subcounty Courts		Subcounty Chiefs
Subordinate Tribunals	Parish Tribunals	Clan and Lineage Tribunals (Inheritance)	Parish Chiefs
	Village Tribunals		Village Headmen
	Subvillage Tribunals		Subvillage Headmen

APPENDIX B

Extract from the African Authority Ordinance (1919)

(as amended)

Power of chiefs to issue orders for certain purposes	7. Subject to the provisions of any law for the time being in force in the Protectorate, any chief may from time to time issue orders to be obeyed by the Africans residing within the local limits of his jurisdiction as follows —

A. Any order which such chief may issue by virtue of any native law or custom in force for the time being in his area:

Provided that such law or custom is not repugnant to morality or justice.

3 of 1942, s. 2.	B. Any order for any of the following purposes —

(1) restricting and regulating the manufacture, distillation, possession, sale or supply of any native intoxicating liquor and, in addition thereto, prohibiting any person from manufacturing, distilling, selling or supplying any such liquor except in pursuance of a permit issued subject to such conditions and on payment of such fees as the provincial commissioner may from time to time approve;

(2) prohibiting or restricting the holding of drinking bouts;

(3) prohibiting or restricting the cultivation of poisonous or noxious plants, and the manufacture of noxious drugs or poisons;

(4) prohibiting or restricting the carrying of arms;

(5) prohibiting any act or conduct which
in the opinion of the chief might cause a
riot or a disturbance or a breach of the
peace;

(6) preventing the pollution of the wate
in any stream, water course, or water hole,
and preventing the obstruction of any strea
or water course;

(7) regulating the cutting to timber and
prohibiting the wasteful destruction of tre

(8) requiring male Africans between the
ages of eighteen and forty-five years, who
are physically fit, to work in the making
or maintaining of any work of a public natu
constructed or to be constructed or maintai
for the benefit of the community;

Provided that no person shall be ordered
or required to work as aforesaid for more t
thirty days in any one year:

And provided that the Governor may by
directions —

(1) exempt any person or class or
persons from such obligation; or

(2) authorise the commutation of such
obligation in any district of the
Protectorate in such manner as may
seem to him desirable;

(9)   (a)   the provision of paid porters
for Government officials on duty and for th
urgent transport of Government stores;

(b) the provision of paid labour for the following public purposes ⸺

(1) building of railways

(2) making or repairing of bridges and telegraphs;

(3) building or repairing of public buildings;

(4) services necessary for the maintenance of public health;

Provided that in the case of (b) the previous sanction of the Secretary of State has been obtained, which authority shall only be sought for a specific work for a specific period:

And provided further that no person shall be required to work under the provisions of this subsection ⸺

(a) for a longer period than sixty days in any one year;

(b) if he be fully employed in any other occupation or has been so employed during the preceding twelve months for a period of three months; employment under paragraph (8) hereof being reckoned towards such period;

(c) if he be otherwise exempted under the provisions of any directions issued by the Governor;

(10) preventing the evasion of any tax or legal duty;

(11) regulating the movement of Africans from the jurisdiction of one chief to that of another;

(12) preventing the spread of infectious disease, whether of human beings or animals, and for the care of the sick;

(13) requiring any African subject to his jurisdiction to report the presence within the local limits of his jurisdiction of any property stolen or believed to have been stolen outside such local limits;

(14) the provision of food for sale to safaris;

(15) preventing the eviction of Africans without good cause from land occupied by them; and

(16) for any other purpose which the Governor may by rule authorise.

Cap.74   C.   Any order which such chief is legally competent to issue by virtue of any Ordinance or by virtue of any bye-law made by a District Council established under the African Local Governments Ordinance.

REFERENCES

Buckland, W.W. and A.D. McNair. (1952). *Roman Law and Common Law* (Second edition revised by F.H. Lawson). Cambridge University Press, Cambridge.

Dicey, A.V. (1948). *Introduction to the Law of the Constitution* (Ninth edition with an introduction and appendix by E.C.S. Wade). Macmillan, London.

Dickenson, J. (1927). *Administrative Justice and the Supremacy of Law in the United States*. Russell and Russell, New York.

Fallers, L.A. (1969). *Law without Precedent: Legal Ideas in Action in the Courts of Colonial Busoga*. Chicago University Press, Chicago.

Friedmann, W. (1967). *Legal Theory* (5th edition). Stevens and Sons, London.

Hart, H.L.A. (1961). *The Concept of Law*. Oxford University Press, London.

Jolowicz, H.F. (1939). *Historical Introduction to the Study of Roman Law*. Cambridge University Press, Cambridge.

Kagwa, Sir A. (1905). *Ekitabo Kye Mpisa Za Baganda* (Customs of the Baganda). Macmillan, London.

Kuper, A. (1971). "Council structure and decision making". *In* A. Richards and A. Kuper (eds.), *Councils in Action*. Cambridge University Press, Cambridge, 1971 (Cambridge Studies in Social Anthropology No. 6) pp. 13–28.

Levi, E.H. (1948). *An Introduction to Legal Reasoning*. Chicago University Press, Chicago.

Llewellyn, K.N. (1962). *Jurisprudence: Realism in Theory and Practice*. Chicago University Press, Chicago.

Llewellyn, K.N. and E.A. Hoebel. (1941). *The Cheyenne Way: Conflict and case law in primitive jurisprudence*. University of Oklahoma Press, Norman.

Maine, Sir H. (1861). *Ancient Law*. Reprinted in World's Classics edition, 1931 etc. Oxford University Press, London.

Maitland, F.W. (1909). *The Forms of Action at Common Law*. Cambridge University Press, Cambridge.

Savigny, F.C. von. (1931). *On the Vocation of our Age for Legislation and Jurisprudence* (English translation by A. Hayward; German original first published 1814).

Savigny, F.C. von. (1867). *System of the Modern Roman Law* (English translation by W. Holloway of first part of German original published from 1840 to 1851).

Shapiro, D.L. (1965). "The choice of rule making or adjudication in the development of administrative policy". *Harvard Law Review 78*, pp. 921 ff.

Smith, S.A. de. (1973). *Judicial Review of Administrative Action*. Stevens and Sons, London.

THE INVOCATION OF NORMS IN DISPUTE SETTLEMENT:

THE TSWANA CASE (1)

John Comaroff and Simon Roberts

I

Gluckman (1955, 2nd ed. 1967, pp. 95, 411) and Krige (1939,
pp. 114-5), both anthropologists with some legal background,
have noted their lack of success in predicting the course and
outcome of dispute settlement processes among the Lozi and
Lovedu respectively. This proved reassuring when, during the
early stages of fieldwork, we encountered great difficulties
in comprehending the logic of similar procedures among the
Tswana. Most perplexing, perhaps, was the extent to which
stated norms, of which it is possible to elicit detailed inven-
tories from Tswana informants (see for example, Schapera, 1938;
Roberts 1972), influenced the actions and decisions of participants (2). In some disputes such norms were expressly employed

---

(1) Comaroff conducted fieldwork among the Barolong boo Ratshidi
(or Tshidi) a southern Tswana people, over a nineteen-month
period in 1969-1970. Roberts acted as Customary Law Adviser
to the Botswana Government between November, 1968 and March,
1970 and in the course of this period conducted fieldwork among the Kgatla. We should like to thank Dr. R.P.
Werbner for reading an earlier draft of the essay. Many of
his suggestions have been incorporated into this version. We
are also grateful to Professor A.L. Epstein and Professor I.
Schapera for their helpful comments.

(2) Epstein (1973, pp. 653-4), in discussing his research on urban courts on the Copperbelt, has noted the same difficulty.

in argument and settlement, in others they were invoked tacitly
by implication, while on other occasions they were not resorted
to at all, although seemingly apposite to the observer. Moreover, on those occasions where norms were invoked, it soon
became clear that they did not necessarily determine the outcome
of the dispute concerned. It is this problem to which we devote
our attention here: is there any systematic pattern underlying
the invocation, manipulation and application of stated norms in
Tswana processes of dispute settlement?

Before turning to the Tswana case, it is necessary to consider
how this question has been handled in the literature of legal
anthropology. Twining (1964, p. 34) in a review of African legal
ethnography, has remarked upon the "enormous diversity of purpose, method and emphasis of different writers" (3). There is no
better illustration of his point than the varied treatment
afforded to norms. In some studies, they have been seen as being
of central interest and providing the sole object of investigation, whereas in others they have been virtually ignored in
favour of an examination of processes of dispute settlement.
More often, though, an intermediate position has been taken (4).
Further, where norms have been the subject of investigation, the
source from which they have been drawn has again varied: they
have been sought in everyday behaviour of members of the group-
ing concerned, in the statements of informants and in actual

---

(3) Comparing six major works of African legal anthropology,
    Twining went on to write: "It is not much of an exaggeration
    to say that if these books had been written about the same
    tribe, each would have still contributed a good deal in its
    own right; certainly if you set out to do a comparative study
    of the Tiv, the Barotse, the Sukuma, and the Tswana, relying
    solely on these books, it would soon become apparent to you
    that it is virtually impossible to find a real basis for com-
    parison from the information provided". (Twining, 1964,
    pp. 34-35).

(4) We do not intend to re-open the debate over whether students
    of law should focus on norms or processes. Moore (1969, p.
    376) has noted a reaction "against sterile citings of rules",
    a reaction which we share. Gluckman (1973), on the other
    hand, has recently felt it necessary to chide Gulliver, in
    our view without justification, for showing too little inter-
    est in norms. We would hope that there is now general agree-
    ment with the view that norms and processes cannot be
    meaningfully comprehended except in relation to each other.

instances of dispute. Nor has there been any uniformity as to the method and purpose of their presentation. Some studies have been concerned simply with the collection and systematic arrangement of norms, whereas others have been primarily concerned with establishing the role which norms play in the society in which they are found. These differences of approach in themselves make it difficult to account systematically for the role of norms in dispute settlement on a cross-cultural basis. Furthermore, the achievement of analytical refinement has been complicated by problems inherent in the material itself. Most of these are well known and are referred to only briefly here.

First, it is apparent that no obvious universal relationship exists between the clarity with which abstract norms are articulated, the way in which they are employed in argument and their importance in decision-making. To begin with, reports suggest wide differences in the degree to which norms are apprehended and expressed: some peoples, it seems, barely perceive or refer to them at all (e.g. Hoebel, 1940, on the Comanches); while in other cases comprehensive and integrated lists are forthcoming (e.g. Schapera, 1938 for the Tswana) (5). Recognising this divergence, the extent to which norms are invoked within the dispute settlement process, the manner of this invocation and their role and significance in decision-making appear to vary independently of one another. The range of variations can be illustrated by comparing Gulliver's description of the Arusha (1963) with Fallers's of the Soga (1969). Gulliver's Arusha material shows that norms are often relied on expressly in the course of a dispute (see, Gulliver 1963, pp. 240-58). Fallers, on the other hand, indicates that norms are seldom explicitly referred to in Soga disputes: instead, argument and decision-making proceeds through reference to facts, the choice of which implies reliance upon a norm that is mutually understood (Fallers, 1969). This distinction between explicit and implicit invocation of norms is an important one, as Fallers notes, and we shall return to it below. Significantly, however, the outcome of an Arusha dispute is rarely determined by the single application of one of the norms invoked, whereas decisions in those among the Soga demonstrate a rigid reliance on norms, reminiscent of the common law. Overall, the picture is one of great comparative variability.

---

(5) The Comanche and Tswana are, of course, polar cases. Bohannan (1957) notes that the Tiv articulate individual norms, without apparently seeing them as organised into a *corpus juris.*

A second problem, which has received considerable attention, arises from the fact that in many societies a number of "normative orders" are found to coexist (see Pospisil, 1971) with the result that it may be difficult to identify those norms of particular relevance in dispute settlement. In western societies efforts are generally made to segregate "legal norms" by arranging them in a discrete sub-system; in small-scale societies, norms are rarely "especially organised for jural purposes" (Bohannan, 1957, p. 58) and hence those important in dispute settlement cannot easily be isolated. Norms tend also to vary in their degree of specificity, so that precise and detailed rules exist alongside more vague and general precepts. Indeed, Gluckman's view that the flexibility of legal conceptions permits the precision of their application in actual cases (Gluckman, 1955, *passim*; Moore, 1969) is founded upon the observation that norms of markedly different order comprise the legal repertoire of the Barotse. We shall consider the Tswana data in the light of these problems below. Related to them is the fact that different systems of norms may be found in operation at different "levels" of the same society (Pospisil 1971; Collier, 1973). At this stage we simply note that stated norms cannot be treated as a series of rules of equal specificity or value.

Thirdly, processes which occur within the legal framework do not always concern the actual settlement of disputes. They may also provide the context for the public enactment of established relations. Gluckman (1955, 2nd ed. 1967, pp. 21-22) suggests this by implication when he reports that Barotse may go to law knowing that they will lose the case or may commit an offence in order to be taken to court. In these circumstances there may be little effort on the part of the litigants to argue the rights and wrongs of the specific suit at hand; they go to court, it seems, to have the state of their relationship recognised. This is even more clearly evident among the Barolong boo Ratshidi. Tshidi sometimes attempt, quite explicitly, to obtain a court hearing in order to make public the outcome of a process, rather than to have an issue decided (Comaroff, 1973, pp. 246 ff.). The role of norms may be expected to be different where the legal process is not directly concerned with the settlement of a dispute.

Fourthly, in many small-scale societies, and the Tswana are no exception, the gravity of a legal issue is not necessarily determined by the material value of the object or right in question. Thus, for example, an argument which ostensibly concerns a household utensil may be treated with the utmost

seriousness by a Tswana chief's court, while the division of a
large family herd may be successfully accomplished by informal
negotiations within the local agnatic segment. Moreoever, the
former may turn out to involve more intricate judicial logic,
frequent appeal to norms and intensely fought litigation. The
reasons for this have repeatedly been made clear; in small-scale
societies, in which the law of persons is significantly more
developed than the law of contract (cf. Gluckman, 1955 2nd ed.
1967 pp. 32), the relationship between two people can rarely be
reduced to one which hinges on the contested object or right
alone. The issue with which courts among the Tswana, Lozi and
others are often most concerned is the relationship itself. The
disputed value is generally of secondary importance — among the
Barolong boo Ratshidi it is sometimes eliminated entirely from
the argument early on in the process of settlement. Hence it may
be necessary to make an analytical distinction between norms
governing access to the disputed value and those directly associated with the relationships involved. They may be intricately
connected in practice but, as we shall show, the distinction may
prove important in accounting for the ways in which norms are
invoked.

These problems have led some writers to direct their attention
away from norms in the effort to comprehend processes of dispute
settlement (e.g. Epstein, 1973 p. 654). Others, however, have
been persuaded to account for the diversity in patterns of norm
invocation and utilization. Thus Bohannan (1965, p. 39), for
example, argues that because cases in stateless societies tend to
be settled by compromise rather than by the handing down of a
decision as in centralized systems, this "leads to very much
less precise statements of norms as law than does the decision-
based unicentric solution". This suggestion seems rather too
general to be of much heuristic value, but even so the great precision with which Arusha norms are sometimes expressed in the
context of a dispute (Gulliver, 1963) casts immediate doubt upon
its validity. Furthermore, the hypothesis is of little help in
relation to those societies, like the Tswana, where a hierarchy
of dispute-settlement agencies includes levels at which settlement by compromise is attempted and ones at which the outcome
involves a "unicentric decision-based solution".

Gulliver (1963; 1969a, p. 17) seeks an explanation in a similar direction. He relates the clarity with which norms are
articulated and the manner in which they are used to the mode of
dispute settlement followed in a given society. Opposing adjudication and negotiation as "structurally different modes", he

puts forward the hypothesis that

> ...on the whole, there is greater reliance on, appeal to, and operation of rules, standards and norms where adjudicatio rather than negotiation is the mode of dispute settlement ... If this hypothesis is viable, it leads to the further hypothesis that standards are both more vaguely defined and more flexible in areas of social life where negotiation procedures occur than in areas where adjudication is the mode (1969a, pp. 18-19).

Given that the taxonomy of modes is viable, the correlation between them and the clarity and the role of norms is not consistently supported by the data. This can be illustrated by comparing two of Gulliver's own studies. His description of the Ndendeuli (1969b), who rely upon processes of negotiation in dis pute settlement, sustains the hypothesis in that their norms ten to be ill-defined and not much stressed in the context of disputes. But among the Arusha, who also employ processes of negotiation, norms are defined very precisely, and are explicitly invoked in argument, even if they are not decisive in the outcome (see particularly the Arusha bride-wealth and land cases which Gulliver cites; 1963, p. 243 ff.). Similarly, in many adjudicated cases among the Barotse, little express reference is made to precise norms. This is true too of the Tswana, among whom both modes are employed; but the ways in which rules are invoked by disputants are not systematically related to these modes (see Case I below).

Moore (1969, p. 376) tacitly accepts Bohannan's assumption con cerning the relative precision of normative statements in stateless and centralised systems, but sees the problem as having nothing to do with modes of dispute settlement. Rather, she suggests,

> ...the more multiplex the social relations, the more contingencies there are that may affect any particular act or transaction. This multiplicity not only makes it difficult to state norms precisely, but sometimes may make it impossible, since the assortment of contingencies can vary so much from one case to another.

While we agree that the precision of normative statements is not necessarily related to the modes of dispute settlement, this alternative hypothesis does not bear empirical examination. In the first place, differing degrees of multiplexity may characterise relations in any one society, so that it is difficult to understand why Moore associates her explanations with Bohannan's formulation. Furthermore, if the degree of multiplexity *is* the determining factor, then the more multiplex the relationship between two litigants, the less precise should be the statement of norms *in any one system* as well. Apart from the difficulties of measuring multiplexity, it will be clear from the Tswana ethnography below that the precision of normative statements may vary over a number of hearings of a dispute between the same people, i.e. the relationship does not change but the nature of norm utilization might. Again, Gluckman's case of the Biased Father is characterised by extremely clear statements of norm, while the case of the Quarrelsome Teacher involves far more vague formulations (Gluckman, 1955). Yet the relationships between litigants in the former case appear to have been more multiplex than they were in the latter. More important, however, is the fact that even if the hypotheses of Bohannan, Gulliver and Moore are valid, correlative statements of the frequency and precision of norm invocation and utilisation do not in themselves explain why rules are (or are not) invoked in the first place.

This brief review of the literature indicates that existing explanations of cross-cultural variation in patterns of norm invocation and utilization are largely unconvincing. The common feature of these explanations is that they begin with the assumption that factors extrinsic to the actual conduct of disputes (such as the political organisation of the society and the structure of its dispute settlement agencies) determine the underlying pattern.

Without denying the importance of explanations of this kind, we argue here that much more has got to be known about the internal detail of individual systems before such explanations can be successfully pursued on a cross-cultural level. In other words, *intrinsic* features have got to be more fully explored and understood before it is worth considering those of an *extrinsic* character.

It is in this light that we reconsider the invocation and utilization of norms in the Tswana dispute settlement process.

II

The procedures followed by the Tswana in the settlement of disputes are well known from the writings of Schapera (1938; 1943a) and need only the briefest introduction here. For political and administrative purposes the Tswana chiefdom is divided into wards, which in turn are sub-divided into local agnatic segments, each made up predominantly of a number of agnatically related households (Schapera, 1938; Comaroff, 1973) (6). The principle dispute settlement agencies are located within these groupings, and are arranged on the same hierarchical basis. A primary attempt at settling any dispute is ideally made within the local agnatic segment (segments) to which the parties belong, and only where this fails is the matter taken up through successive levels.

The ideal procedure at each of these levels is clearly defined. Where both parties are members of the same agnatic segment, the adult males of the unit should gather at their meeting-place (*kgotla*) to discuss the dispute; if the parties belong to different segments, a joint meeting should be held. At this level, the role of the agency is mediatory and, although given solutions may be strongly urged upon the disputants by those present, the members of the segment (s) have little authority to impose or enforce a decision. Where such attempts at settlement fail, the dispute is taken before the headman of the ward within which the first conciliatory efforts were made. Here a different mode of settlement may be employed as the headman has the right to impose a decision and order the parties to comply with it. Should one or both of the parties remain dissatisfied, the matter is then heard by the chief in his *kgotla*. here, a final order in settlement may be made, which the chief will enforce if necessary.

Our observations in a number of Tswana chiefdoms indicate that these ideal procedures are generally followed in practice, although there is much greater flexibility at the first level than the indigenous model reveals. In particular, primary attempts to reach a settlement do not necessarily occur within

---

(6) It should be noted that Schapera (1938) refers to a local agnatic segments as "family groups". Although the hierarchy of progressively more inclusive local units is conceptualise indigenously in terms of the agnatic idiom, the correlation between agnatic recruitment and the actual composition of these units varies within and between different Tswana chief doms.

the local agnatic segment (s) to which the parties belong.
Rather, any senior kinsmen of the respective disputants may be
approached, and when the disputants are themselves related they
will often appeal to kinsmen in a structurally intermediate
position (7). Thus, for example, first efforts to settle a
dispute between the sons of two sisters might well be made by
their mothers' brothers (see Case I below). Similarly, the mode
of settlement attempted at this level is by no means uniform:
while it will often involve a formal meeting of the segment (s)
concerned, the matter may also be resolved through informal
mediation carried out by individual members of the unit (s) without a *kgotla* meeting being convened (8).

The Batswana perceive the regularities of their everyday
lives as being governed by a body of norms collectively described as *melao le mekgwa wa Setswana*, a phrase which has
generally been translated as "Tswana law and custom" (9).
These norms also furnish the criteria and standards whereby
any dispute should be settled. However, the blanket description
"Tswana law and custom" covers a wide repertoire of different
norms, and those that are of critical importance in dispute
settlement do not form a separate or identifiable sub-system.

---

(7) Here we would draw attention to the similarity with the
Ndendeuli procedures reported by Gulliver (1969b).

(8) It should be noted that the dispute settlement process may
be initiated by the disputants themselves who, in approaching
their respective kin, may place the onus on them to expedite
informal mediation. But it may also be set in motion by
these kin themselves or by co-members of the segment concerned who may wish to solve a disruptive conflict.

(9) For comparison with the similar Lozi terms (*mulao* and *mukwa*)
see Gluckman (1955, 2nd Ed. 1967, pp. 164 ff.). Schapera
(1943b, pp. 3 ff.) discusses the semantics of the terms, and
points out that some writers have tried to differentiate
sharply between them. We would, however, agree with his
opinion that "the two terms are really not sharply discriminated in ordinary Tswana usage: the same rule of conduct may
be spoken of on one occasion as MOLAO, and on another as
MOKGWA". (1938 p. 36: quoted in 1943b p. 4). In view of
this, the phrase conventionally used in translating *melao le
mekgwa* is unfortunate. Its effect is to introduce a distinction drawn from an alien system, which Tswana usage
does not appear to support.

Thus the repertoire embraces a range of precepts commencing
with rules of etiquette and polite behaviour, extending through
norms enjoying broad social acceptance, and concluding with man
datory injunctions issued in legislative form by the tribal
authorities (Schapera 1943b; 1970). Related to this continuum,
it should be observed that even among those norms which are mos
important in dispute settlement specificity varies greatly.
Thus, precise substantive prescriptions (e.g. that the youngest
son should inherit his mother's homestead) shade into precepts
of a more general character (e.g. *lentswe la moswi ga letlolwe*,
"the voice of a dead man is not transgressed"), and lastly, int
maxims and principles of a broad abstract kind (e.g. that
agnates should live in harmony with one another). Norms of dif
fering degrees of specificity may, of course, be adduced in suc
a way as to conflict, the normative level at which argument
proceeds may change during a dispute, and the participants may
attempt to impose competing normative definitions upon the issue
under debate.

We will show that, in presenting a case, Tswana disputants
construct and rely upon a "paradigm of argument" (10): that
is, they attempt to convey a coherent picture of relevant
events and actions *in terms of one or more (implicit or explici*
normative referents. Any such "paradigm of argument" is sited
in the requirements of a particular case, and is not fixed or
pre-determined. Its degree of elaboration and integration
depends upon several factors, such as the oratorical ability of
the disputant, his expectations concerning the strategies of hi
opponent and his own strategic intentions. Moreover, the construction of the paradigm may vary over a number of hearings of
the same dispute before different agencies, since the perceptions, expectations and strategies of the opposing parties may
change or become progressively refined. The important point to
note is that the complainant, who speaks first, establishes suc
a paradigm by ordering facts around normative referents which m
or may not be made explicit. The defendant, in replying, may
accept these normative referents, and hence the paradigm itself
under these circumstances he will argue over the facts *within t*

---

(10) The term "paradigm" is used here to convey a pattern, the
     component elements of which may be more or less closely
     integrated and can only be fully comprehended with referen
     to the pattern itself. In other words, we intend a common
     sense usage, rather than one which is consistent with the
     analytical construct of Kuhn (1962) or others who have
     elaborated the concept.

paradigm. Alternatively, he may assert a competing paradigm by introducing different normative referents, in which case he may not contest the facts at all. At the higher levels, where the mode of settlement becomes one of adjudication, the third party responsible for adjudication (a headman or the chief) may order his decision within the agreed paradigm, choose between competing paradigms, or impose a fresh paradigm upon the issues under dispute. We will attempt to demonstrate that the isolation of such paradigms of argument, and the dynamics of their inter-action, is crucial if we are to account for the invocation and utilization of norms in the dispute settlement process.

We now consider two case-histories recorded by Roberts in the course of his fieldwork among the Kgatla. In each instance, the background to the dispute is first outlined. A text of the hear-ings is then reproduced (11), and is followed by a brief discuss-ion of the ways in which norms were invoked and utilized. Finally, we draw together the two case descriptions and examine the patterns underlying the normative aspects of argument and judgment.

CASE I: MMATLHONG'S FIELD

Mmatlhong (12) inherited a tract of arable land from her mother, Kwetse (see genealogy), who had received it from her father when she married (13). Nobody could remember this plot having been cultivated and, by 1960, it was covered by scrub and mature trees (14). On it lay a pan from which water was

---

(11) The texts reproduced here are translations of contemporary verbatim transcripts taken in Setswana by a court clerk in Mochudi. For reasons of space, we have had to edit them, but have attempted to retain the fullest possible version.

(12) At the time of this dispute Mmathlhong was about 80, being a member of the *Kuka* age-regiment (formed 1901).

(13) Among the Tswana, arable land generally devolves from father to son. However, in some cases a man will set aside a field (known as *serotwana*) for a daughter when she marries. This field, which is then cultivated by the woman and her hus-band, devolves upon her own eldest daughter.

(14) As the Kgatla only arrived at their present territory in 1871, it seems unlikely that this site ever had been culti-vated.

perennially obtainable. Kwetse had never used the land, but ha
allowed her brother, Thari, to draw water from the pan. Like h
mother, Mmatlhong never cultivated the plot. She had married
into another ward and had been provided with a field by her hus
band. Following Thari's death, Leoke (his ZSS and MZSS of
Mmatlhong) had been permitted to draw water from the pan.

Some years later, Mogorosi, Mmatlhong's MZDS, asked her to
exchange the field for a beast. She agreed, and the transactio
was witnessed by several people. But in all the visits made to
the field in the course of the exchange it seems never to have
been specified clearly whether or not the pan fell within it.
At the time, Leoke was away from home and did not know about th
agreement. Nor did any of Kwetse's male agnates witness these
events, although they were informed later.

Following his acquisition of the land, Mogorosi excluded
others from it, and prevented the cutting of bark from the
trees. Meanwhile, Leoke had returned. On hearing that his
children had been told not to cut bark, he visited Mogorosi,
taking with him a man to whom neither was closely related. The
argument which ensued is recounted below, but it was serious
enough to persuade the two men to report it to their kinsmen.
Both chose senior members of the agnatic segment into which
Kwetse had been born. Pholoma (see genealogy), who was consul
ted by Leoke, initiated informal efforts at conciliation by
approaching Mmatlhong and Mogorosi. The latter was asked to
allow Leoke to draw water, while Leoke was shown the boundaries
of the field by Mmatlhong. On this occasion it was indicated
that the pan fell within these boundaries. Leoke reacted by
entering the plot and cutting down trees; quite explicitly, he
wished to challenge Mogorosi's right to it.

Some time later, at the request of Mogorosi, the members of
Kwetse's agnatic segment convened a meeting to discuss the dispute. Raditladi, the senior member, questioned Mogorosi about
the terms of the transaction. These appear to have been accepted, although Raditladi expressed regret that none of his agnat
had witnessed it (15). Those present at the meeting emphasized
that while Mogorosi clearly had rights over the land the two me

---

(15) Although the mode of settlement at this level is mediatory,
     some of the discussion (as is suggested also by a later
     statement made during the case itself) proceeded in terms
     of the precise, substantive norms governing the transfer
     of land (see above).

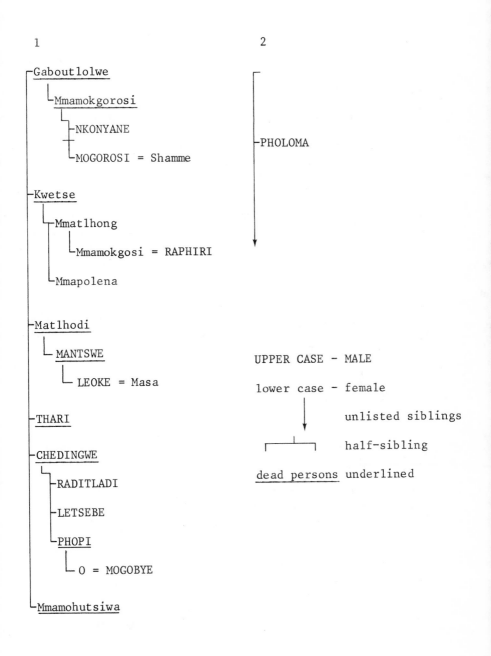

1

2

Gaboutlolwe
  Mmamokgorosi
    NKONYANE
    MOGOROSI = Shamme

PHOLOMA

Kwetse
  Mmatlhong
    Mmamokgosi = RAPHIRI
  Mmapolena

Matlhodi
  MANTSWE
    LEOKE = Masa

THARI

CHEDINGWE
  RADITLADI
  LETSEBE
  PHOPI
    0 = MOGOBYE

Mmamohutsiwa

UPPER CASE - MALE

lower case - female

unlisted siblings

half-sibling

dead persons underlined

should use the pan peacefully together. This, however, did not
satisfy either of them, and their wives, Masa and Shamme, exchanged abuse and blows in the *kgotla*. This convinced members
the segment that a settlement at this level was impossible, and
Raditladi informed the ward headman of the issue (16).

Before further attempts at settlement could be made, some of
Mogorosi's goats wandered over to Leoke's homestead, where Masa
impounded them. Mogorosi sent a child to fetch them, but Masa
demanded that they be collected by an adult. Mogorosi went him
self, and they were handed over. This happened again, and Mogo
rosi again collected them. This time, Masa complained that the
goats had been after Leoke's billy; but most of them were preg-
nant and they were probably attracted to the area by an outcrop
of rock salts. Subsequently, the billy wandered home with Mogo
rosi's goats, and Shamme impounded it. One of Leoke's children
went to fetch it but, like Masa, Shamme insisted that the anima
be collected by an adult. Nobody came, so Shamme sent it off t
wards Leoke's homestead. Some days later, Mogorosi's goats aga
wandered over to Leoke's place. When Mogorosi asked for them,
Leoke refused on the ground that his billy had not yet returned
Soon after, the dispute was heard by the ward headman, Thai Tlha

MOGOROSI:
The dispute began over a ploughing field (*tshimo*). I bought
the field from Mmatlhong. I paid (*dueletse*) a large red ox for
it. I was with Mmusi. I found that Raphiri had cut some bark
from my ploughing field. I told Raphiri not to cut bark again.
I was with Mmamatolala when I issued this warning. One day I
found the sons of Leoke cutting bark again and I told them not
cut bark in my field. I told them to tell their father that I
had stopped them cutting down trees in my field.

Later, Leoke came to me with Mokgakgele. Leoke asked me why
prevented his children cutting down bushes. I told Leoke I hav
bought the field, and I need the trees to fence the field. Leo
said to me that the plot I am talking about is the field of Rad
ladi. I said to Leoke "man" (*monna*). Leoke said: "Do not say
'man' to me. You must say 'man' to my son, not to me" (17).

---

(16) Although the main actors in this case lived in different
     intracapital wards, they occupied adjoining sites at their
     lands between November and June.

(17) *Monna* (lit. 'man') is generally used to address a man who
     junior to the speaker, or a familiar age-mate.

I swore at him: I said *"marete"* (*testicles*). He replied
"mmago mpapa" (your mother's genitals) (18). I tried to catch
his leg, but he moved away quickly. I tried to take a stick, but
Mokgakgele and my wife stopped me. I again swore at Leoke.
Leoke replied and said that I was an illegitimate child and did
not know my father. He went on to say that I was the illegitimate child of Mantswe (Leoke's father). I told Leoke that I would
make him defecate involuntarily on the next day. The following
day I looked for Leoke without success. On the same day, Leoke's
wife came to me. When she asked about our quarrel I refused to
answer her.

When this field was alloted to me, the following were present:
Mmusi, Segale, Mmatlhong, Mmamokhosi, Mmamotalala and Shamme. Raditladi said he wished the Modisana family had been present (19).
When Raditladi and my people were present, Leoke's wife poked my
wife on the head with her finger. Masa challenged Shamme to follow her outside to fight. Shamme refused. Masa then went and
scratched Shamme's face and she bled. Sebopelo and Mmamotalala
separated them.

(One day) Nkonyane informed me that my goats were in Leoke's
enclosure. I actually saw them there. My wife sent a child for
them, but they sent her away; they said they wanted an adult. I
went there and found Masa, Leoke's wife. Masa said my goats were
worrying her billy; they are after it. They allowed me to have
them, and I drove them away. My goats returned there again, being
attracted by the salt-lick. I went a second time, and they allowed
me to have them. I told Masa that my goats were in kid and did
not need a billy.

One day Leoke's billy came along with my goats. I tied it up
to prevent it interfering with my goats, as they were in kid.
Leoke's son came to fetch it. Shamme sent him back to tell his
mother to fetch it herself. She refused to come. Shamme untied
it, and chased it to its owners. My goats were captured a third

---

(18) The utterance of these two obscenities constitutes an almost
stereotyped sequence of abuse. But, except when exchanged
between youthful members of the same age-regiment, they are
taken very seriously and often lead to fighting.

(19) This recalls a statement made by Raditladi at the segment
meeting; 'Modisana' refers to Raditladi's agnatic lineage
segment. Mmusi and Mmamotalala, mentioned in the previous
sentence, were members of the ward into which Kwetse had
married. (All others are included on the genealogy.)

time. I went for them, accompanied by Ditswe. When I was ther
Leoke asked me about his billy. Leoke said that if he did not
find his billy, he would not let me have my goats. Leoke said
should call Letsebe and Raditladi. The goats captured by Leoke
are six in number.

Leoke said he could see I wanted us to fight. He also said on
of us will die. The goats captured by Leoke are still there no

LEOKE:
During the Christmas month I went to the Transvaal. On my r
turn I found that my sons had cut bushes at Leboeng. The childr
said that Mogorosi had stopped them cutting down bushes. They
said Mogorosi came to my place and told them to let me know on
return that he would like to see me at his place. When I came
the boy told me. I waited four days hoping Mogorosi would come
and talk to me; but he did not come. On the fifth day I went t
his place. I was with Mokgakgele, so that he could become a wi
ness of what occurred between Mogorosi and me. When I got ther
I said: "The children say you have stopped them cutting bushes.
He admitted that he had stopped them. He had also stopped Raph
iri and Mogobye (20). I told him he had made a mistake to prevent them. He said it was a field (*tshimo*) and he was going to
plough it. I told him it would be understandable if he had
stopped them because the field was already ploughed (21). He
said that the plot was a piece of arable land. I told him that
the plot belonged to Raditladi's people.

I told him this plot has never been ploughed since before I was
born. He said: "Son, tell me when you have finished." I warne
him I had not come to fight but to ask where I was supposed to
cut bushes. He stood up and looked for a stick. Mokgakgele

---

(20) Raphiri was married to Mmatlhong's daughter. The fact tha
he had accepted Mogorosi's warning was strong evidence for
the latter's claim. For, by the *serotwana* custom accordin
to which the field had been transmitted, it would have bee
inherited by Raphiri's wife on Mmatlhong's death. Hence h
would have had a direct interest in rebutting Mogorosi's
warning if he had thought that the transfer had not taken
place. Mogobye was the husband of the daughter of Raditladi's brother, Phopi.

(21) Tswana distinguish sharply between cleared ploughing field
and bush land, which is usually held to be commonage under
the ownership of the chief. This distinction is later to
a crucial factor in the final judgment.

stopped him. As I went he swore at me. He said: "Your father's
testicles (*rrago marete*), you Mokgalagadi." I told him the man he
swore at was actually his father. He said to me: "Your mother's
genitals". I told him to say it to his mother. He threatened
that if he meets me on my own somewhere he will make me defecate
against my will. I came and asked at the *kgotla* if it was proper
for him to say he would attack me wherever we would meet (22). I
went and cut trees where Mogorosi had prevented the children from
cutting branches. I took the bush away and kept it for a week,
and then used it. I went back and cut down another, and kept
that one for two weeks, then used it.

Mogorosi had not actually seen my children cutting down trees.
When they cut down the trees, Mogorosi was at the cattle-post. It
was the month of Christmas. In February, Mmatlhong sold the field
to Mogorosi and received the ox. When Mogorosi bought the field
I was away; Mmusi told me what had been done. Mmatlhong also
told me that she had allocated the field to Mogorosi. The following day I went to water the cattle and found that the entrance to
my pan had been moved away. I asked Mmatlhong why this was done.
I said the pan was mine, allocated to me by Mmamohutsiwa, where
Thari had dug before.

(Leoke then went on to detail some of the events which preceded the
meeting of the lineage segment. He ended this passage by saying:)

Raditladi asked Mogorosi if he wanted a case (*tsheko*). Mogorosi
said: "Yes, I want a case." Raditladi asked him where his father
Nkonyane, (23) was. Mogorosi replied by saying that Leoke's wife
is worrying his wife.

(Leoke explained that he went away again, and then continued:)

I returned from Oodi and found that my billy was not in the
flock. I heard that it had been serving Mogorosi's goats. Mogorosi caught it and tied it up. When he let it loose it went away.
Mogorosi's goats came to me and I put them into my enclosure. I
asked him why he could not have released it (the billy) when my
wife sent for it. I sent him to go and call Raditladi and Letsebe,

---

(22) This refers to the earlier meetings of the agnatic segment
at which the first conciliatory efforts were made.

(23) Nkonyane was the eldest living sibling of Mogorosi. He was,
however, Mogorosi's half-brother, having been born into a
senior house. As such, he had succeeded to his father's
position as head of the segment.

so that he could take the goats in their presence. I asked my
wife whether she had ever refused to release Mogorosi's goats.
I asked Mogorosi the same question and he said it had never happened. Later Nkonyane came and said he had come for the goats.
I told him they were in the enclosure. He asked me what damage
they had done. I said I did not find my billy where it should b
He asked if Mogorosi had borrowed it from me. I said no, and he
said "a billy, like a bull, has no fence". I said to him that h
could take the goats. Nkonyane asked if I would await them goir
to look for my billy first. They departed, leaving the goats
with me. Mogorosi said to Nkonyane: "I told you one of us (Mogc
rosi or Leoke) would have to move elsewhere or he would die."

(In answering questions, Mogorosi admitted to having started the
exchange of abuse, but added, "I am not to be insulted by reference to my testicles". Leoke confessed that his abuse of Mogorc
si's mother had been wrong, and that he should not have imputed
illegitimacy.)

THAI TLHADI (in judgment):
    Leoke, we have listened to your obscene language with Mogoros
very carefully. You used very obscene language towards Mogorosi
Therefore the *kgotla* finds you guilty. You will receive four
strokes on the back. You, Mogorosi, will receive two strokes.

(After this, the hearing proceeded with a series of statements
made in evidence by Mmatlhong, her younger sister Mmapolena, and
her eldest son Segale. All reported, in a matter-of-fact fashic
the events surrounding the transaction concerning the field, the
demarcation of its boundaries to include the pan, and the report
ing of these events to Letsebe, the younger brother of Raditladi
Segale added that the land had not been ploughed for a number of
years, and that Leoke had drawn water without title to it. Leok
interrupted, claiming that he was allowed to use the pan by Mmam
hutsiwa, a younger sister of Kwetse. Mmatlhong replied that the
trees which were felled had been within the field which she had
had the right to alienate. Leoke and Mogorosi then exchanged
words: The latter argued that he had only stopped the children
from taking trees from his field; the former answered that he ha
cut trees "in order to see what Mogorosi would do". Thai Tlhadi
delivered a second judgment in which he simply stated that the
field had belonged to Mmatlhong, and she had transferred it properly to Mogorosi. The pan was within the field, and it was up
him to decide whether to allow Leoke to draw water. Leoke then
raised the matter of the goats:)

LEOKE:
My billy had not yet been found.

MOGOROSI:
I learn that it was seen by Mothagi and my wife, Shamme.

(Mothagi confirmed that he and Shamme saw the animal in the
company of Leoke's other goats.)

LEOKE:
The billy is now present among my other goats. When it went
to Mogorosi's place it was attracted by the female goats, as most
billies are. It was caught and tethered there. I was advised to
fetch it. I did not fetch it. After that, Mogorosi's goats came
to my place and I decided to detain them as he had detained my
billy. Mogorosi came to claim the goats, but I did not give them
as my billy was astray. I only saw the billy when the matter had
been handed to the *kgotla*.

(Then followed another series of exchanges between Leoke and
Mogorosi. Both reiterated the alleged facts concerning the goats,
and the former admitted that he still held the six animals. Both
accused the other of taking the matter to the *kgotla* without giving due warning.)

THAI TLHADI (in judgment):
Leoke we have listened carefully to the arguments between you
and Mogorosi. You have caused the *kgotla* to deal with an unnecessary problem. You have fought with Mogorosi and detained his
goats. The *kgotla* orders that, from this day, you and Mogorosi
should live together in peace. Mogorosi, you may have back your
goats. You, Leoke, the *kgotla* orders you to pay the sum of
R6 (± £4), which is a fine imposed by the *kgotla*.

(The corporal punishment was administered immediately. After
receiving his fourth stroke, Leoke arose swiftly. This was taken
as a sign of disrespect, however, and a further stroke was administered. Leoke was dissatisfied with this, and with the outcome
of the hearing in general, so he took his grievance to the chief's
kgotla:)

MOGOROSI:
I am complaining against Leoke. Leoke came to my homestead
with Mokgakgele. He said I had chased his children away for
felling trees. I told him it was true. They were felling trees

in my field which I had bought from Mmatlhong. This field has
not been ploughed for some time. I told him they were not the
only ones who I had chased away. Leoke answered by saying the
field belonged to the Raditladi people, not to Mmatlhong's. I
replied, saying I had bought it from the owner, Mmatlhong. Leok
said he would understand if I prevented them from felling trees
in fields that had been ploughed before, not where there has bee
no ploughing. That time, in conversation, he called me 'son'.
warned him not to call me 'son' and swore at him. He swore at r
mother, and I told him I would give him a hiding the next day.
stood up to thrash him, and grabbed a stick. Mokgakgele and my
wife prevented me. He stood outside insulting me and called me
an illegitimate child, saying I was fathered by his father.

(He then repeated the argument concerning the goats, and concluded:)

Leoke and I have not fought. Leoke lost the case of the
goats. I was allowed to receive the goats. I therefore have n
case against Leoke, I have fully settled with him.

LEOKE:
I brought this appeal here because I was not satisfied with
the decision of my *kgotla*. He had a case, and I was ordered to
receive four strokes. After the fourth stroke I arose, and the
men of the *kgotla* caught me and thrashed and assaulted me. Tha
is why I have appealed. I was thrashed unlawfully. When I qua
relled with Mogorosi he had not yet cleared the field which he
says he has bought. The claim that he had bought it is only an
excuse. I disagreed when Mogorosi claimed that the ploughing
field was his because he had not paid the ox for it as he states.

(In answer to questions, Mogorosi reasserted his rights over the
field and the pan. Leoke clarified his statement by saying tha
he thought the field did not include the pan. He also claimed
that the exchange occurred in February, *after* his children had
been chased away. Mogorosi answered that Leoke was not present
at the time of the transaction; it was earlier, when he was in
Johannesburg.)

LEOKE:
I went to the court and reported my disagreement with Mogorosi, and asked the court if it was proper for a man to say to
you that he will make you defecate.

(The remaining discussion was devoted entirely to the details of

the transaction. Mmatlhong and Mmapolena repeated the evidence
they had given at the earlier hearing, and the former stressed
her right to alienate the plot. Leoke claimed once again that he
had received the pan from Mmamohutsiwa. No new evidence was
introduced, and the argument was an almost verbatim repetition of
that heard in the ward court. Finally, judgment was given:)

CHIEF:
   Mmatlhong, I have gone carefully into the case of Leoke and
Mogorosi. According to Tswana law, you can sell a field, not a
plot of land. Land belongs to the chief. You have broken the
law by selling the chief's land. I therefore order you to refund
Mogorosi his beast. Mogorosi must receive that beast from you.
You, Leoke, will receive that pan. It is yours, do not be wor-
ried by anyone about it. The fines imposed on you by the ward
kgotla will remain as they are. You must carry those out, as you
quarrelled with the *kgotla* when found guilty.

                    *   *   *

   At the start of the ward court hearing, Mogorosi - who, being
the complainant, had the right to speak first - began by elaborating a paradigm of argument in relation to an implicit set of
norms. He first established that it was a *ploughing* field which
was at issue, and stated the terms of its acquisition with tacit
reference to a substantive norm governing exchange. He pointed
out, further, that he had warned people who had infringed his
rights over the field, and named a witness who could verify this.
In other words, he stressed that, as far as he was concerned, the
dispute was mainly about title to the land itself. He then recounted the confrontation with Leoke which had resulted, in his
view, from the violation of his rights. He admitted to having
initiated the exchange of abuse, but implied that this was *not* a
separate issue: it was a reaction to his having been wronged. In
organizing his statement in this fashion, Mogorosi was anticipating an argument by Leoke to the effect that it was the confrontation, rather than title to the field, which lay at the heart of
the case. With regard to the confrontation itself, however, Mogorosi tried to offset the fact that he began the swearing by point-
ing out that Leoke has escalated the abuse, and that the defendant's wife had attacked his wife. Finally, he raised the matter
of the goats, claiming that Leoke had impounded his animals for no
justifiable reason. Again he made precise, if implicit, reference
to the norms associated with the infringement of property rights.

   In short, Mogorosi's argument contained no explicit reference
to norms; but it did rely entirely on a series of normative assumptions associated with the substantive issues of control over

land and animals. It was in relation to these that the facts
which he adduced were organised. Both his and Leoke's actions
were to be understood as having resulted from the contravention
of his rights. His primary claim, therefore, was for the recognition of his title to Mmatlhong's field and for the return of
his goats. He was not asking the *kgotla* to pass judgment on his
relationship with Leoke: as he implied in his opening statement
in the chief's *kgotla*, he believed that once the property disput
was settled, there was nothing more general at issue.

In reply, Leoke began by disputing Mogorosi's rights over the
field. He stated that Mmatlhong had no business alienating the
land, as it belonged to Raditladi's descent group. But the logi
behind his argument lay in a somewhat different direction. He
did not, in fact, question the norm governing the transaction as
adduced by his opponent. Rather, he claimed that, when he returned home in December (the dates are important here), he found
that Mogorosi had told his children and others not to cut bushes
Later Leoke emphasized that the transaction between Mmatlhong an
Mogorosi had occurred in February. He also added that, until th
time of the first confrontation at least, the plot was not a
ploughing field, but a bush tract. In other words, he did not
begin by questioning the norms referred to by Mogorosi, but disagreed with him over the *interpretation* of the facts. Nor was
Leoke haphazard in the way in which he developed this: he attemp
ted to construct a picture of Mogorosi as a man who was wont to
do violence to other people and their property rights. In accor
dance with this, he emphasized Mogorosi's verbal and physical
belligerence. The central statement of his argument then followed: "I came and asked at the *kgotla* if it was proper for him
to say he will attack me." This was the first explicit referenc
to a norm in the case (24). Thus Leoke organized his evidence i
such a way as to assert a competing paradigm of argument. This
he made clear in expressly invoking the relevant norm: he wished
to establish control over the proceedings so as to ensure that
Mogorosi's violence became the central issue. The remainder of
his argument reaffirmed this. Mogorosi had chased the children

---

(24) By "explicit reference" we mean a normative statement which
may be understood without reference to the facts or context
of the case. An implicit reference is one in which facts
are adduced in such a way as to be comprehensible only or
directly in terms of an accepted norm. Clearly, explicit
normative statements range from direct ones ("It is the law
that ...") to indirect formulations (such as "I ask whether
it is proper that ...").

away before actually receiving the field, and at a time when Leoke
still believed it to belong to Raditladi's agnates. (After all,
he had been given use of the pan by Mmamohutsiwa.) Finally, in
claiming that Mogorosi had initiated the dispute, and in outlin-
ing the events surrounding the impounding of the goats, Leoke
attempted to reinforce the impression that the complainant was a
violent man who offended people and interfered with property.

In his judgment, Thai Tlhadi carefully distinguishes three
separate issues. He first took the question of the exchange of
abuse, and found Leoke relatively more guilty than Mogorosi. His
judgment which contained no explicit reference to norms, was terse
and to the point. He then heard further evidence on the exchange
of the field and, again without explaining his reasons, awarded
it (and the pan) to Mogorosi. Finally, he allowed discussion
over the goats. Leoke admitted that his billy had returned, but
stressed that this was not the central issue; in any case, it had
not returned at the time that the dispute was reported to the
ward headman. The way that he raised this matter, knowing that
the animal was no longer missing, appears to sustain the suggestion that he viewed it as an integral part of his general argument.
Thai Tlhadi, however, interpreted the question as a straightforward dispute over the seizure of animals, and fined Leoke. The
headman's decision to separate the three issues did not suit the
defendant, who argued them as a single claim. But, as we shall
indicate, this is one of the choices open to Tswana agencies when
dealing with multiple disputes.

In the chief's *kgotla* hearing, Mogorosi again chose to assert
his rightful acquisition of the land. In laying down the normative basis of his argument, and perhaps anticipating that Leoke
would again claim that the plot was not a ploughed field at the
time of the dispute, he explained that it was true that it had
not been ploughed for a long time and implied that he had bought
it with the intention to cultivate. He then recounted the events
surrounding the exchange of abuse and the impounding of the goats,
and ended by saying that he no longer had a case against Leoke.
Leoke's statement, less cogent than his earlier one, appealed
against the "unlawful" extra strokes that he had received. He
also repeated his arguments about the transaction itself, and began building a similar case to the one which he had stated previously. After answering questions, he immediately reiterated his
explicit enunciation of norm concerning the threat of violence.

The judgment in this hearing is significant. The chief dis-
missed Leoke's argument, which focussed upon Mogorosi's alleged

violence, by affirming Thai Tlhadi's decision. In concentrating
on title to the field - to which he reduced the dispute - he
addressed his remarks to Mogorosi's suit. He began by stating a
norm governing the alienating of land which nullified Mogorosi's
claim to have effected a valid transfer, and ordered him to take
back the ox. Thus, in judging the case, the chief selected the
complainant's paradigm of argument for primary attention. He di
this by explicitly invoking a conflicting norm, and awarded
against him. As a result, Leoke's right to use the pan was re-
established.

CASE II: NAMAYAPELA, THE TROUBLESOME SON

This case is typical of those arising out of the transfer of
property across the generations. Mooki was an ailing seventy
year old member of the Manamakgothe ward in Mochudi, the Kgatla
capital, and his mother had been a member of the lineage segment
to which the ward headman, Molope belonged. Namayapela was one
of the Mooki's younger sons (see fig. 2).

FIGURE 2

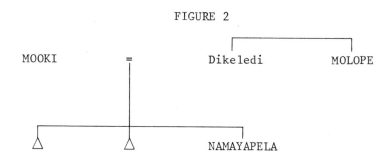

For several years there had been acute tension between him and
his father. Because his other children were away as migrant
labourers, Mooki feared that in the event of his death Namayapel
would seize and waste their portions of his estate. Thus he had
tried to arrange an *inter vivos* allocation to Namayapela. But
the latter refused to accept it. The case is heard by the
chief's *kgotla*.

MOOKI:
    I have come with a complaint. My son, Namayapela, gives me a
lot of trouble. He has been troublesome for a long time.

Recently I told my ward headman, Molope, that I intended to give Namayapela his portion of my estate. The point is to get rid of him, because I fear he would cheat my obedient children in the division of my estate if I did not give him his share now. However, he would not accept it.

I fear that Namayapela may kill me so that he can enjoy my cattle. That is why I want to give him what I think he is entitled to; then I may have nothing to do with him. I want to forestall his chances of doing what he likes when I am gone.

I went to see how the crops were doing after I had reported the case to Molope. When I returned, I went to join a bereaved family. Headman Molope sent Setlhabi to bring Namayapela to him. But Namayapela refused to go. That evening a big noise was heard at my place. Molope sent people to find out the cause of the row. Molope sent people to go and fetch Namayapela, who was causing the row and intended to kill me. When he made the row, he was looking for me; but he did not get me. People sent by Molope reported that Namayapela had a chisel and a hammer. They tried to take these tools away but he refused.

During the night I wished to go home to sleep, but was advised not to go as Namayapela was so unruly that he could have killed me. The following morning I went home to fetch prayer books so that I could lead prayers at the home of the bereaved family. Namayapela told me to sit down; he wanted to tell me something. I refused as I was wanted at the *kgotla*. His mother and Ramakokwana begged me to listen to Namayapela. I complied, and listened to Namayapela. Namayapela asked me whether I enjoyed reporting him to the *kgotla*. My reply was that I could not answer because I was urgently wanted.

When I realised that he was persistent, I ordered him to be quiet. He caught me by the shirt. I lost my temper and gave him a blow. When he tried to choke me I caught his sex organ and he let go. He opened up his thighs. Those who were present separated us. Again I reported to headman Molope that Namayapela was assaulting me. Thus Molope reported to the chief's *kgotla*. Namayapela defies me when I see him and I am therefore appealing to the chief to help me give Namayapela his share of my estate.

NAMAYAPELA:
    Mooki is my real father. I have never fought him. It is true I caught him by the shirt with the intention of beating him.

I caught him in heated passion. My intention was to persuade h
to listen to me. He refused and was persuaded by my mother and
Ramokokwana. The hammer and chisel are mine. When I had them
my hands my father-in-law asked me what I was going to do: was
intention to commit suicide? I took these tools out of their
usual place without thinking of anything in particular.

I have never had any case against my father. My mother said
to my father: "you are troubling Namayapela yet you know his
wife is expecting". She would become ill because of the disput

Machobele came and said he had been instructed to arrest me;
yet he was not aware of the reason. He said I was expected to
report at the *kgotla*. I refused to go. Then I asked my father
to explain why he conspired against me with Molope, without tal
ing to me first. I refused to accept the cattle which my fathe
wanted to give me. I told him that if I am not his son I am no
entitled to the cattle. I told him I did not want them.

MOOKI:
Namayapela sold cattle without consulting me and that is
another thing which annoys me. He benefits from my cattle, yet
he refuses when I send him. That is why I want to give him his
share of the estate. I told Molope and my brothers that I want
to give Namayapela his share so that he may get away from me.

MOLOPE:
Mooki told me that he wanted to give Namayapela cattle from
his estate, but Namayapela refused to accept. I sent people to
call Namayapela but he refused to come to the *kgotla*. I hesita
ted to employ forceful means. When Namayapela refused to come,
he told the people I had said that he would rather they carry h
dead body to the *kgotla* than get him there alive.

NAMAYAPELA:
It is true that I was summoned to the *kgotla* but refused to
go. I told Setlhabi, who had been sent to me, that my wife was
ill. I never said that I would never go there alive. (Answering a question:) On one occasion I was flogged at the *kgotla* f
assaulting a girl who had insulted me. She had referred to my
testicles.

DIKELEDI:
I know the dispute which exists between Namayapela and Mooki
Mooki is my husband. Namayapela troubles his father. Mooki we
with him to the cattle-post to give him cattle which would be h

share of his father's estate. Namayapela refused 20 head of cattle.

Namayapela sold two head of cattle without consulting his father. He spent the money on a trip to Rustenburg to buy roofing material. When he went to Rustenburg, he did not consult me either. He does not respect me as his mother. He regards me as any other old woman. When he had hurled his father to the ground threatening to beat him, I said the best thing was for the two of them to part company. He pointed at me and said: "You aged woman, you will see."

When Mooki called his brothers to tell them that he wanted to give Namayapela cattle, Namayapela refused them on the ground that his elder brother was away. Mooki said that he was not distributing the estate. He wanted to give Namayapela his cattle because he was troublesome.

I told Mooki that it was improper to have a dispute with Namayapela while his wife was expecting because this would make her ill. I was sympathising with Namayapela's wife and not with him.

During the night on which Namayapela had a chisel and a hammer he threatened to commit suicide. He was also asking the whereabouts of Mooki. As he was making a lot of noise I told my last born that his brother was playing the fool with us. He wants to kill your father. No one can use a hammer and chisel to commit suicide. Namayapela said he wanted to see what he could achieve by sunset. He said if he did not achieve anything he would rather die.

NAMAYAPELA:
I am willing to accept the cattle which my father, Mooki, wants to give me so that I may get away from him.

CHIEF:
Namayapela, I have carefully heard the case between you and your father. Your father was very polite to you in discussing with you the fact that he wanted to give you your share. You refused to accept the cattle until you fought him.

You are not supposed to make life uncomfortable for your parents. If you are tired of living you are free to kill yourself rather than make life unbearable for them. You have decided to be rude to your parents. Rudeness, dishonesty and telling lies do not lead to eternal life. You must honour the word of

the chief. Because of your rudeness you refused to respond to
the summons by headman Molope, and did not appreciate the good-
will extended to you by your father. I find you guilty. For
disobeying the summons by headman Molope I sentence you to five
strokes. For refusing to accept the cattle I sentence you to
four weeks imprisonment. The next week you must go with your
father to the cattle-post so that he should give you your cattl

                    *   *   *

 The pattern of norm invocation in this dispute differs
markedly from that observed in the case of Mmatlhong's field.
Mooki, the complainant, opened with a statement to the effect
that his son had been troublesome for a long time. He appears
to have organized his paradigm of argument around the generalized precepts associated with the father-son relationship: He
refers to his son's recalcitrance and his failure to obey or
to inform him of what was being done with family property.
Namayapela was portrayed as being noisy and unruly, and alleged
wishing to kill his father — the ultimate rejection of the
relationship. Throughout, the appeal to norm was implicit and
generalised. Mooki explained his desire to allocate to Namayapela a portion of his estate as an effort, made in desperation,
to sever their tie. Thus, although this aspect of his argument
referred implicitly to a precise substantive norm (a father's
right to divide his estate *inter vivos*) (25), it sought to sum-
marize, in more general (normative) terms the state of the
relationship. Namayapela had refused the cattle, claiming stil
to be Mooki's "real" son. But, because of this, his abrogation
of filial duties was all the more serious. Hence Mooki asked t
court to order Namayapela to accept the cattle in order to ter-
minate his paternal responsibilities. As far as he was concerned, it was the relationship itself which was at issue.
The *inter vivos* allocation was merely a means to achieve the
more general end.

 Namayapela appears to have accepted the paradigm of argument
established by his father, as is indicated by his opening sente
ces ("Mooki is my real father ...."). But, while not disputing
the validity of the norms associated with the father-son tie, h
made consistent efforts to place a different construction on th
facts of the case. Indeed, his refusal to accept the cattle wa
rationalised as an attempt to assert his recognition of this

---

(25) Indeed, Mooki's wife stated in evidence that he had said
  that he was not actually dividing his estate. He simply
  wished to give Namayapela his portion in order to terminat
  the relationship.

father-son relationship, although a succession of witnesses in
support of his father appears to have made him change his mind
in this respect.

In his judgment, the chief distinguished two issues: Namayapela's troublesomeness as a son, and his refusal to respond to
Molope's summons. He introduced each of them with an explicit
statement of norm/s, the first explicit references heard in the
case, and judged Namayapela guilty accordingly.

*   *   *

The two case studies show that argument in the context of
a dispute is organised with reference to one or more established
norms. As the texts demonstrate, such norms may, but need not
be, explicitly invoked. The fact that normative propositions
should give form to the arguments formulated in the course of
a dispute is understandable. The selection and arrangement of
relevant messages must derive from some set of principles and,
because it is "law and custom" which is held indigenously to
determine the outcome of disputes, the normative repertoire provides such principles. Without it, paradigms of argument could
not be constructed and no comprehensible universe of discourse
would be established.

More difficult to understand is the pattern underlying a
choice between explicit and implicit reference to norm. That
norms are frequently invoked by implication is not in itself
surprising, as any Kgatla will consider himself familiar with
"Tswana law and custom" and assume others to be also. Thus,
there is no automatic need for invocation to be explicit if it
is to be understood; the way in which a party arranges the
facts will convey to others present his paradigm of argument.
Nonetheless, there does seem to be a consistent pattern underlying the choice between explicit and implicit invocation and
in order to examine this it is necessary to distinguish between
norm invocation in argument, and that by a judge in giving a
decision.

A complainant seldom invokes norms explicitly in the course
of argument. Because he speaks first, the very manner in which
he presents the alleged facts establishes his paradigm. Consistently with this, neither Mogorosi nor Mooki made an explicit
invocation. Speakers coming later have a fundamental choice:
either they may argue over facts, or they may dispute the norms
to which an agreed set of facts are applied. Thus, Leoke, for

example, did not question the factual basis of Mogorosi's repre
sentation of their confrontation; rather he tried to impose a
different paradigm of argument according to which it could be
assessed. In so doing, he made the only explicit mention of
norms during argument. Namayapela, on the other hand, did not
question the normative paradigm laid down by his father. On th
contrary, he attempted to introduce additional evidence (his
wife's pregnancy) and disputed the alleged facts inferred by
others (e.g., he actually took out the hammer and chisel for no
particular reason; it was not a "fact" that he intended to kill
his father). Thus, in the second case, where the paradigm was
shared by both disputants, no explicit reference was made and
argument proceeded largely in terms of the facts at issue.

Drawing these observations together, it seems that norms are
explicitly invoked by a disputant only when he wishes to questi
the paradigm of argument elaborated by his opponent, and tries
assert control over (or change) the terms in which debate is
proceeding. The complainant has no need to do this in the norm
course of events, because the very manner in which he presents
the alleged facts establishes his paradigm. Although it did no
occur in either of the cases reported above, a Tswana complainant appears to enunciate a norm (or set of norms) only when he
anticipates an effort on the part of the defendant to question
his construction of the dispute itself. (It should be noted th
Mogorosi did not do this; his anticipation of Leoke's point was
over a question of fact. In other cases, however, we have hear
such anticipatory statements.) Thus, while norms are expressly
invoked most frequently by defendants, a complainant may also d
so when he wishes to erode his opponent's prospective paradigm
in advance.

In the process of debate then, express invocation of norms
among the Tswana is associated with efforts to assert control
over the paradigm of argument. If there is no disagreement ove
the paradigm we may expect there to be no explicit reference to
norm — as in the case of Namayapela, and a high proportion of
the Tswana cases with which we are familiar. Under these condi
tions we find a "fact-mindedness" reminiscent of the Soga
(Fallers, 1969).

The invocation of norms in judgment (26) is directly related
to their utilization in argument. In the three hearings report
here, the judges made rather different types of appeal to norm:

_____
(26) On this topic in general, see Schapera, 1966; 1970.

Thai Tlhadi, who distinguished three issues and took evidence
on them separately, simply gave his decisions on the facts of
the case without any reference to legal precept; the chief
treated the same suit as being primarily concerned with the
transfer of land, and passed judgment in terms of a precise
stated norm; and in the case involving Namayapela, he distinguished two issues and expressly introduced the norms relevant
to each one.

In the vast majority of cases, Tswana judges isolate a single
issue within a dispute and hand down a decision in relation to
that issue which makes no explicit reference to any norm. This
occurs predominantly when argument takes place within an accepted
paradigm, and refers mainly to the facts at hand. If, however,
the judge decides that there is a plurality of questions involved
in the dispute, he may do one of two things. He may hear the
whole case, and distinguish the relevant issues in his own final
statement. In such a situation *he* orders the argument into two
or more frames (as did the chief in Case II) and enunciates the
appropriate norms in order to legitimize the distinction and
justify his findings. In so doing, he is rearranging the para-
digmatic structure of the arguments, and is stating the normative basis of his construction. Thai Tlhadi, of course, also
distinguished a number of issues in his judgment (Case I), but
did not invoke norms at any stage. There was, however, a significant feature of his handling of the case: he actually divided the hearing into three parts. In each, he judged on the
facts, and accepted the paradigm shared by the litigants (27).
Had Thai Tlhadi heard the case as a whole, he would have had to
order the arguments before passing judgment, and might have been
expected to clarify and adjudicate between the relevant norms.
This is precisely what the chief did in the same case. In
treating the dispute as a single issue, he was forced to recognise and assign priority to one of the paradigms elaborated by
the respective disputants. In electing to give judgment in terms
of Mogorosi's, he stated a relevant norm concerning the exchange
of land. As it happened, this contradicted the complainant's
argument, and he awarded against him. In short, judges invoke
norms explicitly when they are compelled, or feel it necessary,
to distinguish or adjudicate between a plurality of paradigms of

---

(27) This was made possible by the fact that the disputants did
    not differ over the normative bases of the three aspects of
    the argument when taken separately; rather, they disagreed
    on the norms at issue in the dispute *as a whole*.

argument. These competing paradigms may be presented to them by
the disputants, or they may be constructed for the purposes of
judgment.

The two cases suggest that the invocation of norms varies in
terms of two dimensions. The first dimension, the explicit and
implicit aspect, pertains to ways in which disputants and judges
give form to, and assert control over, the process of argument
(28). We do not suggest, despite having stipulated the distinct
ion between explicit and implicit references, that these are
necessarily absolute categories. In this sense, the distinction
is ideal-typical. But we believe that it is of value in understanding the normative basis of dispute settlement processes.

The second dimension of norm invocation concerns the specificity or generality of the norms employed in dispute settlement.
Case I is characterised by argument in terms of the precise,
substantive norms associated with the exchange of land and the
intention to commit assault. Case II, on the other hand, proceeds with reference to more generalised precepts concerning the
father-son relationship. The significant fact is that, in the
former dispute, the value at issue was emphasized by the

----

(28) Cases among the Tswana vary widely in the extent to which
the disputants are interrupted and questioned by intervening
third parties. When this does occur, however, it appears to
follow the same general principles as those observed in the
discourse of litigants and judges. In most cases, such
questioning proceeds on the basis of the facts as described
and interpreted by respective disputants. Only when a ques
tioner attempts to impugn the paradigm of one of those disputants are norms likely to be expressly invoked. Dr. R.P.
Werbner had described to us (personal communication) a
Tswapong strategy which, in our view, appears to illustrate
this: a questioner begins by eliciting a series of facts
from a disputant and then delivers a *coup de grace* by asking
"Is it not so according to Tswana law ...." in such a way a
to extract a confession of breach of norm. The intervening
party who does this, it seems, is actually constructing a
competing paradigm. He obtains a set of agreed facts and
then imposes order upon them by introducing a new normative
referent. Without the latter, his questions are largely
pointless. It is instructive to note Dr. Werbner's additional observation that norms are frequently invoked by
parties who have a partisan interest *against* the disputants
whom they question.

complainant; explicitly, he believed that the relationship itself was not under scrutiny. Once his property rights had been restored he had "no case against Leoke". Mooki, in sharp contrast, placed his relationship with Namayapela before the court; the substantive issue regarding *inter vivos* property allocation was merely a sympton of the broader problem. This appears to suggest that generalised normative invocations (both implicit and explicit) are associated with arguments in which the relationships themselves are at issue, while substantive, precise ones tend to be a feature of disputes in which the conflict over a right or value is primarily emphasized. In many cases, of course, debate involves both the relationship and the value, and normative invocations reflect this in that both substantive and generalised references are made. Moreover, when disputants appeal to different orders of norm in opposition to one another, we would expect them to state, and argue over, the priority which they assign to competing norms.

III

In this analysis we have looked to factors *intrinsic* to the processes of argument in order to account for the systematic pattern underlying the utilization of norms in the settlement of disputes among the Tswana. We take the strategic constraints and decisions which confront litigants and intervening third parties to determine to a significant degree the manner in which norms are invoked, manipulated and applied. This focus may be contrasted with one which emphasizes *extrinsic* features (e.g. the political organisation of the society or the structure of dispute settlement agencies) as determinants of this underlying pattern. We consider that one reason why the latter approach has so far produced hypotheses that are difficult to sustain is that intrinsic features of the processes compared have been insufficiently understood. Hence, we do not suggest our line of enquiry as an alternative to the consideration of extrinsic factors, but rather as a prelude to further attempts at cross-cultural comparison. Nor do we suppose that the factors applicable to the Tswana case will necessarily prove decisive elsewhere. But we do consider this line of enquiry to be worth pursuing in other contexts.

REFERENCES

Bohannan, P. (1957). *Justice and Judgment among the Tiv,* Oxford University Press, London.

Bohannan, P.   (1965).   'The differing realms of law', *American Anthropologist*, 67, 33-42.

Collier, J.F.   (1973).   *Law and Social Change in Zinacantan*, Stanford.

Comaroff, J.L.   (1973).   *Competition for Office and Political Processes among the Barolong boo Ratshidi*, Unpublished Ph.D thesis, University of London.

Epstein, A.L.   (1972).   'The reasonable man revisited: some problems in the anthropology of law', *Law and Society Review*, 7: 4, 643-666.

Fallers, L.A.   (1969).   *Law Without Precedent*, University of Chicago Press, Chicago.

Gluckman, M.   (1955).   *The Judicial Process among the Barotse of Northern Rhodesia*, Manchester University Press, Manchester (2nd Ed., 1967).

Gluckman, M.   (1973).   'Limitations of the case method in the study of tribal law', *Law and Society Review*, 7: 4, 611-41.

Gulliver, P.H.   (1963).   *Social Control in an African Society*, Routledge and Kegan Paul, London.

Gulliver, P.H.   (1969a).   'Case studies in law in non-western societies', Introduction to Part I, Nader, L. (ed.) *Law in Culture and Society*, Aldine, Chicago.

Gulliver, P.H. (1969b). 'Dispute settlement without courts: the Ndendeuli of Southern Tanzania', *ibid.*, 24-68.

Hoebel, E.A. (1940). *The Political Organization and Law-ways of the Comanche Indians*, American Anthropological Association Memoir, No. 54.

Krige, J.D. (1939). 'Some aspects of Lovedu judicial arrangements', *Bantu Studies*, 12(2): 113-27.

Kuhn, T.S. (1962). *The Structure of Scientific Revolutions*, University of Chicago Press, Chicago.

Moore, S.F. (1969). 'Descent and Legal Position'. *In* Nader, L., ed.), *Law in Culture and Society*, Aldine, Chicago, pp. 374-400.

Pospisil, L. (1971). *Anthropology of Law*, Harper and Row, New York.

Roberts, S.A. (1972). *Tswana Family Law*. Sweet and Maxwell, London (Restatement of African Law Series, No. 5).

Schapera, I. (1938). *A Handbook of Tswana Law and Custom*, Oxford University Press, London (2nd ed. 1955).

Schapera, I. (1943a). 'The work of the tribal courts in the Bechuanaland Protectorate'. *African Studies*, 2: 27-40.

Schapera, I. (1943b). *Tribal Legislation among the Tswana of the Bechuanaland Protectorate*, Athlone Press, London (L.S.E. Monographs on Social Anthropology, No. 9).

Schapera, I. (1966). "Tswana Legal Maxims", *Africa*, <u>37</u>, 121-134.

Schapera, I. (1970). *Tribal Innovators*, Athlone Press, London (L.S.E. Monographs on Social Anthropology, No. 43.)

Twining, W. (1964). *The Place of Customary Law in the National Legal Systems of East Africa*, University of Chicago Press, Chicago,

LAND LAW AND ECONOMIC CHANGE IN RURAL SENEGAL:

DIOLA PLEDGE TRANSACTIONS AND DISPUTES

Francis G. Snyder

INTRODUCTION

Since the nineteenth century most rural African communities
have been part of the world capitalist economy. Increasingly,
scholars question whether these communities may appropriately be
studied as isolated and relatively homogeneous entities. However, neither anthropologists nor lawyers have paid much attention to the effects of capitalist transformation on the legal
systems of rural Africa. Little work has been done to integrate
research in legal anthropology with studies of underdevelopment.
For this purpose land transactions in predominantly agricultural
societies provide especially useful material. In order to examine some of the legal consequences of the penetration of the
world economy into a rural community this study considers certain aspects of the relationship between social and economic
changes, the settlement of disputes, and transaction concepts and
rules among the Bandial subgroup of the Diola of Senegal (1).

Numbering approximately 4,000 people spread over nine

(1) The Foreign Area Fellowship Program (Social Science Research
Council/American Council of Learned Societies) from 1968-70,
the Wenner-Gren Foundation for Anthropological Research in
1970, and the Canada Council in 1973 and 1974 provided financial support for the research on which this paper is based.
I am grateful to these granting agencies, but I alone am responsible for all research findings and their interpretation
in this paper. This article is a substantially shortened version of the paper presented at the 1974 Conference of the
Association of Social Anthropologists held at the University
of Keele, England. The text of this paper was prepared prior
to my field research in Senegal from April to September 1975
so does not take material from that research into account.

villages, the Bandial are sedentary, wet-rice farmers inhabiting the Lower Casamance area of Senegal between the Gambia and Guinea-Bissau. The Casamance River, which flows from the Futa Jalon in Guinea to the Atlantic Ocean, bisects the Diola area, separating the primarily Islamic subgroups on the north bank of the river from the south-bank subgroups, including the Bandial, composed of Muslims, Catholics, and adherents to traditional Diola religion. In addition to religious factors, the extent of its participation in the Senegalese cash economy generally distinguishes the south-bank population from Diola across the river Although these people have long been integrated to some degree i the world capitalist market, south-bank groups such as the Bandial participate less than do other Diola or other Senegalese in producing raw materials for the national export economy. The cultivation of rice constitutes the major economic activity of the rural Bandial. Partly because there is no national marketing system for rice, the distribution and consumption of locally produced rice occurs to a very large extent within Bandial ethnic boundaries. Rice fields have been until recently the pre-eminent form of wealth; in principle, land, particularly rice fields, may not be definitively alienated; and the ecology and cultivation of rice are clearly reflected in Bandial culture and social organization. It is largely through transactions involving rice fields, which underlie a substantial degree of ethnic endogamy, that Bandial ethnic boundaries have been maintained.

The importance of rice field transactions among the Bandial will become evident during the course of this paper. However, the intricate relationship between social organization and obligations or transactions involving land bears stressing at this point. For the most part, *inter vivos* allocation of land occurs today within a generationally shallow group of agnatic collaterals or within the nuclear family and at the time of marriage o younger male and female members of the group. The nuclear famil provides the framework for the principal form of co-operation in agricultural labour. Succession to the same rice fields potentially involves a wider group, comprising dispersed patrilineage sharing a common patronym. In addition to being a member of descent and local groups each person in Bandial society is closely linked by marriage to members of other localized patrilineal or patrifilial groups. The facts that the basic unit in Bandial society is patrifilial, that residence is in principle virilocal and that the basic unit is exogamous imply a circulation of wome by marriage from one localized basic unit to others. To simplify, the social ties thus created include, *inter alia,* the relationship between any male Ego and the members of the basic

unit from which Ego's mother comes and, secondly, the relationship between any male Ego and the members of the basic unit into
which Ego's sister marries. These two relationships are redu-
cible to the relationship between matrilateral and sororilateral
kin (Goody 1969). This relationship is expressed and in large
part created and sustained by a form of land transaction, namely
a prestation in the context of continuing intergroup obligations.
It is frequently invoked to legitimise other forms of transactions, in which individual initiative and agreement play a
relatively important part.

In addition to underlying relationships between matrilateral
and sororilateral kin, periodic land prestations provided until
recently the economic basis for the Bandial ritual kingship or
rain priesthood. Of a type common in Africa, the Bandial kingship seems, on the basis of available evidence, to have been the
result of gradual accumulation by a ritual war leader of prestige
items, mainly women and cattle, during the early nineteenth century. Though this institution constituted a new form of centralized authority, it was partially reinterpreted in terms of categories familiar to Bandial culture, viz. those pertinent to the
relationship between matrilateral and sororilateral kin. In this
context the vocabulary and concepts of kinship served as an ideology which justified and legitimised a new social order based in
part upon the expropriation by royal basic units of the labour of
members of nonroyal basic units and upon the transfer of rice
fields by prestation from nonroyals to royals. From about 1930
to 1960, French colonial military, administrative, and tax policies gradually eroded the institution until today its preroga-
tives are for the most part limited to ritual privileges and
certain manifestations of social deference.

These colonial policies also influenced Bandial land transactions. This paper examines one such transaction, the pledge of
rice land. It first analyzes the concepts, norms, and context of
the pledge; then briefly describes certain economic changes
affecting pledges of land; and, finally, examines the settlement
of rural pledge disputes by urban courts. The discussion has two
purposes: (a) to describe some of the effects of integration
into the world economic system on Bandial land law, and (b) to
show that colonial economic and legal policies led to changes in
Bandial transaction rules and practices without altering the
ways in which these practices were characterized by the Bandial.

DIOLA PLEDGES OF LAND

Strictly speaking, the term 'pledge' belongs to the language of Western legal systems derived from the common law of England. In several respects it inaccurately characterizes the Diola-Bandial land transfer with which this paper is concerned. Both in its original purposes and in its conceptualization by the parties, this Bandial transfer does not correspond precisely to the pledge, the common law possessory lien, or the mortgage known to Anglo-American law (2). However, other authors (3) have frequently used the terms 'gage' or 'pledge' to refer to African or other legal institutions very similar to the particular transaction common among the Bandial. In his classic study Meek (1968:256), for example, states:

Where people have no other form of wealth but their land, and the sale of land is forbidden by native custom, the only means of raising money is by pledging the land or its usufruct. In its main features the pledge of land closely resembles the usufructuary mortgage, that is to say, a mortgage in which the mortgagor delivers possession of the mortgaged property to the mortgagee and authorises him to retain possession until the mortgage money has been paid, and to appropriate the profits accruing from the property in lieu of interest, or in payment of the mortgage-money, or partly in lieu of interest and partly in payment of the mortgage-money...

Unlike the mortgagee of English common law, the pledgee of land in Africa obtains no permanent rights over the land; there is no right of foreclosure; the land remains redeemable for all time, although it is not restored to its owner until the debt has been paid in full.

The term 'pledge' will provisionally be used in this paper,

----

(2) Cf. Cheshire 1967:566-639; Brown 1955:622-679; Fryer 1938: 461-546; Buckland and McNair 1965:314-324; Plucknett 1956: 603-609.

(3) Wigmore 1897; Meek 1968:256-265; Gluckman 1965:98-99; Mauss 1954:59-62; Adegboye 1969; Woodman 1967: Verdier 1968:3.3-3.4; James 1971:339-341; Weber 1966:117-118; Kouassigan 1966:90; Elias 1962:187-191; Obi 1963:120-125; Darmawi 1972: 299-301 stresses the inappropriateness of the term "pledge" for similar *adat* transactions but nonetheless employs the term. Barton 1969:37-38 uses the term 'pawn'.

partly because the Bandial transaction to be described shares
many of these characteristics and partly for the sake of convenience.

Among the Bandial, individual male or female members of a
generationally shallow group of agnatic collaterals, the basic
land holding unit, have access to the unit's rice land upon marriage and at the death of a same-sex member of the basic unit
(i.e., inheritance of rice land is homogeneous). As a result of
changes in population, ecological conditions, or other factors
influencing individual demands for cultivable land in a monocul-
tural economy, it was in the past and is still today frequently
the case that these forms of access to rice land do not suffice
adequately to meet existing demand for this type of land. Hence
as the Bandial express it, 'walɛt ni bijisol wo nakaɛ ambaful
babu:' 'Those [fields which are] not from his *bijis* [allocation
of ricefields upon marriage] have been acquired [by pledge].'
That is, should a person lack sufficient land and be unable to
obtain fields from another member of the same basic unit, he
will seek to meet his demand through transaction with someone
from another basic unit. Conversely, should a person need a
particular item such as cloth, or rice, or a cow, he may, by
initiating the transaction, acquire it in exchange for a rice
field. The Bandial categorize this transaction as *gaiĺɛn* or
pledge.

Categorization of a Bandial transaction as a pledge implies
the existence of principles of inclusion and exclusion. In order
to define a category or segregate one must know the contrast set
of which the segregate is a part (Frake 1969). Like many other
African legal systems (Allott, Epstein, and Gluckman 1969:77),
the Bandial do not have a general model of contract and "view
each transaction as a distinct complex of rights" (Farnsworth
1969:590). All Bandial transactions, with the exception of prestation cycles in marriage or royal — non-royal relationships,
fall into one of five categories: *gɔ̀jii, gamag, gɔ̀luuwaas,
gaiĺɛn,* or *funom.* As Diagram I shows, the pledge transaction
(*gaiĺɛn*) contrasts with other Bandial transactions in terms of
several fundamental components. First, it is a land transaction,
that is, one of its purposes is the transfer of rights with respect to land. In this respect *gaiĺɛn* is normatively similar to
the transactions *gɔ̀jii* and *gɔ̀luuwaas,* which always involve land,
but differs from the transaction *funom,* which, at this level of
semantic contrast, does not involve land; the transaction *gamag*
may concern either land or non-land objects. A second dimension
of contrast, the land or space category involved, further

DIAGRAM I: BANDIAL TRANSACTIONS

	DIMENSIONS OF CONTRAST			
TYPES / TRANSACTION	Good	Space Category	Parties	Time period for which right alienated
Gəjii	land	*Yihin, briteuun*	patrikin	temporary indeterminate
Gamag	land or non-land	*briteuun, galah, fuaoa*	patrikin or non-patrikin	temporary indeterminate
Gəluuəxaas	land	*briteuun, galah*	non-patrikin	temporary specified
Gailen	land	*Yihin*	non-patrikin	temporary indeterminate
Funom	non-land	–	non-patrikin	permanently

distinguishes among the various land transactions. *Gailɛn*
involves rice fields (*uhin,* sing. *n͂ihin*); *gɔjii* may concern
the space categories *n͂ihin* or *biiteuun* (formerly cultivated rice
field now used for harvesting thatch); *gamag* involves *biiteuun,*
galah (fields cleared in the forest for crops other than rice,
particularly peanuts), and *fuwa* (palm groves); and *gɔluuwaas*
involves *biiteuun* and *galah.* As Maine (1963:264-275) suggested,
moral evaluation is implicit in the categorization of property,
and distinguishing among categories of space or property is,
among the Bandial as in many legal systems, a way of expressing
social values and structuring land use and transfer. Thirdly,
the pledge, at least among the Bandial, occurs among parties who
do not share the same patronym. It thus contrasts along this
dimension with the land transaction *gɔjii* and is similar to the
land transaction *gɔluuwaas* and the non-land transaction *funom;*
the transaction *gamag* may involve either patrikin or not.
Finally, these transactions may be contrasted according to
whether the transferred rights or items are considered by the
Bandial to be definitively alienated. This dimension contrasts
funom, which involves the definitive transfer of rights, with
gɔluuwaas which involves the temporary alienation of rights, for
a time period fixed in advance, and all other transactions, which
involve the temporary alienation of rights for an indeterminate
period of time. Thus, three factors determine the conceptual
classification of a land transfer: the category of space or type
of property involved, the social distance between the parties,
and the temporal duration of the transaction. In the case of
each transaction, the denotative nominative term implicitly
specifies the transaction's specific normative components
together with general normative elements which the particular
transaction may share with others.

The Bandial conceptualize the pledge transaction in terms of
three separate ideas, expressed by the lexemes *-ilɛn,* *-mbaf,* and
buuɔl. The lexeme *-ilɛn* is composed of a radical *-il,* which may
be translated as 'to transfer' and of the causative suffix *-ɛn,*
though, to my knowledge, the radical *-il* is never used without
the suffix. I propose therefore to render *-ilɛn* as 'to transfer;' the term 'exchange' may appear inappropriate in a situation in which the transferred land is subject to redemption.
When the lexeme *-ilɛn* is employed, the speaker places himself
always in the position of envisaging the transaction from the
viewpoint of the transferor of the rice field. One may, for
example, designate certain fields as '(*w*)*o n͂ailɛnmɛ*': 'those
which he transferred.' Referring to his transfer of the field
in question, the transferor may say to his transferee,

'*iℓεn̂o ni aɯ*': 'I transferred it to you.' One may also refer
to the field thus transferred by '*n̂ihin n̂an̂u n̂iniℓεn*': 'that
[particular] rice field was exchanged.' Equally from the transferor's viewpoint, the transaction may be referred to by employing another lexeme, *-bεℓεn*, composed of the radical *-bεℓ*: 'to
throw,' 'to lose,' and the causative suffix *-εn*, 'to cause to
be thrown,' 'to cause to be lost.' Thus one says '*nabεℓεnbεℓεn*
n̂ihindoℓ': 'he threw it'; '*aɯ abεℓεn̂omε*': 'you lost it'.
The use of either of these lexemes expresses the transaction
from the viewpoint of the transferor of the rice field. In each
case, a nominative prefix to the radical indicates the transferor, and a nominative suffix is employed to designate the
transferee. The transfer as such is usually referred to by the
nominative form *gaiℓεn* (abstract noun class marker *ga-* prefixed
to *-iℓεn*).

Conversely, from the viewpoint of the transferee, this same
transaction is denoted by the lexeme *-mbaf*, comprised of the
simple subordinate mood marker *mi* (Sapir 1965:34, sec. 4.533.A.
and the radical *-baf*: 'to receive by transfer'. To my knowledge, the radical *-baf* is not employed otherwise than in the
lexeme *-mbaf*. Its use may be illustrated by two examples.
Speaking of a person's acquisition of a field by pledge (*gaiℓεn*)
one may say '*nambabaf*': 'he acquired [it] by transfer.' If a
person wishes to express the notion that he has acquired a field
from someone by this transfer, he may say '*injε imbafℓon̂o ni*
andε': 'I received it by transfer from so-and-so.' Unlike the
lexeme *-iℓεn*, *-mbaf* may be used in contexts other than the particular transaction being considered here to express that one has
received a rice field from another person with whom one stands i
a relationship, such as that between matrilateral and sororilateral kin, involving a land transfer as part of a set of
reciprocal prestations. When *-mbaf* is used, a nominative prefix
is employed to designate the transferee, while a nominative
suffix denotes the transferor. This contrast between the
lexemes *-iℓεn* and *-mbaf* may then be summarized as follows:

DIAGRAM II

DESIGNATION OF RECIPROCATING PARTIES

		Party designated by a prefixed subject-ive pronoun	**Party** designated by a suffixed object-ive pronoun
Lexeme	*-iʲɛn*	transferor	transferee
	-mbaf	transferee	transferor

These two lexemes designate the respective roles of the parties to the transaction not only at the time at which the transaction is concluded but also as long as the 'agreement' is in force. A third term, *buuðl*, refers to the termination of the 'agreement' or to bringing the transaction to a close. Composed of the radical *-al*: 'to redeem' and a prefixed noun class mar-ker, *buuðl* may, for purposes of this paper, be translated as 'redemption.' In this context, therefore, the radical *-al* designates the act of redeeming one's rice field and thereby of terminating the relationship created by the original trans-fer of land. Thus the lexeme *buuðl* refers generally to the pro-cess of redemption shown as the second transaction in the following diagram:

DIAGRAM III

PLEDGE AND REDEMPTION

	Transferor	Object Transferred	Transferee
Transaction I	A	rice field	B
	B	animal	A
Transaction II	A	animal	B
	B	rice field	A

The same term may be used to denote the redemption value of the
rice field concerned in the transaction. Every rice field in
the Bandial area has a value for the purpose, *inter alia*, of th
transaction. Depending on its average yield, a field may be
worth a cow, a bull, a goat, any number of baskets of rice, or,
more recently, a given sum of money. This redemption value of
the field is known generically by the term *buuðl*, a usage which
contrasts with that of the term *'butum'* (mouth, share) to expre
the notion of worth or value in other contexts.

With this conceptual sketch in mind, it is possible to outli
briefly the other normative elements of this transaction.
Together with the four components of *gailɛn* already discussed,
these elements constitute the body of rules governing the Bandi
pledge. The parties must necessarily be married men and belong
to basic units differing in patronym. In other Diola areas the
tend to be related by agnatic ties (cf. Linares de Sapir 1970:
208). In any case, as Gluckman (1965:173) remarked concerning
the Barotse, these "more ephemeral transactions involving previously unrelated people tend to be assimilated to the pattern
of status relationships," allowing room for the sort of manipul
tion of kinship boundaries discussed by Moore (1969; 1972:68-70
Transfer of a rice field consequent to the agreement between th
two parties is in principle subject to the approval of the fath
of each or, if one's father is deceased, of one's brothers or
father's brothers. This precondition is tempered by such facto
as residential proximity of agnates and that the near kin of a
potential transferor will usually attempt to meet the needs of
their kinsman before assenting to the transaction. Much depend
on the circumstances, particularly the unity or fragmentation o
the agnatic group and the purposes of the specific transaction.
A potential transferor of land may need rice to feed his family
an animal for a funeral sacrifice, money for children's school-
ing, or an item to repay another pledge. A potential transfere
may seek additional land for food production or, if he is wealt
in rice, animals, or cash, ways of augmenting his prestige or h
wealth in fields.

The basis of this transfer is the reciprocal exchange of pre
stations, for example a rice field against an animal, and witho
such an exchange there is no transaction. In this the Bandial
pledge, an exchange of use-values, resembles the Barotse transaction of barter, which is considered as a reciprocal conveyanc
of property and in which, consequently, "the legal problems ...
involve not merely what the parties agreed or promised to do,
but what property they exchanged and what rights each has in

that property" (Gluckman 1965:177). It is useful also to recall
Plucknett's (1956:363) statement, in a discussion of the history
of the writ of debt in English law, that there "is fairly old
authority for the theory that a contract consists of 'mutual
grants'" and to note that Pollock (Maine 1963:442-443), though
disagreeing with Maine that contract could have developed from
debt, nonetheless affirms the notion that in medieval English
law debt consisted of mutual conveyances. Weber's analysis of
economic barter makes clear the analytic outlines as well as
the legal consequences of this conception of the pledge transaction:

> Economic barter was always confined to transactions with
> persons who were not members of one's own "house," especially
> with outsiders in the sense of non-kinsmen ... Normally, barter
> enjoyed practically no guaranty, and the conception was non-
> existent that barter could mean the assumption of an "obliga-
> tion" which would not be the product of a natural or artificial
> ·all-inclusive fraternal relationship. As a result, barter at first
> took effect exclusively as a set of two simultaneous and recip-
> rocal acts of immediate delivery of possession ... Thus, the kind
> of "legal protection" accorded to barter was not the protection
> of an obligation, but of possession... (Weber 1966:107-108).

The logical consequence of this conception of the pledge transaction (cf. Weber 1966:120; Gluckman 1965:180-182; Allott,
Epstein and Gluckman 1969:72-73) is the non-enforceability of
bare promises or executory contracts found among the Bandial.

The pledge, once concluded, is of indefinite duration, its
time of termination being specified neither by the parties nor
in relation to an agricultural task. It continues at least one
agricultural year and as long thereafter as the transferor of
the field has not reimbursed to the transferee the prestation
which he received in exchange for his field. During this time
the transferee has the rights to cultivate the field, to appropriate the yield, and to stock the product in his personal granary. He may retain any amount of rice by which the yield before
redemption of the field exceeds the value of the animal or other
counter-prestation, as a village elder explains in the following
text:

> Consider a rice field which has the value of a bull. If you
> cultivate it this year, and you cultivate it next year and the
> following year, and then you cultivate it a fourth year, you
> will have produced [a quantity of] rice which is worth more than

two bulls, but you will continue to eat easily. If after twent
years of this, the other man is rich and comes to see you and
gives you back a bull, you will give him his field. But you wil
have more than him, because you will long since have eaten the
value of a bull and you will have kept all the [rest of the] har
vested rice in your granary. If you show him the rice from th
field during the past twenty year, he will not be pleased.

The transferor of the land acquires the use of the good, typi-
cally cattle, a funeral cloth, or rice, which he receives. In
the case of a transfer of a cow for a field, he is entitled to
keep any subsequent progeny. The rights and obligations of the
parties are transmissible to their respective heirs, and the
right to redeem is in principle never lost. Any man or woman
related by patrifiliation to the original transferor or to his
male agnates may redeem the field.

The mode of redemption, or *buuɔl*, is quite precise. First, the
transferor of the field must notify his transferee of his, (the
transferor's) intention to redeem the field. Notification is
constituted by the transferor's giving to the transferee a sheaf
of rice and telling him of his intention to redeem. To be
effective, such notification of intention to redeem prior to
the cultivating season beginning in June must be given during
the preceding harvest season (*guwɔgen*). A transferor's later
demand risks refusal by the transferee on the ground that the
latter, relying on being able to work the field, has already set
aside a reserve stock of grains (*ɛugit*) for next season's rice
nurseries. In addition to notifying the transferee, the transferor must, prior to the season during which he intends to
recommence working the land, tender to the transferee an animal
or other object of the same type which he himself received.
Though in principle the object must be returned in kind, the
exact object, e.g., a particular cow, need not be returned.

Why termination of the relationship is essentially left to th
initiative of the original transferor of the field is easily see
by considering certain aspects of the social and economic contex
of the Bandial pledge. This transactional relationship presents
striking similarities with the medieval gage of land classified
by Hazeltine (1901:649-650) as a usufruct-gage of the *mortuum
vadium* form in which the gagee was in possession of the land and
had the right to take rents and profits, while rents and profits
from the land did not reduce the debt but were taken in lieu of
interest. Such an arrangement was known to classical law as
antichresis (Eichler 1973:40). Its underlying economic

assumptions emerge if one considers it in the light of the
advantages ascribed by James (1971:340-341) to the Tanzanian
customary mortgage, in which possession of land is not transferred.

First, transferring possession raises the problem of ensuring
continuity of development of the land (James 1971:340-341).
This has not normally been problematic in the Diola case. Diola
economy and society are relatively undifferentiated, sex difference being the principal basis for division of labour. Except
for the ritual king or rain priest, all men engage in approximately the same economic tasks. In the normal course of things
any transferee will perform the same agricultural operations as
his transferor would have, and the assumption that he will do so
has in the past been one reason for a transferor's initiating the
transaction. Wet-rice cultivation requires a substantial initial
investment of labour and, optimally, continuous working of the
same field year after year. A basic unit will therefore seek to
ensure that its rice fields are cultivated each year, preferably
by its own members but, failing that, by someone from another
basic unit. In part, this reasoning lies behind the remark by
Geismar (1933:152) that among the Diola the "feeling of a collective interest is ... pushed to such a point that a rice field
temporarily abandoned must be ceded, without payment, to a cul-
tivator capable of working it," thus spreading agricultural risks
while ensuring continued upkeep of fields. Concomittantly, if a
transferee renders the field unusable and the transferor comes to
redeem, the transferor is in principle entitled to take another
field of equal value belonging to the transferee. As in the
Indonesian *djual gadai* transaction (Darmawi 1972:299), land is
the object of the transaction, and the transferee has no authority to demand reimbursement of the object or sum given for the
land. Thus placing the initiative for *buuðl* on the transferor
obviates problems inherent in an exchange of a moveable object
for an immovable one. It also lends support to the argument
that, unlike the personnel *tidennūtu* contract of Nuzi, the
Bandial pledge does "not represent security for a loan, but
rather a substitute payment for the borrowed capital" (Eichler
1973:44).

Put another way, the pledge was in its original form a legal
institution which served to allocate scarce resources by matching
demand with supply or by adjusting changing demographic factors
to the relatively fixed amount of rice land available. It still
performs this role, though the high rate of labour migration
today tends to reduce its importance in this respect. It also

serves to allocate land between localized basic units by supplementing the land allocation which occurs within these units
on the occasions of marriage and death. Hence in Bandial societ
it performs a role in the distribution of land which in more
politically centralized societies is the task of central political or legal authorities. Though it seems that in the past
priests or ritual kings allocated or periodically redistributed
land in some Diola kingdoms which previously existed in the
Lower Casamance (cf. Thomas 1960:203–205; 1958–1959 I:274–275;
1972:165; 1963:315–317; Pelissier 1966:688), to my knowledge the
Bandial rain priest never performed these functions.

In a society with little centralization of authority and the
economic arrangements which underlie such a political organization, the reasons for social cohesion frequently lie in other
forms of economic organization. Forms of exchange have until
recently been one of the major factors of social cohesion among
the Bandial, as among the Chimbu (Brown 1970). Despite the historical development of a system of economic redistribution
centred on the rain priesthood, reciprocity was crucial in knit-
ting together basic units unrelated by descent. Reciprocal
transfers such as the pledge not only underlie numerous forms of
economic co-operation but they also were used in the past to
create relations of political domination and continue today to
cement and sustain relationships resulting from marriage. The
institution of 'serial pledges' provides one example of the role
of land transfers in fostering social cohesion and makes clear
some of the other characteristics of this transaction.

The term 'serial pledges' refers simply to the conclusion of
a series of pledges with respect to the same parcel of land. Fo
example, A who is a member of lineage W transfers a rice field t
B, a member of lineage X, in return for an animal. B will rarel
if ever, transfer this field to a member of his patronymic group
particularly a co-resident of the same village. Were he to do s
that transaction would fall not into the Bandial category of
gailɛn, or pledge, but of *gɔjii*, or gift, a form of generalized
reciprocity among patrikinsmen, and even this would be unusual.
Should his potential transferee be a patrikinsman, B will refuse
to transfer the field he (B) received by pledge and instead give
his kin a field (*bijis*) which he had received from his father at
the time of his marriage. The transfer of a field subject to
redemption risks spoiling good relations between two parties
whose co-operation may be crucial in other activities. Should B
give his brother, for example, a pledged field and B's pledgor
redeem the following year, B's brother will be obliged to return

the field, probably with little improvement in his own situation.   Hence the transferee of a pledged field will only in rare instances use that field in a *gɔjii* transaction with a kinsman. B may, however, pledge the same field to C, a member of lineage Y.   In order to do so he must, preferably without revealing C's identity, advise A of the possible transaction between himself (B) and C and offer A the option of redeeming the field.   If A is unwilling or unable to exercise his option of redemption, B may then transfer the field to C for appropriate prestation, one equivalent to that which B transferred.   This second transaction renders A's later redemption of the field more difficult, since in order to recover his field A must reimburse B and then persuade or coerce B to reimburse C, so the field may be returned from C to B and then to A; A may not request the field directly from C.

For another reason also this second transfer renders A's eventual redemption more difficult.   In the event that prior to B's transfer to C, A fails to exercise his option to redeem, C is not obliged, except by courtesy, to consult A should he (C) wish to transfer the field to D.   Diagram IV illustrates the inverse relationship between the knowledge of the original transferor and the length of the chain of transactions:

DIAGRAM IV

SERIAL PLEDGES

Transferor	Transferee	Person who must be consulted by transferor
A	B	near kin of A
B	C	A
C	D	B
D	E	C

Though it is extremely difficult to trace empirically these transactional chains, the Bandial state that a chain might include three transactions at most; it may also involve pledges to redeem pledges or be linked with other pledge chains.   In such cases, it is easy to understand why, in entering into a pledge transaction, an original transferor risks losing his field. Nonetheless, one of the principal consequences of this land transfer is to link by economic interest or transactions persons unrelated by kinship. Considered as an entirety composed of two transactions, the pledge is a type of balanced reciprocity in which, as "for the main run of balanced exchange social relations hinge on the material flow" (Sahlins 1965:148) It nonetheless includes substantial room for manoeuvre and sufficient possibility for the use of calculation and guile for the Bandial clearly to distinguish it, conceptually and practically from the transaction of *gəjii* between persons classified as patrikin, either generally or for the purposes of the transaction.

James' analysis of Tanzanian materials raises a second point a pledge involving transfer of possession is not a "suitable transaction for loans by co-operatives and governmental agencies which would not normally want to enter into possession of the land" (James 1971: 340-341). This indicates possible conflicts arising from the Diola pledge as the Bandial are increasingly drawn into the capitalist economy. It also suggests that, as with contractual relationships among the Barotse (Gluckman 1965:172-176), pledges of land among the Bandial have in the past served primarily to supplement the intricate network of obligations found in kin relationships, whether through filiation or marriage, by which the distribution of most goods, including credit, took place. In this respect, and within certain limits, the pledge permits an individual to transfer fields in order to meet other, immediately pressing needs such as food or funeral goods which he or his patrikin are unable or unwillin to satisfy. Even then a potential transferor may prefer to rely on more distant kin (cf. Linares de Sapir 1970:208). That transactional relationships created by pledging rice fields are ideally supplementary and essentially short-lived and that in some respects "the economic relation tends to be a simple negation of kinship reciprocities" (Sahlins 1965:150) are evident also in the measure of value or equivalents. As suggested by the informant's text already quoted, only a fool or a man poor i rice, cattle, or kin would, as transferor, allow the pledge relationship to endure more than a few years.

Nonetheless, a person wealthy in fields and sufficiently skilled in or otherwise capable of manipulating legal institutions may use this transaction in order to increase the number of persons indebted to him. Since rice fields are the most highly valued goods in rural society, individuals may seek to acquire them as a form of wealth immediately translatable into prestige and power. However, since the transferor of the field has the initiative for terminating a transactional relationship created by pledge, prestige and power and other attributes acquired in this way remain, to a certain extent, dependent upon the good will of the original transferor.

Depending on the circumstances, factors which are equally if not more powerful lead individuals and groups to retain fields or to redeem them once transferred. Kin lands are more highly valued than those acquired elsewhere, so all other things being equal, a person will not have recourse to pledges if he can satisfy his needs otherwise. Likewise, early redemption by kinsmen of the original transferor may allow the fact that a parcel was ever pledged to be obscured (cf. Leach 1968:173-174). Though women may redeem a kin field and are in principle allowed to pledge their own fields, in practice a woman who pledged one of her fields would be considered lacking in common sense. If she wishes to transfer or is approached by a potential transferee, she is expected to consult her father or brother who may take the field in question and give her the item she needs, the assumption being that she would not consider transferring a field unless she needed something. As the use of the term *-bɛlɛn* (to throw, to lose) to denote the pledge suggests, any transfer of rice fields outside one's kin group runs the risk that the field may be lost because the original transferor or his kin are unable to redeem the field, because the transferee may refuse to relinquish the field and become unamenable to remedial measures, or because in the course of time the original oral transaction unintentionally or intentionally escapes the memories of the heirs of the original parties or any witnesses. Consequently, a person who transfers fields too frequently risks kin and public censure of his irresponsibility and wastefulness. In addition, he may, as a result of meeting short-run needs, find himself confronted with land shortage in the long-run, for example as his children reach the age of marriage.

A final factor favouring retention or redemption of fields is that, according to Bandial notions of personal success, a person acquiring a field is thought to be more advantageously placed than one giving up a field. This value reflects in part the fact that the longer the duration of the pledge relationship, the greater the difference between the value of the rice produced and the reciprocal prestation, e.g. a cow, involved in the transaction, since the pledgee is not required to account for or return profits in kind resulting from his working the land.

In a community with a strong egalitarian ideology and in which
levelling mechanisms and witchcraft accusations still inhibit
the accumulation of wealth, such a notion of success constitute
a powerful logic for holding on to kin fields, or, if transfer
by pledge is unavoidable, for redeeming them as soon as possibl

TRANSACTIONS AND ECONOMIC CHANGE

Certain sources of potential inter-party and inter-group
conflict are therefore inherent in the pledge. This transactio
also reflects broader social conflict and illustrates certain
facets of the contemporary transformation of rural Senegal. Th
economic changes which most directly affect land transactions
are labour migration and the increasing use of all-purpose mone
Both of these have influenced the Bandial pledge.

Labour migration in the Bandial area resulted primarily from
French colonial tax policy and encouragement of the cultivation
of peanuts for the world market (Snyder 1973). Together with tl
establishment of a local administration, the improvement of
transport, and the construction of infrastructure by forced
labour under the *indigénat* system and in lieu of tax payment,
these policies were the forms in which the international capitalist economy penetrated into rural Bandial villages. They
linked the Bandial to the colonial Senegalese version of peri-
pheral capitalism (cf. Amin 1970, 1971b). Although, partly for
reasons similar to those leading other Senegalese peasants to
continue millet cultivation (cf. Amin 1971a:26), rice remains
the predominant Bandial crop, two consequences soon followed.
First, male agricultural labour-time was partly diverted from
food to non-food crops and activities. Secondly, female non-
agricultural labour was converted into a market commodity. Thu
French colonial policy gradually transformed into market commodities labour expended for certain purposes and specific product
of forest and agricultural land.

"[L]abour and land," as Polanyi wrote, "are no other than the
human beings themselves of which every society consists and the
natural surroundings in which it exists. To include them in the
market mechanism means to subordinate the substance of society
itself to the laws of the market" (Dalton 1968:31). Among the
Bandial, one of the consequences of labour migration was the
increased importance of all-purpose money. This was dependent
only partly on the transformation of labour into what Polanyi
(Dalton 1968:32) called a fictitious commodity. It also rested
on the sale of local products, such as fish, fruit, palm wine

and kernels, and peanuts, to townsmen or to government co-operatives. The marketing of both types of commodities resulted, in turn, in more readily available all-purpose money and more transactions involving all-purpose money. Though an increase in the volume of all-purpose money and an increase in transactions involving all-purpose money may differ in their social and economic consequences (Postan 1954), they were closely related so far as changes in Bandial land transactions are concerned.

Perhaps the major distinction between the Bandial transaction described in this paper and the pledge sketched by C.K. Meek (1968:256) is that, in the past, the former was not conceptualized by the parties as a means of providing collateral security for a loan but, at each of the two stages (pledge and redemption) of the transactional relationship, as a "mutual appropriative movement of goods between hands" (Dalton 1968:170). Like the institution of equivalency exchange described by Polanyi (Dalton 1968:109-111), its purpose was to ensure access by all to the means of food production in a society without centralized political authority. In this respect the pledge of rice land was a form of balanced reciprocity between non-kinsmen and complemented the transfer known as *gǝjii* which performed an analogous function among patrikin. It was a direct transfer of a good desired by one person and 'possessed' by another in exchange for a good desired by the latter party and 'possessed' by the former. This view of the transaction was not dependent on an absence of credit, as some legal historians (Hazeltine 1909: 647; Wigmore 1897:322; Plucknett 1956:603) might maintain. As Mauss (1954:35) and Firth (1964) have shown, "[e]ven in the most primitive and non-monetary economic system the concept of credit exists — the lending of goods and services without immediate return against the promise of a future repayment" (Firth:29). Both the Bandial transaction of *gǝjii* and prestations between matrilateral and sororilateral kin involve credit in this sense, though its social meaning and the structural relations it entails differ from those in capitalist market economies (Godelier 1965:75-77). Such a conception of the pledge depended on the exclusion of all-purpose money from rice land transactions among the Bandial. In the Anglo-American social and legal context, pledging enables the pledgor by providing security to acquire desired goods with the (all-purpose) money he receives. Among the Bandial the pledge transaction enabled the pledgor to have access to other goods but without using the medium of all-purpose money. In both cases the legal institution, from the pledgor's viewpoint, functions *inter alia* to convert one (scarce) resource into another. However, it does so, in one case, through the use of all-purpose money, and in the other, by mutual transfers or the use of special-purpose money. Only within the past twenty years has all-purpose money entered at all into Bandial land transactions, and until very recently its use has been restricted to transactions involving categories of land which are less highly valued than rice fields.

The Bandial have long had forms of special-purpose money, that is, objects which serve one or several, but not all, of the functions of money, namely exchange, payment, storage, and standard of value. Rice land, rice, and cattle were the principal prestige goods, and certain other goods were also used as special-purpose money. When French money first became available to the Bandial in labour or agricultural commodity transactions, it was integrated into the Bandial rural economy as simply another kind of special-purpose money. In 1882, for example, Bour (1882:342) remarked that French money, once distributed, rarely remained in general circulation but was often used for women's jewellery. Cash was later employed as a means of exchange, first, in the transaction *funom* (cf. Koelle 1854:60: *funom*, pl. *kunom*: market) involving the transfer of subsistence goods to non-kin and, secondly, in the transaction *gǝluuwaas*, from the French louage, or rental, which in the immediate area of Ziguinchor concerned peanut fields and today in the Bandial area may involve the right to cut (*-rus*) thatch grown on abandoned rice fields (*biiteuun*). It first entered rice land transactions indirectly by being used to purchase a prestation for redemption, such as a cow, and then directly as a means of payment on redemption, here merely as a substitute for other forms of special-purpose money when these were not available to the pledgor and when the pledgee was willing to accept cash.

Cash, however, differs profoundly from the forms of special-purpose money for which it was substituted as a means of payment. Marx remarked that in immediate exchange "the equivalent form is applied sometimes to one commodity, sometimes to another ... The exchange article therefore acquires no form which is independent of its use-value" (cited in Meillassoux 1971:69, n. 3). By contrast, cash leads to commodity exchange. It "is in the nature of a general-purpose money that it standardizes the exchangeability value of every item to a common scale" (Bohannan 1967:133). The Bandial economy remains, in Barth's (1966) terms, a minimally integrated set of values, but all-purpose money is becoming, especially for younger people, a means of storing wealth and is used by all for different purposes in different types of transactions. It is a means of exchange and a standard of value in the transaction *funom* involving subsistence goods, such as peanuts, fruit, and palm wine and kernels, which are sold in the market. It is a mode of payment in the renting of peanut fields and thatch fields. Although no national marketing structures for rice exist in the Bandial area and rice is rarely sold for cash, rice is occasionally pur-chased in town. Cash is frequently used as a mode of payment for the wage labour of youth associations working on rice fields; co-operation between husband and wife remains the dominant mode of production for rice. Finally, cash is a mode of payment in the redemption of pledged rice fields and, though rice land is not sold, cash is becoming a means of exchange in the creation of pledges. These changes in pledge practice are closely related to labour migration and the gradually increasing use of all-purpose money during the colonial period. The three factors converge in the translation of migrant-earned cash into rural agricultural land, partly through the pledging of rice fields. One consequence of this is greater economic and social differ-entiation in rural areas. The apparent range of economic choices open to Bandial villages has increased at the same time as traditional controls on the accumulation and retention of wealth break down. As the use of cash increases, and as labour migra-tion reduces the supply of labour potentially available for recruitment by kin ties and balanced reciprocity, a wealthy man may acquire more land than he or his kin are able or willing to cultivate and may hire wage labour in order to benefit from his transactions. In this incipient form of agrarian capitalism, labour and, more gradually, land are being transformed into marketable commodities. In this context, land transactions systematize values, foster the sharing of values, and modify shared values in the direction of greater consistency (Barth 1966: 14-15), both among the Bandial and between Bandial and outsiders. Their consequences are the increasing use of cash, the altera-tion of transaction rules and practice, and the transformation and integration of the Bandial economy into the periphery of the international economy.

TRANSACTIONS AND THE SETTLEMENT OF DISPUTES

Conflicts inherent in these economic changes frequently brought litigants to colonial courts. In turn, colonial dis-pute settlement institutions influenced the extent to which economic changes altered Bandial transaction concepts, rules, and practices. To begin to assess this influence, this section examines four disputes involving pledges of rice land, three in or near the Bandial area and one from the Fogny sub-group of the Diola on the north bank of the Casamance River. The cases

are drawn from a total of approximately 130 land disputes heard
in the Ziguinchor primary courts and by the local administratio
between 1934-1968 and for which written records exist. Undoubt
edly many cases went unrecorded, particularly prior to Senegalese independence in 1960, while records of others have been los
Not all of the local colonial administrative documents have yet
been classified in the National Archives so it is possible that
other cases may eventually become available. Existing records
fall roughly into three categories: judicial conciliation
agreements (*procès-verbaux de conciliation*), first instance or,
more rarely, appellate decisions, and administrative conciliation hearings. Compared to case files from African countries
influenced by the English common law tradition of judicial
decision-making and case reporting (cf. Abel 1969; Fallers
1969), even the fullest records, those of courts of first
instance, are relatively brief. The most useful part of the
file is witness testimony, at best simultaneously translated
more or less verbatim into French by the court clerk. The form
of judicial decisions reflects French practice (cf. Lawson
1962:233-234), and reports contain relatively abstract statements of law mixed with the court's summary of facts. The contrast with lower court reports in English-influenced African
countries should perhaps not be over-emphasized, however, since
the lack of a full exposition of judicial reasoning seems typical of many primary courts in Africa and elsewhere.

These case records do not include disputes settled by villag
dispute settlement agencies. Most land cases did not reach
either the courts of the local administration. During the
colonial period several factors made the Bandial reluctant to
take disputes to the local courts. The nearest court was about
25 kilometres from the nearest Bandial village. Courts were
part of the alien colonial administrative system, and a French
colonial administrator presided over the lower court. He was
assisted by two African assessors who in principle represented
the customary law of the parties (Pautrat 1957:28-30), but this
guideline was not always followed in practice. In any case Dio
assessors, consulted notables, or the interpreters, whose role
was especially significant (cf. Alexandre 1970), were usually
drawn from the numerically dominant Fogny subgroup of the Diola
and not from smaller groups such as the Bandial. In many cases
it was to the mutual advantage of the parties not to go to
court because of the moral values expressed in the Bandial adag
'one who requests something should not argue' or because when a
dispute did arise parties preferred a mediated or negotiated
settlement within the community rather than an alien, adjudicat

or administratively determined one. Beginning in this period
Bandial law may be characterized as customary law according to
Faller's (1969:3) useful definition, since it was henceforth

> not so much a kind of law as a kind of legal situation which
> develops in ... contexts in which dominant legal systems recog-
> nize and support the local law of politically subordinate
> communities.

In this situation the general French colonical principle of
respect for local law was not seriously adhered to (Diarra 1973:
97-101), and transactional concepts explicitly or implicitly
employed by the courts (cf. Badets 1954-55) frequently differed
from those of the Bandial. It is nonetheless useful to focus
here on colonial courts since, as the lowest official legal
institutions during the colonial period, they were the primary
institutional vehicle by which the legal foundations of peri-
pheral capitalism penetrated into rural areas and, together
with social and economic changes resulting from colonial policy,
began subtly to alter Bandial transaction rules and practice.
Although part of the apparatus of colonial domination, they were
thus partly analogous to the second force described by Weber
(1966:145) when he wrote:

> The ever-increasing integration of all individuals and all
> fact-situations into one compulsory institution which today,
> at least, rests in principle on formal "legal equality" has
> been achieved by two great rationalizing forces, i.e., first,
> by the extention of the market economy and, second, by the
> bureaucratization of the activities of the organs of the
> consensual communities.

With the institution of village chief created by the French in
the Diola area, these courts were the principal legal institutions
mobilized by the Bandial and other Diola in support of legal
change, but, unlike chiefs, colonial courts present the very pragmatic advantage of having left a number of written records.

By the Decree of November 10, 1903 the French colonial
administration established a dual hierarchy of courts (cf. Diarra
1973:91-105), thus extending the reach of the administration into
rural areas and expanding the options open to disputants unamenable to or unsatisfied by rural dispute settlement. The 1903
decree, supplemented by ministerial orders of 1910, constituted
within the African court hierarchy a *Tribunal de Cercle* in
Ziguinchor, which by 1909 was hearing appeals from civil cases

from seven *Tribunaux de Province* (ANS,G, 1G343:102), including
the one located at the circumscription or *Résidence* of Ziguinch
which had jurisdiction over the Bandial. A decree of August 16
1912, substituted the *Tribunaux de subdivision* for the
Tribunaux de province. By 1923 the Ziguinchor *cercle* comprised
one *tribunal de cercle* and three *tribunaux de subdivision*,
several of the latter having been abandoned because of lack of
cases (cf. ANS, G, 2G23, 35). The *subdivision* and *cercle* court
were replaced by first and second degree courts established by
the decree of March 22, 1924. This decree also instituted a
form of mandatory judicial mediation, maintained by the organic
decree of December 3, 1931 (Chabas 1953; 1954:122-129), accordi
to which the court of first instance was obliged, before hearin
the case judicially, to attempt to mediate the dispute. The
following cases illustrate both adjudication and judicial media
tion.

Case I:

Redemption of a pledge is a
reciprocal exchange of prestations

Recorded as case no. 7 of June 15, 1952 (4), this case
involves judicial mediation of a pledge dispute and provides a
straightforward example of redemption of a pledge. A forty-yea
old man, whom I shall call Anafan (all names are fictitious),
claimed against Boila, aged thirty, to recover a rice field
which Anafan's father had pledged for a pig at some unspecified
time in the past, and which Boila apparently refused to return.
So far as one can surmise from the case file, the parties were
not kinsmen, though they lived in different wards of the same
large Bandial village. The dispute arose in May or June 1952,
just at the beginning of the rice cultivating season and follow
ing a royal rain ceremony, *garumo*. In addition to opening the
period of preparation for intense agricultural labour, this
ritual signals the return to rural villages of people who durin
the dry season have been engaged in migrant labour or otherwise
travelling in nearby towns or other parts of Senegal and also
marks the transfer from wife to husband of responsibility for
feeding their children. According to the royal holder of the
shrine propitiated during the ritual, *garumo* "is celebrated in

---

(4) File entitled: *1950-1960. Tribunal de premier degré de
    Ziguinchor. Registre des procès-verbaux de conciliation.*
    Not paginated; handscript and typescript, Archives of the
    Justice de Paix, Ziguinchor.

order to show that the rainy season is approaching and that each
man should begin to think of cultivating." Hence it explicitly
signals a change in economic activities away from dry season
occupations such as palm wine harvesting, hunting, gathering of
wood, and repairing tools and houses and toward rice cultivation.
As the shrine holder explained, this reorientation focusses
attention very specifically on rice fields and on one's particular claims with respect to particular parcels of rice land:
"This ceremony is done to remind people that each must remember
his rice fields. You occupy a place, and it is yours alone.
You have your rice field, so you know that each should go cultivate his field during the rainy season ... This is not to say
that you can work any fields you like ... You must not cultivate
other people's rice fields." *Garumo* thus divides the season of
social interaction from the season of production (Labouret
1941:160) and, as one would expect, is followed by numerous
land disputes in densely populated areas. Though the Bandial
area has a relatively low population density of about 35 persons
per square kilometre, it is during the period just before and
immediately after the rains that most disputes over rice fields
arise.

In this case, following mediation by the Ziguinchor first
degree court composed of a French colonial administrator as
President and two African assessors, Boila agreed to return
the field to Anafan, and in turn Anafan agreed to transfer a
pig to Boila. The file contains only identification of the
parties and the basis of their agreement. No indication is
given of party or witness testimony or of any discussion between
the parties and the court, though a note indicates that the conciliation agreement was executed the following month. Despite
the straightforward nature of this dispute and the brevity of
the file, the case is useful for two reasons. First, it indicates that the local court shared with the Bandial the conception of the pledge relationship as consisting of two transactions
involving the reciprocal exchange of equivalents, as being
capable of succession by descendents of the original parties, in
this instance of the pledgor, and as being terminable, within
limits, at the initiative of the pledgor. Secondly, it suggests
that, if persons are unable to obtain satisfaction of their
claims within village dispute settlement agencies, they may
resort to the local town courts in order to reach an agreement
which will be committed to writing and regarded as a "judicial
contract, that is, an authentic act made before a judge and
having executory force" (Pautrat 1957:53), in other words, to
mobilize the local court system in support of claims arising

from rural agricultural disputes.

Case II:

A pledgee cannot refuse the pledgor's legitimate
exercise of his right to redeem.

This case, number 199 of August 13, 1934 (5), provides an
even more striking example of the mobilization of urban legal
institutions by rural villagers, since the complainant was able
to obtain a judgment in his favour against a defendant who fail
to appear in court. Paul's father pledged a rice field for a c
with one Charles of the same village. Following the pledgor's
death, Paul, his son and sole heir, requested the return of the
field and tendered to Charles a cow, which Paul tied near
Charles' house. Charles cut the rope by which the animal was
attached, and the cow strayed into the surrounding forest where
it was found by Duri. Paul then brought the matter to the chie
of the village in which all three parties resided, but the chie
was unable to settle the dispute so Paul, probably employing th
services of a local scribe or relative literate in French,
addressed a written complaint to the *commandant de cercle*.

The case file lists the complaint as being brought by Paul
against Duri for return of the cow but, as will appear, Paul's
complaint was in substance directed primarily against Charles.
Called to present his case, since legal counsel was not allowed
in African courts, Paul related the pledge transaction between
his father and Charles, his own return of the cow and request f
the field, and Charles' refusal to accede to the demand. He sta

I am bringing a complaint against him [Charles] in order
obtain my rice field. The cow which I returned to [Charles]
was picked up by [Duri] who now has the animal and does not
want to return it.

Called to speak next, Duri replied that when Paul returned the
cow to Charles, the latter refused to accept it and cut the rop
tying the cow, which wandered into the forest. Duri came upon
the cow and, recognizing it by its markings as belonging to Pau
led it to Paul's house. Duri continued:

---

(5) File entitled: *Année 1934. Tribunal de premier degré de
    Ziguinchor civil et commercial,* 100 pp. Signed April 23,
    1934. Handscript, Archives of the Justice de Paix,
    Ziguinchor.

[Paul] told me to take it again to [Charles] and to keep it for myself if, after all this, Charles refused once again to take it. Charles again refused to accept it and told me to keep it for myself if I wanted. That is why I am still keeping it.

The court was confronted with contradictory testimony concerning Duri's claim over the cow, a conflict which only Charles, who failed to appear in court, could resolve. This contradiction, however, is relevant only to the complainant as it formally appears and not to the issue of substance underlying Paul's complaint against Duri for the cow, which is the legitimacy of Paul's exercise of his right to redeem his rice field from Charles. Disregarding the question of form, the court goes to the principal issue and, after deliberating, renders its judgment as follows:

Whereas it is established by the debates that during his lifetime, the father of Paul pledged his rice field against a cow belonging to Charles of [the same village],

Whereas the father of Paul now being deceased, his son Paul who is his sole and unique successor and heir returned the cow in question to the said Charles in order to enter in possession of his rice field,

Whereas Charles refused to accept the cow which was tendered to him by Paul,

Whereas the cow in dispute was found wandering in the forest by the said Duri who holds it by order of the said Charles,

Whereas Diola custom provides that if a pledgor returns the object, thing, or animal pledged, he should retake possession of his rice field or other pledged object,

Considering that the said Paul is well-founded in his complaint and that he should re-take possession of his rice field.

The court decides that, following the harvest of this year, the said Charles must return to Paul the rice field he holds [and] that Duri will return the said cow to Charles, from whom he received it.

The court employs several means to resolve the problem posed by conflicting testimony as to the facts relevant to the complaint formally before the court and to reach the issue of substance involved in the case. No doubt drawing from Charles' failure to appear inferences unfavourable to him and favourable to Paul, the court first resolves the disputed question of fact by accepting Duri's testimony as to how he came into possession of the cow, thus placing on Charles principal responsibility for the formal dispute between Paul and Duri over the cow. Secondly,

the court evokes the well-known principle of the Diola pledge
to the effect that a pledgor may redeem his field by returning
the prestation which he received. Together with Charles' fail
ure to appear and his actions as they appear from the parties'
testimony, this principle is only one of several factors influ
encing the decision. But while the inferences drawn by the co
from Charles' failure to appear remain implicit and unstated a
the parties' testimony is restated by the court as a basis for
findings of fact, the principle of Diola customary law is presented as the normative rationalization and legitimation of th
decision. Its explicit invocation in Case II distinguishes th
judgment from the process of judicial conciliation in Case I,
in which legal principles remained implicit. Explicit stateme
of principle is a major factor distinguishing adjudication fro
judicial mediation, both of which take place before the full
court. The invocation of a rule, without which a lower court
decision risks being nullified on appeal (Pautrat 1957:56), ma
the court judgment appear as an authoritative decision rather
than a settlement based on agreement by the parties (cf. Pautr
1957:51), even though the rule invoked as a consequence of
institutional requirements may have as little bearing on the
outcome in this setting as in mediation. Finally, the court
does not implement its decision woodenly but specifies that,
though Paul's demand for the field cannot ultimately be refuse
Charles may this year harvest the crop he has planted. It thu
resorts to implicit considerations of equity to resolve an iss
which might have been addressed according to rules of 'customa
law if the dispute had been amenable to settlement by the vill
chief.

Case III:

All-purpose money is a legitimate means of exchange
and mode of payment in a pledge transaction.

This case, briefly reported as judicial conciliation case
number 6 of August 20, 1956 (6), demonstrates judicial recogni
tion of the increasing use of all-purpose money in pledges of
rice fields in the immediate area of Ziguinchor. The parties
were neither Bandial nor resident in the Bandial area. One,
Bass, was a fifty-six year old resident of a ward of Ziguincho

---

(6) File entitled: 1950–1960. *Tribunal de premier degré de
    Ziguinchor. Registre des procès-verbaux de conciliation.*
    Not paginated; handscript and typescript, Archives of the
    Justice de Paix, Ziguinchor.

a city of approximately 45,000 people which is now the capital
of the Casamance Region, and the other, Emanding, a farmer aged
28 and resident of a village about ten kilometres from Ziguinchor.
The conciliation agreement states simply that:

> [Bass] will cultivate the rice field in 1956, and he will re-
> turn if to [Emanding] after the harvest. [Emanding] will re-
> imburse to [Bass] the sum of 2,500 francs [CFA] which Bass
> gave in order to have the field.

The report indicates that land pledges are one means of
linking rural villages to urban centres by providing cash to
rural farmers who may produce few crops for the market but who
are increasingly dependent on imported goods, including food, and
need cash to acquire these goods. Conversely, pledges allow
permanent or temporary urban residents continued access to agricultural land. In this instance Bass apparently worked the field
himself, as many Ziguinchor residents do on weekends or holidays.
However, the same transaction may be used by permanent labour
migrants as a form of social security, as a means of maintaining
an economic stake in their home villages, or as a form of investment in guaranteed food production using wage labour. The case
also illustrates the use of all-purpose money as a means of
exchange and a mode of payment in rice field pledge transactions. Although this dispute involved a Ziguinchor resident and
a non-Bandial villager, the analysis in the preceding section
suggests that the use of all-purpose money in pledge transactions will not, in the long run, be limited to this particular
social situation. In this respect the case exemplifies the role
of the urban court, first, in supporting and sanctioning new
definitions of familiar rural transactions; secondly, upon being
mobilized or invoked by a party to the transaction, in redefining
social and economic relationships between rural and urban
dwellers; and, finally, in recognizing new pledge practices and
legal rules within a continuing conceptual framework.

Case IV:

Defining the pledge as a security transaction enables
the pledgor to deal directly with a sub-pledgee.

This case (7), recorded as number 1 of February 25, 1957, was

---

(7) File entitled: *1955-1966. Judgments du Tribunal de 2eme
degré de Ziguinchor.* Non-paginated, typescript, Archives
of the Justice de Paix, Ziguinchor.

appealed from the first degree court at Bignona to the second
degree court in Ziguinchor. The relationship among parties
involved was as follows:

DIAGRAM V

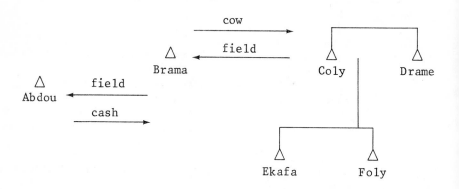

Coly borrowed a cow from Brama and died before paying the debt.
To guarantee eventual repayment of the cow, Drame, the brother
of the deceased, agreed with Ekafa and Foly, sons of the
deceased, to pledge one of Coly's rice fields to Brama as security. The record implies, but does not confirm, that Ekafa and
Foly were unmarried. Generally throughout the Diola area, inclu
ding the Fogny (cf. Pelissier 1966:692-694; Touze 1963:200), a
decedent's brother is responsible for acting as trustee of the
goods of the deceased until the latter's minor sons marry.
Following the pledge, Brama pledged the same field to Abdou for
9,000 CFA francs. Although the lower court record is not available, it appears from the brief appellate file that the dispute
arose when Drame claimed from Abdou the rice harvested from the
field.

Overturning the lower court holding, the appellate court rule
that Abdou could cultivate the field and take the product until
the field was properly redeemed and that he should be reimbursed
for any rice which he had handed over to Drame. The court expli
citly cited the rule of Diola 'customary' law that a creditor ma
transfer the pledged object. In the guise of stating that this
second pledge had met reasonable standards of publicity since
Ekafa showed Abdou the field, it also implied the original
pledgor's heirs' acquiescence (cf. Fallers 1969:284-290) in the

second pledge. Finally, and most important in this context,
the court stated that

> consequently, reimbursement of the cow should be made directly
> to Abdou as long as Brama has not repaid the 9,000 francs which
> he received in exchange for the pledge.

Working explicitly with a concept of pledge, the court
treated the cow, the rice field, and the sum of cash involved as
equivalent. Here the complete substitutability of cash for
cattle, a Bandial prestige good and form of special-purpose
money, is recognized and sanctioned by the court. Furthermore,
the original pledgor is allowed to deal directly with the sub-
pledgee in order to reclaim his land. Such a procedure contra-
venes Bandial notions of pledge, which tend to isolate each dyad
in a chain in order to maintain the privacy of each transaction,
but here its recognition is consistent with a greater development
of the market economy and the more widespread use of all-purpose
money in the Bignone area. It also accords with Drame's and
Brama's explicit use of the pledge as a security transaction,
Drame having originally pledged the animal solely to guarantee
repayment of the debt owed to Brama. Taken in conjunction with
the interchangeability of cash and cattle, it emphasizes the
exchange-value rather than the use-value of the goods involved,
though the latter is predominant in the ideal notions of the
Bandial pledge already described. Although not clear from the
record, it appears that in this situation such an emphasis risks
doing particular violence to the expectations of one of the
parties involved, for Abdou, the sub-pledgee, transferred cash
for the field but may be compelled to give up the land when the
original pledgor presents him with a cow. This case thus illustrated judicial willingness to enforce a transaction in which
balanced reciprocity is minimized and market factors predominate.
It also lends further support to the view that, in addition to
dispute settlement, one important albeit indirect consequence
of town court processes during the colonial period was to create
potentially authoritative alternative rules for land transactions
and new definitions of social relationships without altering the
conceptual classification of land transactions. In this specific
instance as in Case III the outcome also served to foster the
increasing penetration of the capitalist economy into rural
areas.

CONCLUSION

This paper has described some of the processes during the

colonial period by which the Bandial of Senegal were brought int
the capitalist world economy and how this economic transformati
affected aspects of Bandial law. Colson (1966) has demonstrate
how, among the Valley Tonga of Zambia, changes in social and
economic circumstances affected the ways land was obtained and
rights in land but did not lead to any change in legal rules.
In contrast, I have tried to show that, in the instance of the
pledge of rice land among the Bandial, economic changes and the
channelling by colonial courts led to changes in transaction
practice and in specific transaction rules without any change i
legal concepts.

With increasing labour migration and the penetration of the
capitalist market economy into rural areas, the function of the
pledge in the Lower Casamance now lies in providing a means of
security and investment in land for those able to invest as wel
as in supplementing the allocation of land within and among kin
units. Writing with hindsight of an empirically similar gage o
land in medieval England, Plucknett (1956:603) stated that:

> The primitive gage was capable of development in two direc-
> tions: first, the gage may become a slight object whose trans
> fer is treated as a binding form in a contract for future pay
> ment; or, the transaction may take its modern aspect of sec-
> urity only for the future payment of the principal debt.

Plucknett (1956) and Hazeltine (1909) ascribed these changes in
the medieval English transaction essentially to three factors:
the development of judicial execution for debt; the development
of other forms of obligation and of means for enforcing them;
and the increasing use of credit, particularly (cf. Hazeltine
1909:664-666) the increased activity of moneylenders. The
history of analogous legal institutions at other times and
places does not, of course, necessarily indicate eventual change
in the Bandial pledge, and this is especially so if one consider
that medieval England was undeveloped but not underdeveloped
(Frank 1969). However, two points concerning changes in the
contemporary Bandial pledge bear stressing. First, the rice
field pledge, once a transaction involving relatively symmetrica
transfers and conceptualized as a reciprocal conveyance of equivalents, is now sometimes considered a means of providing collateral security for the repayment of cash loans. This practice
is specifically related not to the development of credit but to
the increasing use of all-purpose money as a result of the penetration of capitalism and to new legal means of enforcing transactions. Secondly, while the pledge remains in principle a

transfer for an indeterminate but temporary duration and the
Bandial do not admit the sale of land, the practice of forfeit-
ure now offers a practical means of escaping the stringencies
of principle, either, as in the medieval Kentish custom of
gavelet (Hazeltine 1909:661-662), by setting the equivalency
of land so high that for all practical purposes the pledgor is
unable to redeem or, more probable in an area with an oral legal
system and a high rate of labour emigration, by the pledgor's
or his successors' failure ever to redeem.

In the cases examined here, disputing parties, most of whom
were from rural areas and whose transaction practices were
changing, mobilized urban courts in situations of conflict.
These institutions treated cash as equivalent to forms of
special-purpose money. The use of cash was sanctioned in pledge
transactions from which it had previously been excluded. A
pledgor was permitted to deal directly with his sub-pledgee.
The notion of a pledge was extended to cover a security transaction. At the same time as these changes in context and content
of Diola pledges occurred, Bandial conceptual classification of
rice field transactions among non-patrikin remained intact.
Empirical variations in such transactions did not lead to changes
in the definition of the pledge through modification of the
principal components distinguishing *gaiɪɛn* from other land
transactions, or to inclusion of rice land transactions in
another transaction category such as *funom*, or to the development of a new transaction type. Rice land transactions thus
differed from transactions involving land suitable for the cultivation of peanuts, since the growth of peanuts as a cash
export crop resulted in a transformation of the transaction type
gɔluuwaas.

That changes in rice land transaction rules and practice co-
existed with continuity of conceptual classification was due to
the unevenness and inconsistency of penetration of the capitalist mode of production in the Lower Casamance. Two aspects of
this penetration have been examined here. By its very nature as
well as by its volume and the increasing frequency with which it
was used in land transactions, cash tended to dissolve some of
the social functions of the Bandial pledge and to emphasize
exchange-value rather than use-value. Colonial courts tended to
treat land as a commodity and stress similar aspects of the
pledge, thus facilitating the economic changes which were under-
way. Several reasons explain why colonial courts affected
pledge practice, rules, and concepts to a somewhat different
extent.

First, though relatively few cases came to town courts, it is
likely that this group of cases comprised those in which rural
notions of pledge were particularly disturbed and which consequently were not amenable to settlement by village institutions.
Secondly, urban courts handled disputes between parties of different villages or between rural and urban residents, both
instances in which no other institutions existed to settle disputes. Cases III and IV suggest that such disputes involved
pledges especially likely to be oriented toward the cash economy
Thirdly, French administrators presided over these courts, and
they tended, in the Lower Casamance as in Mali (Pollet 1972;
Cohen 1971) to be relatively removed from and ignorant of the
intricacies of rural agricultural life, values, and legal concepts. Consequently, these officials tended to decide cases on
an *ad hoc*, empirical (cf. Robert 1955:170-175), or political
basis, invoking relatively specific rules with little conceptual
analysis. This manner of processing disputes was accentuated by
the frequent use of court mediation rather than adjudication.
The blending of administrative discretion, mediation, and adjudi
cation characteristic of French low-level colonial courts contributed to the development of a style of dispute settlement
oriented toward facts and rules rather than the manipulation of
concepts. In such a situation, dispute settlers resorted implicitly to their own values and notions of the purposes of land
transactions derived from experience in France and in colonial
service. Only to a limited degree did they explicitly articulat
the conceptual and normative aspects of their decisions and, in
so doing, reinterpret 'customary' concepts.

In addition, French colonial officials were heavily dependent
upon interpreters and other intermediaries. Much of responsibility for the formulation of 'customary' norms and the authoritative determination of facts in dispute settlement processes in
colonial Ziguinchor rested with a court interpreter from the
relatively commercialized Diola-Fogny area near Bignona. One
result of his substantial influence was the elaboration of a
fairly uniform and necessarily very general Diola 'customary'
law. However much its conceptual categories and rules may
have differed in other respects from those of the Bandial, it
included a concept of pledge or *gage* (cf. Badets 1954-55: 33-
34) closely resembling the Bandial concept of *gailɛn*. Thus in
the cases discussed in this paper the conceptual category
employed by colonial courts substantially coincided with that
of the parties.

The conceptual continuity of the Bandial pledge is due

finally, and perhaps most importantly, to the relatively limited extent to which, even today, Bandial rice land and rural social relations have been integrated into the capitalist market economy. In principle land is not sold. With one exception outside the Bandial area, Senegalese national marketing struc- tures in the Casamance purchase peanuts but not rice. Wage labour is frequently employed for rice cultivation, but workers are recruited from among Bandial youth and not from non-Bandial Diola or other ethnic groups. Wage labour for rice production is still supplementary to co-operation between husband and wife.

This paper has treated legal concepts primarily as dependent rather than independent variables. It is probable, however, that the structure of Bandial transaction categories has hindered the growth of rural capitalism to some extent. In general colonial economic and legal policies tended to foster and facilitate such changes. It remains to be seen in what way Senegalese policy concerning land transfers and dispute settlement will affect Bandial agriculture and the conceptual categories bound up with it.

REFERENCES

Abel, R.L. (1969). "Customary Law of Wrongs in Kenya: An Essay in Research Method," *The American Journal of Comparative Law*, 17, 4, pp. 573-626. Reprinted as Yale Law School, Studies in Law and Modernization, No. 2.

Adegboye, R.O. (1969). "Procuring Land through Pledging of Cocoa Trees," *Journal of the Geographical Association of Nigeria*, 12, 1-2, December, pp. 63-76. Reprinted as Land Tenure Center Reprint No. 94, Land Tenure Center, University of Wisconsin at Madison, n.d.

Alexandre, P. (1970). "Chiefs, *Commandants* and Clerks: Their Relationship from Conquest to Decolonisation in French West Africa," In Michael Crowder and Obaro Ikime, eds., *West African Chiefs: Their Changing Status under Colonial Rule*

and Independence, pp. 2-13 (trans. B. Packman). Africana
Publishing Corporation, New York; University of Ife Press,
Ile-Ife, Nigeria.

Allott, A.N., Epstein, A.L. and Gluckman, M. (1969). "Intro-
duction," *In* Max Gluckman, ed., *Ideas and Procedures in
African Customary Law* (Studies presented and discussed at
the Eighth International African Seminar at the Haile
Sellassie I University, Addis Adaba, January 1966), pp. 1-96.
Oxford University Press, London, for the International
African Institute.

Amin, S. (1970). *L'accumulation à l'échelle mondiale. Cri-
tique de la théorie du sous-développement.* Editions Anthro-
pos, Paris.

Amin, S. (1971a). *L'Afrique de l'Ouest bloquée. L'économie
politique de la colonisation, 1880-1970.* Les Editions de
Minuit, Paris.

Amin, S. (1971b). "La politique coloniale francaise à l'égard
de la bourgeoisie commerçante sénégalaise (1820-1960)",
In Claude Meillassoux, ed., *The Development of Indigenous
Trade and Markets in West Africa* (Studies presented and dis-
cussed at the Tenth International African Seminar at Fourah
Bay College, Freetown, December 1969), pp. 361-376. Oxford
University Press, London, for the International African
Institute.

Archives Nationales du Sénégal, Série G, sous-série 1G 343:
Monographie de la Casamance, 1911 (mise à jour de la

Monographie de la Casamance, 1903).

Archives Nationales du Sénégal, Série G, sous-série 2G23,35: Rapports périodiques, mensuels, trimestriels, semestriels et annuels des gouverneurs et chefs de service. Justice indi- gène, Rapport annuel 1923. 22 feuillets, 5 tab. stat.

Badets, J. (1954-55). *Du problème foncier en Pays Diola Casamançais — Tentative d'application du Décret du 8 Octobre 1925.* Paris, Mémoire de l'Ecole Nationale de la France d'Outre-Mer, typed.

Barth, F. (1966). *Models of Social Organization.* (Royal Anthropological Institute Occasional Paper no. 23.) Royal Anthropological Institute of Great Britain and Ireland, London.

Barton, R.F. (1969). *Ifugao Law.* University of California Press, Berkeley and Los Angeles. Orig. pub. as University of California Publications in American Archaeology and Ethnology, 15, 1, 1919.

Bohannan, P. (1967). "The Impact of Money on an African Subsistence Economy,"In George Dalton, ed., *Tribal and Peasant Economies: Readings in Economic Anthropology,* pp. 123-135. Natural History Press, Garden City, N.Y. (Orig. pub.: *The Journal of Economic History,* XIX, 4, 1959, pp. 491-503.)

Bour, C. (1882). "Etude sur le fleuve Cazamance", *Revue maritime et coloniale,* <u>75</u>, pp. 330-358.

Brown, P. (1970). "Chimbu Transactions, " *Man,* n.s. 5, pp. 99 117.

Brown, R.A. (1955). *The Law of Personal Property*. Callaghan & Co., Chicago, 2nd edition.

Buckland, W.W. and McNair, A.D. (1965). *Roman Law and Common Law*. Cambridge University Press, Cambridge, 2nd edition.

Chabas, J. (1953). "La conciliation devant les tribunaux de droit local de l'Afrique occidentale française." *Revue juri dique et politique de l'Union française,* 7, pp. 333-349.

Chabas, J. (1954). "La justice indigène en Afrique occidentale française," *Annales Africaines,* pp. 99-151.

Cheshire, G.C. (1967). *Modern Law of Real Property*. Butterworths, London, 10th edition.

Cohen, W.B. (1971). *Rulers of Empire: the French Colonial Service in Africa*. Hoover Institution Press, Stanford.

Colson, E. (1966). "Land Law and Land Holdings among the Valley Tonga of Zambia," *Southwestern Journal of Anthropolog* 22, 1, pp. 1-8.

Dalton, G., ed. (1968). *Primitive, Archaic and Modern Economics: Essays of Karl Polanyi*. Doubleday and Co., Garden City, Anchor Books.

Darmawi, H.   (1972).   "Land Transactions Under Indonesian *Adat* Law," *LAWASIA*, 3, 2-3, August-December, pp. 283-316. Reprinted as Harvard Law School Studies in East Asian Law, Indonesia: No. 2.

Diarraj, M.   (1973).   *Justice et développement au Sénégal.* Les Nouvelles Editions Africaines, Dakar, Abidjan.

Eichler, B.L.   (1973).   *Indenture at Nuzi: The Personal Tidennūtu Contract and its Mesopotamian Analogues.* Yale University Press, New Haven and London.

Elias, T.O.   (1962).   *Nigerian Land Law and Custom.* Routledge and Kegan Paul, London, 3rd edition.

Fallers, L.   (1969).   *Law Without Precedent: Legal Ideas in Action in the Courts of Colonial Busoga.* University of Chicago Press, Chicago and London.

Farnsworth, E.A.   (1969).   "The Past of Promise: An Historical Introduction to Contrast," *Columbia Law Review*, **69**, pp. 576-607.

Firth, R.   (1964).   "Capital, Saving and Credit in Peasant Societies: A Viewpoint from Economic Anthropology," In Raymond Firth and B.S. Yamey, eds., *Capital, Saving and Credit in Peasant Societies*, pp. 15-34. Aldine, Chicago.

Frake, C.O.   (1969).   "The Ethnographic Study of Cognitive Systems," In Stephen A. Tyler, ed., *Cognitive Anthropology*, pp. 28-41. Holt, Rinehart and Winson, Inc. New York.

F. G. SNYDER

Reprinted from *Anthropology and Human Behaviour* (Anthropological Society of Washington, 1962, Washington, D.C.)

Frank, A.G. (1969). "The Development of Underdevelopment," In *Latin America: Underdevelopment or Revolution*," pp. 3-17. Monthly Review Press, New York.

Fryer, W.T. (1938). *Readings on Personal Property*. West Publishing Company, St. Paul, 3rd edition.

Geismar, L. (1933). *Recueil des coutumes civiles des races du Sénégal*. Imprimerie du Gouvernement, Saint-Louis.

Gluckman, M. (1965). *The Ideas in Barotse Jurisprudence*. Yale University Press, New Haven and London.

Godelier, M. (1965). "Objets et méthodes de l'anthropologie économique," *L'Homme*, 5, pp. 32-91.

Goody, J. (1969). "The Mother's Brother and the Sister's Son in West Africa," In *Comparative Studies in Kinship*. pp. 39-90 Stanford University Press, Stanford.

Hazeltine, H.D. (1909). "The Gage of Land in Medieval England," *Select Essays in Anglo-American Legal History* (compiled and edited by a committee of the Association of American Law Schools), vol. 3, pp. 646-672. Verlag Sauer and Auvermann KG, Frankfurt.

James, R.W. (1971). *Land Tenure and Policy in Tanzania*. University of Toronto Press, Toronto.

Kaplan, I. (1965). "Courts as Catalysts of Change: A Chagga Case," *Southwestern Journal of Anthropology,* <u>21</u>, pp. 79--96.

Koëlle, S.W. (1854). *Polyglotta Africana; or a Comparative Vocabulary of Nearly One Hundred Words and Phrases in more than One Hundred Distinct African Languages.* Church Missionary House, London.

Kouassigan, G.-A. (1966). *L'homme et la terre: Droits fonciers coutumiers et droit de propriété en Afrique occidentale.* Editions Berger-Levrault, Paris.

Labouret, H. (1941). *Paysans d'Afrique occidentale.* Gallimard, Paris.

Lawson, F.H. (1962). *Negligence in the Civil Law.* Clarendon Press, Oxford, reprint of corrected first edition.

Leach, E.R. (1968). *Pul Eliya, A Village in Ceylon: A Study of Land Tenure and Kinship.* Cambridge University Press, Cambridge, reprinted, orig.pub. 1961.

Linares de Sapir, O. (1970). "Agriculture and Diola Society," In P.F. McLoughlin, ed., *African Food Production Systems,* pp. 193-227. Johns Hopkins Press, Baltimore.

Maine, H.S. (1963). *Ancient Law: Its Connection with the Early History of Society and Its Relation to Modern Ideas.* Beacon Press, Boston; orig. pub. 1861.

Mauss, M. (1954). *The Gift: Forms and Functions of Exchange in Archaic Societies,* trans. I. Cunnison. London, Cohen and West. Originally published as "Essai sur le Don" in *Sociologie et anthropologie* (Presses Universitaires de France, Paris, 1950).

Meek, C.K. (1968). *Land Law and Custom in the Colonies.* Frank Cass, London, reprinted 2nd edition; prog. pub. 1946.

Meillassoux, C. (1971). "Introduction," *In* Claude Meillassoux ed., *The Development of Indigenous Trade and Markets in West Africa* (Studies presented and discussed at the Tenth International African Seminar at Fourah Bay College, Freetown, December 1969), pp.3-86. Oxford University Press, London, for the International African Institute.

Moore, S.F. (1969). "Descent and Legal Position", In Laura Nader, ed., *Law in Culture and Society,* pp. 374-400. Aldine, Chicago.

Moore, S.F. (1972). "Legal liability and evolutionary interpretation: some aspects of strict liability, self-help and collective responsibility," *In* Max Gluckman, ed., *The Allocation of Responsibility,* pp. 51-107. Manchester University Press, Manchester.

Pautrat, R. (1957). *La justice locale et la justice musulmane en A.O.F.* Rufisque, Imprimerie du Haut Commissariat de la République en Afrique Occidentale Française.

Pélissier, P. (1966). *Les paysans du Sénégal. Les civilisations agraires du Cayor à la Casamance.* Imprimerie Fabrègue, Saint-Yrieix (Haute Vienne).

Plucknett, T.F.T. (1956). *A Concise History of the Common Law,* Little, Brown & Co. Boston, 5th edition.

Pollet, E. (1971). "Du pluralisme juridique dans le droit colonial: Etude d'un cas en République du Mali," In *Le pluralisme juridique* (Etudes publiées sous la direction de J. Gilissen), pp. 273-288. Editions de l'Université de Bruxelles, Bruxelles.

Postan, M.M. (1954). "The Rise of a Money Economy", In E.M. Carus-Wilson, ed., *Essays in Economic History* vol. I, pp.1-12. Edward Arnold (Publishers) Ltd. London. Reprinted from *Economic History Review* XIV, 2, 1944.

Obi, S.N. Chinwuba. (1963). *The Ibo Law of Property.* Butterworths, London.

Robert, A.-P. (1955). *L'Evolution des coutumes de l'Ouest africain et la législation française.* Editions de l'Encyclopédie d'Outre-Mer, Paris.

Sahlins, M.D. (1965). "On the Sociology of Primitive Exchange." *In* Michael Banton, ed., *The Relevance of Models for Social Anthropology,* pp. 139-236. Tavistock Publications, London.

Sapir, J.D. (1965). *A Grammar of Diola-Fogny.* (West African Language Monographs, 3). Cambridge University Press, Cambridge.

Snyder, F.G. (1973). "French Colonial Policy, Law, and Diola-Bandial Society, 1815-1915: Background to Legal Change in

Rural Senegal," *Rural Africana*, 22, Fall, Special Issue on "Law in Rural Africa."

Thomas, L.-V. (1958-59). *Les Diola. Essai d'analyse fonction-nelle d'une population de la Basse-Casamance*, vol. I. (Memoires de l'Institut Français d'Afrique Noire, 55.) Institut Français d'Afrique Noire, Dakar.

Thomas, L.-V. (1960). "L'organisation foncière des Diola (Basse-Casamance)," *Annales Africaines*, 1, pp. 199-223.

Thomas, L.-V. (1963). "Essai sur quelques problèmes relatifs au régime foncier des Diola de Basse-Casamance (Sénégal)," In D. Biebuyck, ed., *African Agrarian Systems* (Studies presented and discussed at the Second International African Seminar, Louanium University, Leopoldville, January 1960), pp. 314-330. Oxford University Press, London, for the International African Institute.

Thomas, L.-V. (1972). "Les 'rois' diola, hier, aujourd'hui, demain," *Bulletin de l'Institut Fondamental d'Afrique Noire*, 34, B, 1, pp. 151-174.

Touze, R.L. (1963). *Bignona en Casamance* Editions Sepa, Dakar.

Verdier, R. (1968). *Terre et Femme dans la pensée juridique négro-africaine: Introduction à l'étude anthropologique d'un système juridique africain*. Laboratoire d'Anthropologie Juridique, Paris, roneo.

Weber, M. (1966). *Law in Economy and Society.* (Rheinstein, ed.; E. Shils and M. Rheinstein, trans.) Harvard University.

Wigmore, J.H. (1897). "The Pledge-Idea: A Study in Comparative Legal Ideas," *Harvard Law Review,* 10, 6, January, pp. 321-350; 10, 7, February, pp. 389-417; 11, 1, April, pp. 18-39,

Woodman, G.R. (1967). "Developments in Pledges of Land in Ghanaian Customary Law," *Journal of African Law,* 11, 1 Spring, pp. 8-26.

INDIVIDUAL INTERESTS AND ORGANISATIONAL STRUCTURES:
DISPUTE SETTLEMENTS AS 'EVENTS OF ARTICULATION'

Sally Falk Moore

Courts and other institutions of dispute settlement often
represent their task as the disinterested enforcement of normative rules, or of general ideas of justice, proper behaviour, and
the like. This self-description is sometimes taken as literally
true and as the whole story. In contrast, when an anthropologist
hears a ritual expert describing his purpose in communicating
with the spirits, he listens to the statement as a piece of evidence in itself, and is appropriately analytical. It may be useful to treat the statements of agencies of dispute settlement
with the same detachment.

One way to do this is to treat proceedings of dispute settlement as ceremonies of situational transformation (Moore, 1975).
Looked at this way, the hearing of a case can be seen to have
many layers of meaning beyond those most immediately evident.
This paper will treat rules as part of the material used in the
course of such ceremonies, and organizational aggregates as among
the "interested" parties.

A dispute that arose between two Chagga in 1968 will serve as
case material. The dispute was heard twice. Since the underlying circumstances of the quarrel are constant and only the
forum changed, it is instructive to notice the differences in
rules, interests and "facts" that were relevant in the two tribunals. The two hearings of this dispute also will be analysed
to show the ways in which a hearing whose declared purpose is
the settlement of a *particular* quarrel is simultaneously a
general event of articulation between levels and kinds of
organization. Chagga society has a variety of organizational

forms, some quite old and "traditional," others quite new and
"planned."

In the 19th century, there were many Chagga chiefdoms on Mou
Kilimanjaro. They varied very much in size and power, each
having dominion over a separate strip of lush green banana gardens watered by mountain streams. The general organizational
structure of these chiefdoms was a three level one: lineage,
mtaa, chiefdom. At the bottom were the localized corporate
lineages of the various patriclans, each with a discrete territory. A local aggregation of several unrelated lineages formed
a *mtaa*, which was a political unit under a headman (*mchili*).
A chiefdom consisted of several *mitaa* under the leadership of a
chief (*mangi*). The whole was cross-cut by an age-grade organiz
tion of military and political importance.

Skipping a hundred years, and innumerable changes on the
macro-level of organization which have had loud echoes on the
micro-level, we come to socialist Tanzania in 1974, and the fac
that localized lineage branches and the *mitaa* are still signifi
cant social units. Officially, on local government charts, the
do not exist. What is consequently of organizational interest
about the localized lineages is that in some ways they are very
much like segmentary units in Durkheim's model of a mechanicall
solidary society. They also resemble units in an acephalous
society, because the lineages are not attached as such to any
generalized organization. They are many parallel social bodies
not formally linked into any superordinate administrative syste
This Chagga situation suggests the importance of the dimension
of *detachment* in complex societies in general. It suggests the
utility of looking at a centralized system of political adminis
tration as existing on top of a great variety of organized soci
fields that exist within its geographical domain, but which are
normally outside the zones of its strongest direct pull or
effectiveness (Moore, 1973). On occasion, as when two Chagga
lineage-brothers take their case to court, persons in such soci
fields may plug into the national system. And the reverse, as
when TANU (the Tanzanian one-party) set up ten-house cells, the
central administration may try to invade the furthest corners o
its geographical domain. But in neither case is the lineage, a
an organization, attached to the official central system.

In contrast, the Tanzanian national system of courts is a
centralized, specialized, hierarchical-bureaucratic organizatio
It has full-time salaried officials, levels of courts higher an
lower, modes of appeal, with rulings of superior courts binding

on inferior ones, and the like. It was legislated into existence during the period of British colonial rule, and has been reorganized a number of times, most recently since Independence (see Allott, 1970, and Georges, 1973). As a consciously constructed, legislated edifice, the national court system is a creature of rules. Conventionally these are classified into two kinds: those having to do with its own *organization* (jurisdiction, powers, relationships internal and external, financing, procedures, and the like) and those having to do with the *grounds on which it makes decisions* in the cases that come before it. In the decision of particular cases, both kinds of rules are always involved, though most of the time most of the rules are not "issues."

Such a system of courts is a bureaucratic animal whose only food is cases. It lives only to process to cases. It prospers and fattens when there are many cases (but not too many). There is no other justification for its existence. It has an internal life as an organization of judiciary officials. But it depends for its cases on an external source of supply. Some events outside the courts must turn into cases, or the courts are out of business. Some individuals, or groups, or agencies (such as the police or administrative agencies) must use the courts as the way to mobilize the power of the state on their behalf or there are no cases.

In contrast to such a specialized and centralized organization are the many separate and varied arenas of action in which disputes actually arise and wrongs occur, but in which people are primarily engaged in activities other than dispute settlement and rule enforcement. The normal activities of an agricultural community would be an example. These social fields also may have internal techniques of rule-making. Frequently they also have their own modes of enforcement quite apart from those offered by the state (Moore, 1973). But the handling of all such matters is incidental to other enterprises.

This paper will follow a dispute that arose between two classificatory brothers in a Chagga patrilineage in 1968, from its inception through its "informal" hearing before lineage elders and neighbours, and beyond, through its rehearing and disposition in a Primary Court. All the persons involved in the two hearings were Wachagga. All were using the same fund of Chagga "customary" law and other common understandings as a general resource for rules and models of proper behaviour. However, the organisational implications of the hearings at the two levels were entirely different, and concomitantly, so were the *place* or rules and "interests" and the *kinds* of rules and "interests" that were brought into play. On both levels rules were the only legitimate idiom in which "interests" could be argued.

The facts of the case are simple. The two lineage brothers have contiguous coffee-banana groves which used to have a common boundary. The line between their properties was marked by a living fence of *masala* (dracaena), a plant traditionally used for such purposes. One brother, Richard, is a bright-eyed, educated, prosperous young clerk who works in the nearby town of Moshi (25 miles away). The other brother, Elifatio, is a tattered, moustachioed, uneducated farmer in his forties.

Along Richard's side of the boundary there is now a fairly wide path. It was cleared and made a public village-way a year or two before the dispute arose by a team of development worker (farmers doing one day a week corvée labor). Formerly the path had meandered through the middle of Richard's coffee grove. He preferred having it on the boundary, and had had something t do with the decision of the TANU leader of the public works tea to move it. He may have gained a few inches of land that way, and some privacy. In any case, the path was on Richard's side of the hedge-like line of boundary plants that marked the edge of Elifatio's property.

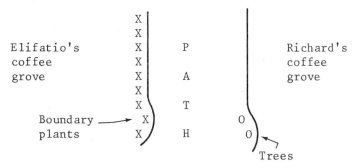

There is a shortage of land on Kilimanjaro, and a population explosion. To try to increase the productivity of his plot, Elifatio uprooted a number of yards of the boundary plants and replaced them with seedlings of a fruit tree, *helimu*. Not only is their fruit delicious, but their leaves make very good goat food. On his side of the path, Richard had made analogous use of the edges. He had planted *asteria*, a low-growing grass-like plant used for animal feed, and it did well.

One fine morning, soon after Elifatio had planted the seedlings of *helimu* trees, Richard came along and pulled them up. He threw them on the path and left. Those were the facts to which everyone agreed (at least for a while). Elifatio soon went to his neighbour, the ten-house leader, head of the lowest unit in the TANU party organization, to complain. He said that he wanted to bring a case against Richard for the damage he had done. The ten-house leader said he would see to it, and a date was fixed for the hearing.

In order to understand the significance of what followed it is necessary to know a little more about the Chagga, past and present. The Chagga people now number about 350,000 and are settled primarily in a wide green belt on the high slopes of Mount Kilimanjaro. Being coffee growers, they have been involved in a cash economy since the 1920s. It was their fate to be energetically missionized from the late 19th century (Europeans like the climate) and they are among the most ambitious, educated and prosperous of Tanzania's peoples. Much of their indigenous culture is gone, but some very important elements persist, particularly certain aspects of local and kinship organization and the customs associated with these. Because they irrigated and manured and grew bananas and kept cattle in pre-colonial times, the socio-economic base of their society has always been the permanent occupation (over generations) of particular plots of land.

Each household lives in the midst of its permanently cultivated gardens of bananas and coffee, the *kihamba*. In the areas of older settlement, the gardens of patrilineally related men are likely to lie next to each other in localized lineage clusters. Richard and Elifatio are two members of a local cluster of 23 patrilineally related households. These local lineage branches are usually small parts of larger patrilineal clans whose member branches are widely scattered around the mountain. The gardens of each local group are interdigitated with neighbouring lineages at their boundaries. Also, here and there, are gardens of other, unrelated individuals who settled locally, some as affines, some as borrowers of land, and more recently some as buyers of land. Also, in some places, peppered among the original settlers, are descendants of the local chiefly lineage, since there was a period when chiefs appropriated any unoccupied land they could get their hands on for their myriad children and kinsmen.

Today there is no organization at the clan level at all. But

localized lineage clusters are organized internally. The
descendants of each great-grandfather form a separate sub-branc
The whole local group recognizes a ranking of all males in orde
of birth. This is the order in which portions of meat are distributed at collective slaughtering feasts for men and boys.
Thus any kinsman of Richard and Elifatio could without a moment
hesitation rattle off a list of the men of the localized lineag
in order of birth. Slaughtering feasts including the whole of
the localized lineage are few nowadays, since the group is larg
and cattle are costly. But collective beer drinking is quite
frequent. And smaller slaughtering groups, including all the
male descendants of one grandfather, or one great-grandfather,
continue to assemble several times a year. At the invitation o
one of their number, the men and boys get together to kill and
divide a goat or two provided by their host. These small group
also always attend the life-crisis rites of all members and the
children. Frequently so do most members of the larger lineage
group. In short, the local lineage branches feast and drink,
celebrate and mourn together, regularly reiterating their collective existence. Members assist each other in work, in times
of illness, in times of need. They guard each other's wives,
homesteads, and gardens. They take responsibility for the aged
and the infirm among them. All land interests are individually
held, but are subject to strong contingent claims of kinsmen.

The lineages have lost some of the qualities of corporatenes
which they once enjoyed. But they continue to be important as
firmly consolidated social groups with strong emotional ties,
groups that are coherent over time and place, and that control
the access of most of their members to land in the lineage area
When there are disputes between lineage brothers, the lineage
elders and some of their neighbourhood cronies hear the case,
and decide it. In 1968 and today, in 1974, it is mandatory tha
they include in such a hearing the neighbour who is head of the
ten-house cell concerned. But the cell leader is a contiguous
neighbour (and not infrequently a lineage brother himself)
chosen by his constituents, he is the sort of person who might
well have been included at a neighbourhood hearing even before
there were TANU cells. He is seldom the most influential man i
the neighbourhood since one of the requirements of the job is
that he be around and available most of the time. That virtual
eliminates all the salaried men from candidacy, as well as the
shopkeepers. He is normally a farmer without outside employmen
One may well ask whether the neighbour's identity as TANU cell
leader is stronger than his identity as long-term neighbour,
affine, or whatever else he may be. His prior connection with

the local lineage is likely to be strong and of long duration.

It is true that there formerly were more matters that were
regarded as entirely private lineage business than there are,
perforce, today. But since he is bound by his myriad local ties
the presence of an unrelated ten-house leader probably does not
greatly alter the outcome of a lineage hearing. Ordinary local
hearings at present often consist of an *ad hoc* assemblage of
patrikinsmen with a few neighbours present for good measure.

It was just such a group that Elifatio was to face the day of
the hearing of his case, on August 16, 1968. The appointed place
was a junction of footpaths in the midst of the lineage homeland.
First to appear was the ten-house leader, an affine of the two
"brothers." He carried a rather bent stick with the Tanzanian
flag tied to it on one end — a drooping bit of green cloth.
He stuck the stick in the ground and called to a child who was
watching to bring chairs. The child duly fetched a few from a
nearby house. The chairs were for the principals. Most people
sat on the ground. After a while Elifatio arrived, clutching his
271 dead seedlings, dry as a bunch of twigs.

Elifatio was then in his early forties. His clothes were very
worn, his trousers patched, his shirt torn. He is the father of
three sons and five daughters: many mouths to feed. In 1968,
before schools became free, he had many school fees to pay.   As
indicated earlier he has had little education himself, can barely
read, and makes his living exclusively out of his land. Like all
other local Chagga, he grows coffee and bananas, the one for cash,
the other for food and beer. He is considered poor by his brothers though he has about three acres of his own, because a three
acre plot scarcely takes care of his needs and those of his many
dependents. These include two adult members of his extended
family in addition to himself, his wife, and their many children.

Richard, the brother whom Elifatio was accusing, has about
the same amount of land, three acres, which he will eventually
have to divide with his as yet unmarried younger brother, a
schoolboy who lives with him. In Richard's household are the
young brother, their mother, Richard's wife and five daughters.
Yet he is considered a rich man. That is because in addition to
his *kihamba* he has a salaried job in Moshi Town. He is educated,
having passed one part of the way through secondary school. He
reads and writes Swahili well. And he can type. These accomp-
lishments, together with some contacts, got him a job as a clerk-
secretary which he has had for a number of years. Normally

Richard wears the white shirt, dark trousers and pointy black shoes of an office worker. (A clerk could be defined as a man who wears Sunday clothes every day.)

At the place chosen for the hearing, people arrived little by little. Eventually Richard appeared. Nothing in the neighbourhood (nor anywhere else) ever takes place at the time it is normally scheduled. For one thing, few have watches, and for another, every day holds unexpected encounters as well as routine tasks. Being on time is not urgent. Nothing can start without the principals, hence they can be late with impunity. As for the spectators, they are not really needed, so they can arrive when they please. And so it always is. When Richard finally turned up, there were about eight people waiting, a cluster of kinsmen the wives of two of them, and I.

They were ready to begin. The ten-house leader made a little speech about why we were all assembled and then called on Elifatio to make his complaint. He did so, very simply and tersely "On the 28th day of last month I got up and was working in my *kihamba* and I heard Richard talking to someone and saying that I had interfered with the boundary between our *vihamba*. I had planted these seedlings," he took up his pathetic bunch of dried twigs, holding them rather lovingly and then dropped them to the ground in their dry worthlessness. "Richard was the one who pulled them up. I went to the ten-house leader and complained.

Richard answered, "I deny it. I did not uproot your trees." This answer surprised me, because Richard had not only admitted uprooting the plants in the days previous, but had boasted of having done so. No one else seemed in the least surprised. It seemed to be what was expected. It later developed that Richard argument was that the boundary was a common boundary, belonging to him as much as it did to Elifatio. Hence, according to local customary rules, nothing could be done to it without mutual approval. Thus Richard could pretend that a mysterious someone whose identity he did not know had interfered with their mutual boundary, and that he, Richard, had rectified the situation by pulling up the seedlings. In fact, the boundary *had* once been a common one. The situation had changed, however, because of the village path, which now lay between Richard's land and the boundary of Elifatio's. If one were to state the central legal issue, it was whether the existence of the path changed the boundary from a common boundary to one that belonged to Elifatio alone.

As Richard seemed to be denying pulling up the seedlings, the ten-house leader asked Elifatio whether he had any witnesses. Elifatio answered that his wife and son both had seen Richard uprooting the seedlings. A discussion following about moving the whole company to the site of the planting, since the wife and son were not at the hearing but at home. Meanwhile, various people appeared on the path, passing by. One man carried a coffee pulping machine. A cheery albino walked through and smiled broadly. No one greeted him. Richard repeated his denial of having uprooted Elifatio's *helimu*.

Elifatio became visibly angry, "Whose trees were the trees that you uprooted?"

Richard answered, "I have not interfered with your trees."

At this point one of the senior men said he would like to hear Elifatio's wife and son say that they saw Richard pulling up the plants. The ten-house leader agreed that it would be a good idea, and that as the witnesses lived precisely where the trees had been uprooted, and an inspection of the boundary was necessary, we should all proceed there. Everyone would have a chance to look at the site and hear further evidence. There was some talk about this and then an elder on Elifatio's side shouted at Richard, "Have you ever uprooted trees anywhere, in your *kihamba* or anywhere else?"

Richard answered cagily, "Yes, I have uprooted trees somewhere." His strategy was now plain. He was going to prove that the seedlings were on his own property, hence that he had not disturbed anyone else's.

After more discussion, we all got up and walked to the edge of Elifatio's garden, eventually reaching the path that divided it from Richard's coffee grove. It was a ten-minute walk. As it was toward noon, it was very hot, and everyone was uncomfortable. We all looked at the *masale*, the boundary plant along the edge of Elifatio's property and we saw the gap and loose earth where he had pulled them up to replace them with *helimu*. Evidently he had done something of the sort once before as there were a few well developed coffee trees planted among the *masale* a bit further down the hill. No dispute had arisen at the time of the planting of those coffee trees.

Richard became more voluble, "These *masale* were not planted by Elifatio, but by our grandfather, and this is a new path.

The path that was here before went into my *kihamba*." An old
man, a neighbour, who was walking by approached, listened a
while, and joined in, saying, "Part of this path has been here
since the grandfathers of grandfathers. This case could have
been settled, but it was not. It is just because of the path,
which is the property of the Government. The dispute is not
about the *vihamba*. It is about the path.

As if on cue, Richard picked up this direction of argument.
"I don't know who planted the trees I uprooted. I uprooted them
after I saw that they were planted in the land of the
Government."

Another elder, the one of Elifatio's side, said, "Three years
ago, the path was not there. There was another path, a small
one, that cut in through Richard's *kihamba*. The path was
changed at Richard's request and put along the edge of his land
instead of through the heart of his coffee."

Elifatio then began arguing that the land on both sides of the
new path was his in places, and pointed to two trees. "Those
trees," he said, "used to be at the edge of my property, and now
they are on the other side of the new path. The path is partly
on Richard's land, but it is also partly on mine. Some of mine
was taken away."

More people gathered. There were now about fifteen. All
were residents of the immediate area, neighbours, patrikinsmen
and their wives, except for two of Richard's white-collar
friends. Several newcomers began to put their views forward in
excited voices, "If Richard's father had planted trees along the
masale of Elifatio, would Elifatio have had a valid claim against
him? If the road were closed now, the *masale* planted by our
grandfathers would remain where it is."

A woman pitched in, "The trees Elifatio planted were on
Richard's side." The tide seemed to be turning toward Richard.
All speakers became increasingly vociferous and excited.

A young, educated official of the local co-operative made a
long and vehement speech on Richard's behalf. "All the land on
this side (the path side) of the *masale* is Richard's land."
He went on for fifteen minutes looking furious, gesticulating
wildly. He was one of the three white-collar workers there
besides Richard himself. All four men are daily drinking com-
panions and have close links of friendship that transcend the

fact that two of them are not of Richard's lineage. They are of the same general age-group and of the salaried "class."

The ten-house leader thought it was about time for him to say something. He was plainly no longer in charge of the meeting, and was simply present, not in control. He said, "The *masale* were removed by Elifatio himself in order to plant useful things in their place. The boundary was correct because it was set by the grandfathers. There has never been a dispute about this boundary. There is a rule about a common boundary that if a tree is on a boundary and its branches are useful for building, the owners on each side can cut them, one cuts one year, the other the next." The sense of what he was saying was that Elifatio had lost his case by analogy, that as it was a common boundary Richard could even have claimed some rights to his trees.

Richard, who had been very quiet, then showed us where Elifatio had uprooted the *masale* to plant *helimu*. We had all seen it already, but he seemed to think that walking us all up and down would increase our horror at Elifatio's temerity in disturbing that boundary. At this point the arguments went on in little knots of twos and threes. There was no longer a single proceeding with one person speaking at a time. All participants were arguing vigorously. By now many of the neighbours who were not members of the ten-house cell had come out and joined us.

There ensued a lot of talk about who should pronounce a decision. The ten-house leader tried to defer to the most prestigious of the educated men present. He declined, deferring to the elders and the ten-house leader. There was a great deal of "after you Alphonse" thereafter, some of which was doubtless caused by my presence and the wish to be correct, lest I report critically to the authorities. The general conclusion was that someone from the ten-house cell had better do it.

Taking advantage of the temporary distraction afforded by this discussion about who should decide, an old man on Richard's side said, "As the *masale* were planted by our grandfathers, Elifatio had no right to touch the boundary. And it was perfectly all right for Richard to uproot the *helimu*."

In despair, Elifatio tried to make a "modern" argument, "I just planted the *helimu* against soil erosion." But it was plain that the *masale* itself would have been effective for this purpose.

An elder on Elifatio's side spoke up, "It was also wrong of Richard to uproot the plants. One must not tear up the plants of others. He should have told Elifatio to uproot them, or he should have gone to the cell leader to complain. He had no business taking matters into his own hands and doing the uprooting himself."

The argument that self-help was wrongful in the circumstance set the co-operative society man off again. "But it was Elifat who started this dispute because he planted trees between the boundaries of two *vihamba*. Richard did not commit any offence when he uprooted the trees because the trees were in his own *kihamba*. You say Richard committed an offence when he uprooted the trees. *I* say Elifatio committed an offence when he planted them."

A moderating voice was heard. The senior man of the lineage said, "What remains is to reach some agreement, to make some ki of settlement."

The ten-house leader reprimanded him. "No. We have to say properly who was right and who was wrong. An elder cannot do that. Only the cell leader can. I am following the opinions of the elders for two have said that Elifatio did in fact plant the trees in the land of Richard, and that is what I say. Now, in the future, when you want to plant trees between the boundaries of the *vihamba,* those on both sides should come together and make some agreement." The cell leader had spoken. That was it. He had been willing to defer to the prestigious young educated man but not to the farmer-elders. If the choice were to be between himself and the elders, *he* would pronounce judgment. This acute concern to lead in fact as well as in name was, I was told, enhanced by my presence.

Although everyone had been told that the proceedings were ove as far as the cell leader was concerned, the people present wen on sitting and arguing as before. An elder on Elifatio's side said, "The path had been here for some time. The path divides the *vihamba*. Each should keep on his side. Richard also committed an offence when he planted *asteria* grass along his side the path."

The co-operative society man, seeing the anger on Elifatio's face, seemed to want to push him just one step further. He pressed on, "There had better be some reconciliation between these two as they are brothers. It is not good for brothers to

fight about such things. There have been no previous quarrels
between these two. There is no need to impose a fine. Anyone
may have a quarrel. And if Elifatio wants to plant trees now,
he can *arrange* with Richard to do so."

An elder on Richard's side remembered a pertinent rule,
"Years ago if a banana plant growing on the edge of a property
fell into a neighbour's yard, the bananas became the property
of the neighbour. This path should be well maintained and kept
wide. People should not plant on the sides of it." He disclosed
his own worries, "It should be kept clear, because if someone is
sick, perhaps a car might have to come to collect him from his
house and take him to the hospital. The paths should be kept
open and wide.

The cell leader asked Elifatio if he accepted the decision
and if he would shake hands with his brother. Elifatio answered,
"If I am defeated, how am I to accept? How am I to shake hands
with him?"

Richard shrugged, "If he doesn't want a reconciliation, that
doesn't matter. It is up to him."

Elifatio replied, "I am thinking about whether I will
appeal. I am not satisfied."

This account is, of course, a selected portion from notes
made of several hours of talk. But it suffices to give the
sense of what went on. Before going on to describe the retrial
of the case in the Primary Court, it may be useful to note some
things about this proceeding, first, with regard to the pertinent explicit norms, and second, from the point of view of the
"interests" at work in the hearing. Some of the principal
normative arguments could be set up in pairs of opposites as
follows:

A new village path can change previous boundaries.	A path through someone's *kihamba*, even if made by the village, may be closed as easily as it was opened. Thus in appropriate cases a village path is just like a private path as far as boundaries are concerned.

It is all right to uproot and replace one's own boundary plants.	It is wrong to disturb a common boundary except with the consent of both parties.
It is wrong to use self-help and to destroy your neighbour's plants. If you think he has planted improperly, you can accuse him and have a hearing.	There is no harm in taking peaceful action when there has been wrongdoing. The inviolability of boundaries must be maintained. One may take action to protect one's own property.

As far as these normative grounds were concerned, a decision either way could have been supported. (There were of course, many other norms "in the air" and finding them is rather like the children's game of looking at a puzzle picture to see how many faces you can locate in the bushes.) In effect, the ten-house leader's decision was that the new path did *not* change previous property rights. The path, though it passed along the boundary and seemed completely continuous to it was still, by implication, in some sense in Richard's *kihamba*. The path was treated more as a right-of-way than as village property. By ignoring the self-help issue, the ten-house leader implicitly approved Richard's action.

But it would be difficult to argue that the decision had been determined by "the rules," or that generating general rules was the objective of the hearing. Rather the result was sufficiently *associated* with general rules to legitimate it. By "general rules" I not only mean norms applicable beyond the particular case, but also norms not specifically associated with a special organizational setting. TANU rules do not pertain to the boundaries of *vihamba*. The nucleus of white-collar workers does not constitute a rule-making body. The fact that the lineages are unattached as such to any political centre means that lineage rules could not play the same connective role that they do in bureaucratic structures. Nor were the lineages closed autonomies which might have made use of special rules to reiterate organizational closure. Instead, the rules mentioned in the hearing came from here and there, were argued by this one and that one, and the decision in Richard's favor was not explicitly attached to any particular rationale emmanating from any particular organizational quarter.

The question of interest is, of course, intertwined with the norms of kinship and friendship behavior, as well as with matters

of individual gain. This hearing was a situation in which, in
the absence of any special factors, it was expected that senior
kinsmen would take sides with the protagonists according to their
closeness of genealogical relationship. They all did so. The
kinship relationship between Elifatio and Richard is that of 6th
or 7th cousins. They come from the two major branches of the
localized lineage. There is no one who is considered equally
related to both. Since this was a case in which there was great
uncertainty about the legal question whether or not the boundary
was still to be regarded as a common boundary because of the
interposition of the path, it was the kind of case in which
"interest" might be expected to operate strongly.

However, it must be emphasized that even though "interest"
deriving from relationship made certain alignments highly probable, the discussion of such cases is always carried on by
everyone in normative terms. No one would ever say, "I am on
his side. I am his older brother. I know he is right," without
offering a normative reason. And, of course, there are many disputes, such as those between "true" brothers, or father and son,
in which the matter of closeness of relationship cannot settle
the question of "interest." Also, it is clear from other cases,
as well as being shown by later events between Elifatio and
Richard, that especially good relations or especially bad relations with a particular individual can modify the normal alignments of kinship.

Given all these caveats, it is generally evident to the parties when they sit down to a discussion of this kind, which persons will certainly come forward and side with them. A *display*
of partisanship is mandatory on certain persons, such as very
close kinsmen and their wives. Women tend to align themselves
with their husbands, since in many respects they are socially
dependent persons. There is no expectation of any general display of impartiality. Whoever "chairs" the meeting makes some
temporary show of neutrality, but the others are expected to
take sides, and to do so early in the discussion. Kinship, then,
is one of the "interest" factors. But it is an "interest" factor
itself ordinarily governed by the rules of lineage organization.

Past social relations with the parties is another "interest"
factor. These past social relations can include long-term connections such as Richard's with the three other educated men who
were present. Late every afternoon the men assemble and have a
drink of banana beer with their cronies. The men with salaried
jobs drink at a different establishment from that patronized by

these who are exclusively farmers. There are, in short, nascent
ties of class, and these cross-cut lineage loyalties. These,
too, predispose those present at a hearing to certain alignments.
Thus the vociferous co-operative society man was sitting with
Richard, his friend, his daily drinking companion, his not very
distant neighbour. He was more excited than any of the older
men, and spoke with a certain arrogance. This was at least in
part a matter of individual personality and exuberance. The two
other educated men were a decade older and spoke much less,
partly, I believe, because in the situation they were aligning
themselves with me, as observers, rather than as active participants. We had had other contacts, and they were aware of my
work.

Perhaps some of the neighbours who wandered in and out
started out without any strong bias in the direction of one or
the other of the parties, but that is unlikely where there is
such a long common history. It is possible that some of the
people who were there were present for the "show" because such
events are an interesting distraction in a world of endless numbers of routine tasks. But however neutral their motives for
appearing, they were likely to have had some past transactions
either with Richard and Elifatio, or with the men who spoke for
them.

There is vaguely in the background of all of this a general
bias toward men like Richard. There is a feeling that men like
him may be a good contact in the future. He is young, person-
able, educated, and times are changing fast. Perhaps he would
be useful if one needed a loan, or a witness, or an introduction
if not for oneself, for one's son. This kind of "interest" is
extremely hard to get at, or be sure of. It is embodied in the
remark of one of the educated men who said to me afterwards,
"Rich men always win." Yet the same individual had told me
before the hearing started that he had no idea how it would turn
out.

The elements of "interest" which have been discussed thus far
have all been presented in terms of the individual social relationships of the casehearers with the parties. These have
included the genealogical closeness of the kinship relationship,
friendship, educational-occupational status, age, sex, or other
ground for identification. Also included was the situational
factor that is often strategically important in a close group of
this kind, indebtedness because of transactions in the past, or
the wish to build up credit because of anticipated transactions

in the future. It will readily be seen that in particular cases, these determinants may be contradictory. Consequently, to produce choices, some criterion of selection or ranking among determinants must be operative at any particular moment. An analysis of the social characteristics of the persons at this hearing is not difficult to produce. But if their mutual transactional history is also to be taken into account, only a novel could do the case justice. Moreover, one also would have to take into accounts the events during the hearing itself, the force of personality and argument of the various speakers, their efficiency at manipulating symbols and soliciting support, the use of the hearing as a forum for the interplay of individual competition relating to matters quite extraneous to the immediate case, and the like.

However, these causal questions are especially complicated when put in terms of individual choice. If the perspective is changed, and the questions posed are in terms of the organizational implications of the case, much more generalization is possible. A localized lineage is an organization, a traditional one with many cultural elaborations, including norms of solidarity in internal dispute, and norms of ranking in terms of seniority. However, today the lineage exists only unofficially. Its formal competitor on the micro-political level is the local TANU organization with its ten-house leaders. Its informal competitor, which also does not exist officially, is the tight network of prosperous educated men, each of whom has a business or a job, most of them in government agencies.

This case brings all three of these durable organizational forces on stage together. When the senior elder of the lineage said, "What remains is to reach some kind of agreement," obviously intending to propose the terms of such a settlement as behooves a senior elder, he was at once cut off by the ten-house leader. The TANU man said it was a matter of who was right and who was wrong and that this was for him and him alone to declare. After this power play, it is interesting that he felt it necessary to legitimate his decision by saying, "I am following the opinions of the elders." That is, in fact, what the ten-house leaders generally do. They do not act contrary to the judgment of local senior elders. However, the fact that there was a question about who was to pronounce the decision suggests that there is a latent struggle going on between the lineage and the TANU organization about autonomy at the lowest local level.

However, as indicated earlier, both the ten-house TANU man and

the lineage elders are by definition relatively uneducated farmers who are not salaried. Both recognize the social power and
public respectability of their educated, employed kinsmen and
neighbours, and the greater mobility and outside contacts which
they have in the Big World. From the point of view of the Big
World these men may be clerks, but on the mountain they are the
very epitome of modern city people.

The norms of lineage prescribe that the lineage elders are
the ultimate authorities in all matters. The norms of African
Socialism proclaim the primacy of its Party functionaries as
representatives of The People. The realities of economic and
social stratification suggest that as far as the farmers are
concerned, the clerks and teachers, and other low-level white-
collar workers are the prominent citizens of the neighbourhood.

Richard's winning was more congruent with the interest of
each sector than his losing. From the point of view of the
lineage elders, only those on Elifatio's side of the lineage
could be said to be in a position to gain social strength if he
had won. But unfortunately for them, the present configuration
of the lineage is such that the most senior man of the whole
local branch is on Richard's side of the family, and he is a
respected man. The second eldest is on Elifatio's side, but he
is "a man of quarrels" and is not generally liked. Moreover,
the most senior man has two sons who are salaried clerical
workers, and one who is a government driver, while the senior
man on Elifatio's side has sons who are farmers only. The thir
ranking elder is again on Richard's side, and again is a respec
ted man with a number of educated sons. In fact, the weight of
lineage prestige is altogether on Richard's half on the local
lineage. Thus even in terms of internal considerations regardi
the relative strength of lineage sub-branches and the tradition
deference to seniors, the scales were tipped in Richard's favou

The ten-house leader is an affine of the lineage. He has ma
dealings with its members both in his capacity as TANU man and
a private individual. It is in his interest to be on good term
with "everyone," but if he has to choose among them, it is wortl
noting that his father's brother's wife was from one of the
branches of the lineage on Richard's side, and that the *kihamba*
he occupies was inherited from that father's brother, who had
himself obtained it from his wife's kinsmen. His stronger connection with Richard's side of the family is thus more than a
generation old. If that were not enough to tip the balance, th
there is the additional consideration that the salaried men, wi

their connections outside the local *mtaa* are very useful contacts for him, not only in his private dealings, but in his official ones, for example, when he must collect funds for TANU that are "voluntarily" presented by his constituents toward one campaign or another, a not infrequent circumstance. It is much easier to collect from them as they have more cash, than to squeeze shillings out of their impecunious farmer brothers. The clerks need him to give them a clean bill of health in the Party, but he needs them to maintain his political well-being as well.

As for the local white-collar network, it obtained from the case an essentially symbolic gain, a reinforcement of the ranking system in which they rate higher than their farmer brothers. What they got out of the case was a good laugh. It need not have been a case at all. Richard chose to make it so. He could have left Elifatio's seedlings in place, and simply warned him that if he went an inch further and crossed the boundary line, there would be trouble. But he didn't. He engaged in a show of bravado instead, performing a hostile act of force, and throwing down the gauntlet. It was an act of warning and boastfulness on the part of a young man in relation to an older one. It said, "I am a man to be taken seriously. How dare you cross me?"

Both kinds of questions raised in connection with this case, those having to do with norms and those having to do with organized "interests" by their very nature emphasize that a disagreement between two individuals can become a public issue, i.e. that its settlement can involve the customs and organized social relations of a particular body public. The lineage, neighbours, friends, and the ten-house leader were drawn in at the request of individuals, Elifatio and Richard. But every such request, every use of these organizational nexus for the settlement of dispute provides an opportunity for certain public collectivities to come into competitive contact, to act authoritatively, to demonstrate and to reaffirm local relationships of superordination and subordination. The persons mobilized are part of the networks of individuals, but they also are aligned in other organized collectivities. Dispute settlements of this kind sort out and give strength to those organizational structures. They give them some of their life by providing occasions for them to act. There are many other occasions, of course, when these neighbourhood bodies are mobilized, which range from mutual assistance to common celebration. But very few of these occasions may be compared with dispute settlement in the explicitness with which the exercise of community authority is expressed.

When a case moves from this local neighbourhood scene to the Primary Court, the lowest court in the national judicial system of Tanzania, it can also be said to be feeding an organization with the material on which it acts. But since the Court is a specialized agency whose working life depends on a steady flow of cases, the place of the "case" in the life of the Court is very different from its place in the local neighbourhood aggregations which serve many other purposes as well.

Cases not only serve the court as its daily business, but in so far as they are appealed or reviewed or decided on the bases of precedents set by superior courts, cases as well as rules serve as one of the links with the higher levels of the national judicial system. The Primary Courts are in the rural areas of Kilimanjaro, one per village. They are the successors of what were formerly Chief's courts. Appeals lie from the Primary Courts to the District Court in Moshi Town (25 miles away) and thence to the High Court of Tanzania. The Magistrates of the Primary Courts are paid out of a national budget for the judiciary, and are, in theory at least, supervised by superior magistrates in Moshi. The Primary Court Magistrates are without formal legal training, though all have had a course of some months at the Local Government Training Centre at Mzumbe.

The law the magistrates were supposed to be applying is partly statutory, partly customary law. No attorneys or other representatives of the parties are allowed in the Primary Courts. Magistrates act as court recorders as well as judges. They write down whatever they think necessary of the testimony and discussion, and the reasons for their decisions, as well as recording the opinions of the two elders (called assessors) who are an official adjunct of the Court. The rules, the book-keeping, the forms, the scale of fees, the fines and costs, the jurisdiction of the Court and the formal framework in general are laid down in statutes and departmental rules.

In short, in 1968, the Magistrates on the mountain, though al were Chagga, were all members of a national corporate group, res ponsive to its regulations as well as to local ideas of justice and proper behaviour. Since Magistrates were assigned to sit in villages other than their natal ones in order to assure impar-tiality, whatever biases they might have had (for example in favour of their white-collar brethren) were likely to be of a generalized rather than a personal nature. They did sometimes receive individuals in their private offices, and discussed case business with them. Whether they were thus reached by local

networks of influence or not is hard to say. In particular
cases, they probably were, but on the whole, the impression one
had was that they were quite indifferent to most of the parties
who came before them.

It was to such a Court that Elifatio flew when he lost his
case against Richard in the neighbourhood hearing. On the
clerk's advice, he filed a criminal complaint for the malicious
destruction of property. What he really wanted was reimbursement
for the value of his seedlings, and an opportunity to defeat his
"brother" Richard in a public forum. A civil litigation would
have cost him a filing fee. A criminal complaint cost nothing.
The Magistrates have considerable statutory freedom to give what
we think of as civil remedies in criminal cases when they see
fit. Elifatio risked nothing and might gain.

Within less than a week after the neighbourhood hearing, Elifatio's case actually was heard in court. He thought he was sure
to win because Richard had ultimately admitted pulling up the
plants in the neighbourhood hearing. Everyone had heard him say
so. Furthermore, the day before the hearing in Court, the ten-
house leader had agreed to come and testify to that effect for
Elifatio. There seemed no way in which Richard could wriggle
out. He would pay for having used self-help!

But as it turned out, when the day came, the ten-house leader
did not appear at all. Elifatio did not ask for a postponement.
Whether he did not ask because he did not know he could (unlikely),
or whether he did not ask because there was no point in trying to
push the ten-house leader (likely) was not made explicit. In any
case, Elifatio simply went on to present his grievances without
his expected star witness.

In the Primary Court the Magistrate sits up on a raised platform about three feet above the floor at the front of the room.
His chair is behind a table on which there are papers and writing
materials. He faces "the audience." On the platform to one side
of him there is a backless bench on which the assessors sit.
Below, at floor level stand the complainant and the respondent,
one on the left side of the front of the room, one on the right.
They stand throughout most of the proceedings, backs to the audience, facing the Magistrate, unless a witness is testifying. The
room itself is long, and has a centre aisle with benches on
either side for anyone who wants to listen. The courtroom has no
walls, and is simply a tin-roofed open structure, public in every
way. The crowing of roosters provides background noise.

The procedure in the Primary Court is to have the complainant make his statement, and then to allow the respondent to question him. Then the complainant's witnesses testify and may be questioned. Thereafter, the respondent makes his presentation, and brings in his witnesses, all of them subject to questioning by the plaintiff. The Magistrate and the Assessors ask questions and interrupt when they see fit.

Elifatio made his statement and then was asked by Richard, "Why don't you produce any witnesses?" He answered that he thought it unnecessary since Richard had admitted pulling up the plants. Richard then denied doing so. (In the questioning period Richard was not yet under oath, as the oaths are usually sworn just before each party makes his formal statement.) The Magistrate peered at Elifatio rather severely, and asked, "If you saw him pull up the plants, why didn't you make an outcry and rouse the neighbours?" Elifatio made two answers, "I didn't think it was necessary. I was afraid because Richard had a big dog with him."

A number of questions followed from the Magistrate, the gist of which were, "How can you *prove* that Richard pulled up your seedlings?"

Elifatio finally said, "My son saw him pull them up." Elifatio's statement was read back to him, from the beginning, as the Magistrate had taken it down. He was asked whether he agree to the contents, and was then made to sign it. This routine procedure is cumbersome and slow, since everything is recounted at least twice, and if there are corroborative statements by wit nesses, again and again. But it is a procedure that turns a simple conversational account into a formal charge, or response.

Elifatio's son then stood up to testify. He was a thin, sad and timid looking boy of seventeen, who appeared, as many Chagga adolescents do to American eyes, very much younger. He was tall and his thin wrists stuck far out of his too-small threadbare cotton jacket. He said that he had seen Richard pull up the seedlings. Richard barely let him finish his statement and said fiercely, "You did not see me. You were told by your father wha to say in this court." Richard was using his "question" period rather irregularly to make statements rather than to ask questions, but this is not uncommon, and the Magistrates only intervene when they want to.

The boy seemed terrified by Richard's outburst. Sternly the

Magistrate said to him, "Did you actually see the seedlings in Richard's hand?"

"No," he replied. His statements were read back and he signed.

The Magistrate then asked Elifatio if he had any other witnesses, and he said, "Yes, there are the people who heard the case before the ten-house leader."

"No," said the Magistrate, "I will not hear them. I want people who saw Richard uprooting the trees." There were no others.

Richard was then put under oath and asked to make his statement. "I have no statement," he said. Later his lineage brother told me that Richard had said nothing because he did not want to lie under oath.

It was Elifatio's turn to ask questions, but he, poor fellow, was no match for his sharp young kinsman. "What," he asked Richard, "What did you say before the ten-house leader?"

"I denied doing it," said Richard. And that, of course, was true, as Richard had both denied and ultimately admitted it at various stages of the earlier proceedings.

Elifatio's questions turned against him. He kept insisting helplessly that Richard had admitted everything before the ten-house leader. "Then why," asked the Magistrate, "did you fail to win that case?"

One of the assessors put in a word, "If Richard had admitted it, you would not have lost before the ten-house leader. What is the relationship between you?" The Magistrate did not allow the question. He said it was not relevant since no statements had been made about any enmity between the brothers.

Richard offered no witnesses. The case was at an end. The Magistrate acquitted Richard forthwith. Was the Magistrate biased in favour of Richard? Possibly he was from the start, inclined to favour another white-collar man. But probably more significant, just before the Court session started, I saw one of the educated men who had been at the neighbourhood hearing enter the Magistrate's office with him. It is unlikely that they did not discuss the case.

In any event, Richard had taken what precautions he could to
see that he would win. He had approached every single local pe
son who had been at the neighbourhood hearing the day before hi
appearance in the Primary Court, and had asked each one not to
testify in Elifatio's favor. In fact, I later found out that h
had tried to send a message to me to the same effect. While th
ten-house leader had told Elifatio he would appear, he had no
doubt pledged secretly to Richard that he would not. Thus Elif
tio's best witness melted away just when he was needed.

The case in the Primary Court was very different from the sa
case in the neighbourhood. There had been no need for the test
mony of the son in the neighbourhood hearing because of Richard
admission of guilt. Faced with the Court, Richard lied and won
Moreover, the issues which were central in the neighbourhood, a
might be said to be central to the case altogether, the questio
in whose property the seedlings were planted, and about the pat
were questions which simply were not raised nor were they considered in the Court. Yet from the point of view of an outside
such as an appellate judge or supervisory magistrate (had eithe
had occasion to look at the record, which they didn't) coming t
the case with no background, the record would hardly have seeme
distorted. Quite the contrary. It seemed entirely justified
that the Magistrate should have refused to allow the accusation
to stand, when the plaintiff's only witness was his minor son,
against the denials of an apparently respectable well-to-do
brother. Justice was apparently done, whether or not it was
really done. The Court upheld the law regarding the presumptio
of innocence in criminal cases and regarding the plausibility
of evidence, though the Magistrate did not state it explicitly
those terms.

When parties come to a Primary Court on Kilimanjaro, from th
point of view of the Court, the most important thing is that
their situation becomes a case, in other words, that its dispos
tion should fit into one of the general categories from which p
scribed consequences flow. A highly personal and idiosyncratic
situation from the point of view of the parties is easiest to
deal with if it can be classified as an instance of a general
category so that it can be dealt with efficiently. Thus a complaint like Elifatio's becomes in the hands of the court clerk
case of malicious destruction of property. The issues for the
Magistrate then become: Was property destroyed? Whose propert
was destroyed? By whom was it destroyed? And procedurally, he
asks for the proof of each of these matters. Once the issues a
narrowed in this way, there is no need to inquire into the

general situation, the background, the relationship of the
parties, the motives, and the like. On the whole, the Primary
Court Magistrates show great reluctance to inquire very deeply
into motives. Most of the time it is as if they prefer not to
know *why* anything has happened, but rather *what* occurred, or even
more narrowly, what can be *shown* (persuasively) to have happened.
This is all part of their way of de-particularizing a situation,
so that it will fit into the rules "everyone knows." One of
those rules is that normally no one has the right to destroy the
property of another. There is nothing subtle or complex there.
All that remains is the proof. If that is lacking, then the disposition is indisputable. If there is proof, the only issue is
what must be paid in fines or compensation.

Of the Chagga cases about which I know the "inside" story, a
very large percentage appear in Court at least as distorted if
not in even more fictitious a form. What one reads in the records
and in the decisions of the Magistrates is always fairly plaus-
ible. But a knowledge of Chagga life makes one very sceptical
about whether the facts as presented have much to do with "what
really happened in the particular case." In the Chagga Council
Minutes of 22 February 1962, Minute 5, no. 37a Bwana Male said,
"...when people are sent to court to be charged you cannot know
who was wrong and who was right and sometimes justice is and
sometimes is not done." If this is so, not in all, but even in a
substantial number of law cases, what then is going on in the
Court? What function do such hearings have and for whom?

Tribunals such as these are in an important aspect spokesmen
for the government. Formal legal institutions contribute to
the regular demonstration of the corporate qualities of the
state. In their professional acts the Courts give support to
the general political-ideological thesis that a government
through its laws is the ultimate custodian of the boundaries of
public and private morality. This expository function is ful-
filled even if the courts make errors in the decisions of particular cases. What is essential for such representational
purposes is that the errors should never be apparent on the
face of any decision, and should not be apparent in any other
way, even if they occur. Litigants may lie and not be found
out. Witnesses may feign illness and fail to appear, or plead
faulty memory when they remember perfectly well. If the court
gives this credence, then for the purposes of the hearing, what
they have or have not said is as effective as if it were true.

If a court is known to be prejudiced or influenced or a trial

is rigged, it may still be extremely effective for political pur
poses. What greater show of power than to contravene all public
conceptions of "fairness" in a public ceremonial? Thus public
acceptance of judicial decisions may rest on either (or both) of
two foundations: the judicial decision as a non-resistable
application of state power and/or the judicial decision as an
enforcement of local ideas of justice. Even in so minor a tribunal as the Primary Court on Kilimanjaro these twin elements
are prominent and intertwined. Those who like a decision perceive it as "just." Those who do not like it perceive it as an
exercise of power that must be accepted. The Court's ceremonial
proceedings are designed to support both theses, and many symbolic statements are made about power and justice in the course
of sorting out disputes and punishing minor violations of law.

Another political purpose that is served by the existence of
these Courts is to furnish an avenue by which individuals may
appeal to the state to intervene in their affairs. Technically
the Primary Courts give every resident direct access to the
state, which he can try to mobilize on his behalf. This open-
ness to all depends for its smooth functioning on being used by
few. But the political message is for all, and is built into
the very existence of the Court.

There is no doubt that rules and interests were both involved
in the neighbourhood hearing of the case, and were also both
involved in the Primary Court. But despite some overlap, there
were also some notable differences in the content and significance of the rules and interests in the two tribunals. The rule
of procedure in the Court drama have no precise parallel in the
neighbourhood hearing. The ceremonial performance in the Court
is one which is an everyday matter for the Magistrate and an
occasional event in the lives of the parties. This familiarity
with the organizing rules of the judicial ritual makes the
Magistrate more comfortable than the parties and gives him a
situational authority. He can and does use that situational
authority not only to run the proceedings in an orderly way, but
indirectly to make symbolic statements on a small scale that
hint at his substantial powers. Most but not all of the substan
tive rules applicable in the Primary Courts are the rules that
"everybody knows," whether customary or statutory. But the
parties are always aware that the Magistrate knows more rules
than they do and that this esoteric body of knowledge is one
source of the power of his office. Most Magistrates take some
opportunity during the proceedings to remind their audience of
this either through the tone of their questioning, or in their

management of what is allowed to be said and what is cut off.
In the Court one speaks only with permission of the Magistrate.
The non-verbal signs are equally impressive and also are governed by a set of rules. Everyone present is at least sublimi-
nally aware of the connection the Court has with the awesome
powers of the state, and some of this sense is conveyed by the
considerable display of rules and rulings that are pertinent to
almost everything that transpires in the courtroom. It is as if
it were being said, "There is nothing improvised or accidental
about what goes on here. We are keepers of order." Rules have
an enormous utility in the Court, both in dramatizing what is
taking place, and in linking those events with a larger organizational system, the hierarchy of courts, the government, and in a
diffuse way with the whole idea of a social and moral order.
Thus in the course of settling particular disputes and enunciat-
ing standards of behavior, the Courts are conveying many other
connected messages. The use of rules and rulings is an intrinsic
part of this complex of activities.

Normative rules about boundaries were very much in the air in
the neighbourhood hearing, but it could be argued that in this
case, at least, they were to a great extent the rationale of
partisanship. In the neighbourhood hearing the show of partisanship was not merely expected, it was mandatory on certain close
relatives and friends. In the Court, by contrast, any show of
partisanship or "interest" in the parties or outcome was a dis-
qualifying circumstance. Elifatio's son was not a credible witness because he was so closely related and was a young person
under his father's aegis. His testimony was disregarded. Had
the Magistrate been provably an "interested" party, he too would
have been disqualified. In the Court apparent partisan interest
was anathema, and the legal rules pertinent to the case were
treated as a self-evident set of categories and consequences.
In the Court, the statutory category under which a criminal complaint is filed with the Court Clerk preclassifies the case under
given rules about wrongdoing. The Court is at liberty to re-
classify matters if it chooses, but it is usually far easier to
let matters stand, as was done in this case. For the Court, the
prime issue was what had happened, that being very narrowly
defined by the legal category "malicious damage to property."
By contrast, in the neighbourhood, what had occurred was settled
fairly quickly. Everyone really already knew what had happened
before there was any hearing. Interests were also far from con-
cealed. Yet in the neighbourhood, the issues of what behaviour
was proper in the circumstances, and what rules were pertinent,
were treated as no simple question, but as a subtle matter, and

a complex one.   Rules about paths, boundaries and self-help wer
all stated and discussed and weighed. But the outcome of the
hearing was the settlement of two particular issues rather than
the development of general rules: 1) that Richard had had the
right to uproot the plants, and 2) that the TANU man had the
right to pronounce the decision.

There is no doubt that the Court had much more *potential*
power than the neighbourhood aggregations, and displayed it.
But in the end, in this case as in many others, it was the
neighbourhood social nexus that controlled the result in the
Court, by withholding testimony. The Court has police power at
its beck and call, but the neighbourhood social relationships
control the witnesses.

What one might call the hidden ruling of the case was that
ordinarily in internal matters individuals must submit to the
decisions of the lineage-neighbourhood in which they live out
their lives. They challenge it at their peril. For the most
part they must accept its organizational structure and the
instance by instance consequences of its internal political
alliances. They must accept its "interested" decisions. With
some elders, the ten-house cell leader and the clerks all agains
him, Elifatio was finished, even in the external forum that
trafficks in impersonal rules.

From the point of view of the parties and the society at
large, the dispute was "settled." That is, two ceremonies of
situational transformation had turned Elifatio's private quarre
into a public ruling he hated but had to accept. He had to
recognize that it was useless to go on, that he could not win.
That is what the ceremonies meant for him. But in a less particular sense, from an outsider's long-term view, these were
events on which various durable organizational interests
impinged, and in which they competed for effectiveness. These
were events of articulation between levels and types of organiza
tion. As such they reflect the extreme localism of social control that still dominates the lives of rural Chagga farmers.

POST-SCRIPT

The dispute was ended but the anger was not. Elifatio and
Richard ceased to be on speaking terms. They did not attend
beer drinks at each other's houses (for example when celebratin
the baptisms of their children) and remained in this state of
avoidance and anger for five years. However, through the

accident of a death and various surrounding circumstances, Elifatio recently has gained access to some land that Richard wants. Suddenly in 1973, everything changed between the two men. Richard was ready to help Elifatio in all matters. Elifatio was arrested for assault after beating up a woman who had to be hospitalized as a result. Richard bailed him out, and has since succeeded in manipulating the Court calendar in such a way that the case will never come to trial and the charge will soon be dropped. Richard is Elifatio's friend and protector. Thus do temporary individual alliances cross-cut the more durable clusters of "interests" that are currently operative in rural Chagga neighbourhoods.

REFERENCES

Allott, A.N. (ed.). (1970). *Judicial and Legal Systems in Africa*, Butterworth, London.

Georges, T. (1973). "The Courts in the Tanzania One Party State." *In* ... James and F.M. Kassam (eds) *Law and its Administration in a One Party State*, East African Literature Bureau, Kampala, pp. 9-32.

Moore, S.F. (1973). "Law and Social Change: the Semi-autonomous Social Field as an Appropriate Subject of Study," *Law and Society Review* Summer, 1973, pp. 719-746.

Moore, S.F. (1975). "Ritual Concord and Fraternal Strife: Kilimanjaro 1968-69". In S.F. Moore and B. Myerhoff (eds.) *Symbols and Politics in Communal Ideology* Cornell University Press, Ithaca.

ACKNOWLEDGEMENTS

The work, both field work and library study, which made the preparation of this manuscript possible, was done in two periods, in 1968-69 under a grant from the Social Science Research Council of New York, and in 1973-74 under a grant from the National

S. F. MOORE

Science Foundation, which grants are hereby gratefully acknow-
ledged. A preparatory year spent as a Research Fellow at the
African Studies Center at the University of California, Los
Angeles (1967-68) and a year as Honorary Research Fellow at the
Department of Anthropology, University College, University of
London (1973-74) and two periods as a Research Associate of the
University of Dar es Salaam (1968-69 and 1973-74) have also been
of invaluable assistance, and the author is duly grateful.

LAW-CODES AND BROKERAGE IN A LESOTHO VILLAGE (1)

J. A. G. Perry

INTRODUCTION

It is...often a mistake to assume that all Basotho know their customary law in detail, especially the younger generation from among whom, no doubt, future court presidents will be chosen. Moreover legal practitioners are not permitted to appear in civil causes before the Basotho courts...and thus the courts are without the benefit of their argument and research (Palmer and Poulter 1972:127).

The first concern of this paper is to debate to what extent the ordinary litigant or disputant at village level in Lesotho apprehends the laws to which he is subject and the procedures that govern the administration of those laws. Drawing heavily upon Paine's discussion (1973) of Bernstein's concept of 'restricted' and 'elaborated' linguistic codes, I will show how the law operative in two courts in a Lesotho village constitutes a code that is in the process of change, and how villagers have differing degrees of access to and command of the various modes of the law-code.

In so doing, it is necessary first to construct a model of traditional jural activity in the past as being conducted in terms of a restricted code which, says Bernstein,

_____

(1) For the theoretical underpinning of this paper I am heavily indebted to Paine, whose ideas (1973), enabled me to rework material that I have published previously on the broker, and who gave me permission to quote from an, as then, unpublished paper.

'will arise where the form of the social relation is based upon
closely shared identifications, upon an extensive range of share
expectations, upon a range of common assumptions...where the
culture or subculture raises the "we" above "I".' (1972:476)

This will be followed by the contention that the progressive
encapsulation and consequent modification of the tribal system
saw the introduction of a different order of properties to the
law-code so that the law operative in village courts today is a
compound of elements of both the restricted code and a code that
may be likened to the one Bernstein labels 'elaborated', one
which

'...is not concerned primarily with the maintenance of consensus
and solidarity and...is likely to be used where consensus is
either absent or not an issue. Its concern is the communication
of "specific referents" of a situation or a problem.' (Paine
1973:38, citing Bernstein 1965:156)

Further, attention will be directed to what Paine terms a
'disjunction', in this case between the peasant and his grasp of
the law on the one hand and, on the other, the law as administered by the courts. This disjunction is not confined to law-
codes, but is part of a more general problem of inadequate chan--
nels of communication between the local community and the encapsulating structure.

Where disjunctions such as these exist, there will emerge men
to bridge them, and the second part of this paper explores the
role of a broker who has this ability. The broker's command of
the codes operative in the village courts serves as a starting
point for an appraisal of his role for, as Paine points out,

'The operational strength of a broker lies in his command of a
repertoire of codes, both R[estricted] and E[laborated].'
(1973:30)

The broker's fluency in law-codes enables him to enter into
transactions with clients in which his role may be seen as purveyor of legal expertise. It will be shown that the efficacy
of the broker's code-utilization is a function of a more complex
role repertoire. His articulation of law-codes is simply one of
the connections he is able to make for a client. Others have
their source in his involvement in local-level politics and in
his long association with the chieftainship. A notion of the
law at village level as a code is inseparable from viewing the

courts that control and define that code as embedded in the ongoing decision-making processes of the society. Successful
brokerage in this context depends on the broker's securing and
maintaining access to decision-making channels and information.

PART I

The Law-Code of the Lekhotla

This section develops an analogy between, on the one hand,
the operation of law at a traditional level in Lesotho villages
largely unaffected by change and, on the other, Bernstein's concept of the restricted code. My model of traditional tribal law
and its operation is, of necessity, an ideal one, adopted for
its explicatory value. Many of the elements in the model are
adumbrated in the description Jones gives of the 'traditional
judicial system' of the Basotho.

'Each village group formed a close knit community and looked
to one person as their head, in the Basuto idiom they turned the
doors of their huts towards his, and the open space before his
huts formed the *khotla*, the place where the men of the village
met together to talk, to do any sedentary work they might have,
and while doing it assist with their comments and advice the
head of their community in his administrative and judicial
business.

'The Basuto traditional judicial system was also designed for
such small units. Disputes and breaches of the community's peace
were dealt with by the chief or headman in the *khotla*. Justice
was free and the main objective was to get to the bottom of the
trouble and to bring about a settlement of it. The parties and
their witnesses gave their evidence before the *khotla* subject to
the comments of their fellows and to the cross-examination of the
chief who gave his judgment before them, either directly or after
consultation with some of the older and wiser men. The main
function of the judge was to determine whether or not the "law",
that is the tribal usage, had been broken in which case those
who had broken it, it might be either or both of the parties,
paid the customary fine; he had also to determine what compensation if any should be paid to the person who had been most
wronged. Compensation and fine were usually paid in livestock,
normally in cattle, and the fine went to the chief as head of
the community. Justice under such a system was normally speedy
and satisfactory and was accepted by the parties, for it was
subject to effective public sanctions — neither judge nor

litigants could afford to disregard the opinion of the rest of their community who were listening to the case.'(1951:8)

In tracing an analogy here with Bernstein's restricted code, I focus on the social determinants of the code, and largely ignore its linguistic aspects. This is not to do violence to Bernstein's model, for:

'The codes themselves are functions of a particular form of social relationship or, more generally, qualities of social structures.'(1965:153)

The key elements of the restricted code for our purposes are: that it is based on common social assumptions, that status is a important determinant of the code, and that the code reinforces the form of the social relation.

Concerning the first point, Bernstein suggests that the restricted code will arise in a closed community (1964:61), and th it will be 'played out against a backdrop of assumptions common to' the users of the code,

'...against a set of closely shared interests and identificatic against a system of shared expectations; in short, it presuppos a local cultural identity...'(1964:60)

Bernstein's criteria for the emergence of a restricted code presume a social milieu similar to that in which Jones places the traditional men's *lekhotla*, i.e. in a small, closed, lineage-based village. The law-code in such a community, it is reasonable to assume, was firmly ensconced in a familiar framework: both the customs and norms regulating behaviour and the procedures involved in enforcing the code were known to participar in the judicial process.

The routine of judicial activity will establish in such a co munity what Bernstein calls 'predictability at a high level of consensus'(1964:59). The nature of the judicial process will be both predictable to the participants and consensual in tone and objective, since the social relations between disputants ar ongoing and clearly defined. Assuming that the bulk of tribal dispute-settlement rested on a process of arbitration, it follo that there would be a high level of consensus too in acceptance of the norms invoked by the *lekhotla*

The second step in our explication is that

'The consensus is obtained by making the status aspect of the social relation salient.'(Bernstein 1964:59)

The composition of the traditional *lekhotla* reflected the status structure of the community, consisting as it did of the adult males presided over by the chief. Acceptance of the court's decision was acceptance of a body in itself representative of the community. The chief stood for the enduring values of the group and expression of consensus by him was a symbolic reaffirmation of communal values. In this sense, the chief *was* the law.

A disputant before the *lekhotla* was viewed as a total social personality, whose structural position in the ongoing status relations of the community was known to both the chief and the men of the *lekhotla*. This background knowledge of a disputant's place in the social order was brought to bear upon his case. Gluckman makes this point, writing on the Barotse:

'In order to fulfil their task the judges constantly have to broaden the field of their enquiries, and consider the total history of relations between the litigants, not only the narrow legal issue raised by one of them.'(1955:21)

In social situations in which the restricted code obtains then,

'Individuals relate to each other essentially through *the social position or status they are occupying*.'(Bernstein 1965:154)

Thus the restricted code is status rather than person oriented, and 'the individual is transformed into a cultural agent' (Bernstein 1964:58).

To take this one step further, one might postulate that a disputant or litigant would be judged in the restricted tribal code by the norms directly relevant to his status, and that decisions of the *lekhotla* would reflect status relations and obligations. Detailed communal knowledge of the status positions and relations of disputants would lead to their being classified as, say, 'recalcitrant younger brother', or 'reasonable neighbour'. In Bernstein's terms, the individual's 'discrete intent' would be 'implicit' and identifiable. It follows that there would be a close congruence between role expectation and norms applied, and that

'The range of discretion of the role is confined to the area of common intent and, therefore, the role receives explicit support

from the status components of the relationship.'(Bernstein
1964:64)

This brings us to the third element in Bernstein's restricted
code model that is of importance here, namely that

'The code symbolizes and reinforces the form of the social relation and controls the channel through which new learning is made
available.'(1964:59)

Gluckman is again pertinent, about one of the tasks of Lozi
judges:

'...as they have to maintain the law, they expound in public the
rights and duties of headman, villager, father, son, brothers,
husband, wife, etc., and these form units which are the nuclei
of the substantive law.'(1955:81)

There is a sense in which the law-code is didactic, enjoining
the disputant to 'go back and behave like a good father', etc.
More than this, each time the injunction is given, it defines
more exactly just what a 'good father' is. There is a feedback
process then between the code and the social relations that give
rise to it, and this process is self reinforcing.

This is inseparable from a view of the *lekhotla* as a socializing agent, inculcating a knowledge of the judicial process in
members of the social order. The *lekhotla* was not separated fro
the main stream of village life. Boys from an early age were
drawn into an awareness of what was going on in the *lekhotla*, in
which they were expected to perform such tasks as the fetching o
firewood. A young man growing up in the confines of these close
communities, with male activity centred as it was on the
lekhotla, could not but absorb, by a process of cultural osmosis
the law-ways of his community.

Change and the Lekhotla

The small, closed communities which generated the form of

a restricted law-code are now rare in Lesotho (2). Wallman writes of village life:

'It appears from historical reports that the Basuto once led a closer community life than they now do. The chief and the men under him spent much of their time in court...together. It was the duty and the habit of every man...who could not attend to call "at the Chief's place"...on the way to and from the day's tasks...He would then hear the latest news, discuss the cases of the day, and generally catch up with current affairs...

'Nowadays the men do not automatically stop by "the Chief's place" every day...Those who have not migrated to work, probably regard themselves as temporarily at home and tend to be occupied with their private affairs.'(1969:18-19)

The changes that effectively transformed village judicial life had their roots in a historical process affecting the lives and status relations of both chiefs and commoners. By 1937, the ways of closed community life had been undermined by social and economic change. The relations of reciprocity between rulers and subjects, based on mutual obligations and services, had been eroded by the growing desire to satisfy new economic needs. The chiefs' involvement in a cash economy had made them unwilling to redistribute to the people, while education and rising political aspirations caused the commoners to resent the continuing demands made by their rulers. The course of alienation early affected the judicial system. In the traditional men's *lekhotla*, fines levied had often been used to feed those present, expressing the unity of the group imposing the sanction. This custom was falling into desuetude and, as Hailey has written,

'...it was a common complaint that the Chiefs were exploiting their Courts by giving the people vexatious orders and fining them heavily for disobedience...'(1953:81)

These trends, in conjunction with the fact that each chief had

---

(2)   Some informants maintained that 'behind the mountains' there can be found villages where integrated community life still exists, and where a more traditional kind of *lekhotla* can still be found. I was unable to check the veracity of these statements, and they may well have been a wishful assertion on the part of lowlanders that the mountains still provide a repository for traditional forms of Sesotho culture.

his own court and that, under the 'placement system', petty chie
had proliferated, all contributed to a wide-spread desire for
reform.

1938 saw the beginning of a series of reforms that was to
beget a process wherein the chief's administrative and judicial
functions were progressively separated. This marked the start
of increasing centralization and encapsulation. The chief's
administrative role was to be dictated in growing measure by
central government, while his effective judicial function was
to be superseded by a system of Local Courts.

The Law-Code of the Chief's Court

Rural life is still dependent on the Chief, but it no longer
revolves around him. A man attends the khotla *if he is involvec*
in a case, normally not otherwise. While there are certainly
informal gossip and discussion groups, these cannot be expected
to keep people informed of and participating in community affaix
in the way of a regular khotla *meeting.* (Wallman 1969:19)

I turn now to give an account of legal processes in the village where my fieldwork was carried out. The broker's area of
operations was based in a principal chief's village and centred
mainly on litigation in two courts: the chief's court of arbitration and the Local Court. The chief's court resembled in no
great measure a traditional *lekhotla* (3). It was presided over
not by the chief himself, but by a series of representatives ane
functionaries in his administration. He himself seldom appeare
in court, and only occasionally were messages sent to inform hir
of a particularly troublesome case. He was often absent from t
village and, even when he was home, petitioners might be fobbed
off repeatedly with such euphemisms as 'The chief is sick/busy/
sleeping'. By no stretch of the imagination could it be said
that the chief was either the 'father' or the 'law' in this
village.

---

(3)   This was the court of a principal chief, hearing cases at
      first instance from the area immediately under its jurisdi
      tion as well as cases on appeal from the courts of chiefs,
      sub-chiefs and headmen under its broader jurisdiction. It
      possible that these lower courts had more in common with a
      traditional *lekhotla* than the principal chief's court did.

Over a period of three years (4) a number of men succeeded each other in representing the chief in his court. Each representative was assisted by various other functionaries who, in the absence of the representative, presided over cases. Two of these authorities were forced to leave office during the fieldwork period, the one for alleged malpractices in land allocation. The second man aroused wide-spread antagonism because of persistent neglect of his duties: he worked irregular hours and sometimes kept people waiting for days. He himself was a sub-chief and, so it was alleged, he tended to support fellow authorities in disputes. Accusations of political partisanship were also levelled against him. Particularly in connection with these two men, the chief was censured for having allowed them so much latitude.

There was a strong view that some of the men in the administration were outsiders, lacking concern about local problems, who did not represent the interests and values of the community. Certain of these men did reflect the status hierarchy of the ward in that they were chiefs or headmen; others, however, had been chosen for certain skills (literacy, familiarity with administrative procedures, and so on). These men were thus not representative of the community as the *banna ba lekhotla* (men of the court) had been, but bore rather a resemblance to a group of bureaucrats. Because of lack of co-ordination, the administration was riven by political and personal factions, all of which contributed to delays and confusion for the people it was there to serve.

Procedure in the chief's court today is quite different from the traditional community-based consensus and debate that characterized the *lekhotla*. The court now hears only those directly concerned in the case. Men do not normally attend the court as spectators as part of their daily round of activity. There is little sense of community participation. The chief's representatives sometimes reach their decision only once they have sent the parties and their witnesses out of the courtroom, after which they are called back to have the decision announced to them. Notes are kept of most cases and, should it prove necessary to forward a case to the Local Court, a docket is sent to that court.

The chief's representative did play an inquisitorial role in eliciting and investigating evidence, but the object of such probing was not always to assist parties in cross-questioning or to

---

(4) A total of sixteen months was spent in this village over a period of three years (1969-71).

discover common grounds for reconciliation. Instead, on some
occasions, the questions were designed to discover whether ther
were grounds, according to the letter of the law, for forwardin
a case to the Local Court. The fact that the court was aware
that some disputes under investigation were likely to appear in
the Local Court as criminal cases coloured the tone and content
of its inquisitorial function. So although it is commonly agre
that

'...the traditional authorities...conduct proceedings in the
nature of arbitrament with a view to settling disputes out of
court...'(Palmer and Poulter 1972:500),

the chief's court also functions as a clearing house for litiga
tion in the Local Court.

I would suggest that there has been a shift in emphasis in t
type of norms selected and applied by the court away from those
that, based on consensus, used to define role expectations, and
corresponding tendency towards judging the individual's actions
in terms of the law. This might be so partly because status
relations are no longer as clearly defined as they once were, a
partly because the law-code in operation is no longer defined
exclusively by customary usage. One of the points Bernstein
makes about role expectation in the context of an elaborated co
applies here, namely that

'The form of the social relation which generates an elaborat
code is such that a range of discretion must inhere in the role
if it is to be produced at all...The range of discretion which
must necessarily inhere in the role involves the speaker
[litigant] in a measure of social isolation.'(1964:64)

The difficulties facing the chief's court arising out of
changing status relations are illustrated by cases where norms
applying to traditional role expectations are obscured by, or i
conflict with, recent legislation. Formerly, for example, a
chief or headman had fairly wide latitude in control over land
and other resources in his area. His power and position have r
been made ambiguous by, for instance, legislation that lays dow
that he must consult with an elected land advisory board. Dur
the fieldwork period the chief's court was often faced with cor
plaints brought by members of land advisory boards against the
authorities they had been elected to assist, or by villagers
against authorities who had not had land boards elected. In th
type of case, the chief or headman had allegedly not complied

with the provisions of the *Land (Procedure) Act* (5). The chief's court seemed reluctant to investigate these disputes further. On occasion they delayed the hearing with repeated postponements until the complaints petered out, or they attempted a type of rough and ineffectual arbitration: 'Headman, these are your subjects — go home and hear their complaint; people, this is your headman — go home and respect him'. I did not record any instance of the court's forwarding a case in which a chief or headman was obviously guilty of contravening the terms of this legislation to a competent authority for further action.

I would suggest that the ineffectual nature of these decisions was conditioned by ambiguity regarding status relationships. There is considerable uncertainty in Lesotho among tribal authorities in particular about the exact function of a land advisory board and about the precise degree in which it shares authority with them. With the election of land boards so often serving as a testing ground for party-political strength, it might happen that a chief or headman and his land board were opponents in the party-political arena as well.

Thus the chief's court may be faced with a headman who sees his traditional function threatened (land allocation is one of the few powers left to tribal authorities), and a land advisory board which views the headman's reluctance to consult with them as arbitrary, reactionary and unconstitutional. In trying to balance out these conflicting sets of expectations, the court often satisfied neither party. Headmen would ask 'Who owns the village - them or me?' From the board's side, the court decision could be seen as partisan, designed to shore up the position of authorities.

Court decisions in cases like these, then, far from reflecting and reinforcing status relations, served to show up and sometimes to aggravate the potential conflict inherent in the strained structural position of the disputants. This is congruent with an element of the elaborated code, that

'...role relations receive less support from shared expectations.'(Bernstein 1964:64)

This is not to suggest that the court lost sight of the aim of conciliation; indeed the bulk of its cases was concerned with this process, and in areas where the conflict of interests was

---

(5) Act 24 of 1967.

not so marked, the court was often a successful arbiter.   This i
an area in which the restricted code retains force.   Another is
that the court also served to instruct in new laws, and in this
sense the court did 'control channels of new learning and reinforce the form of the social relation'.

But the quality and effectiveness of the court as a socializing agent are questionable.   As it is no longer a community
gathering place, knowledge of the law is not absorbed informally
as it were.   Nor does it constitute a debate forum: decisions ar
not discussed communally, but given.   When it suited them, the
representatives of the chief were able to adopt a tone and
bureaucratic style that served as a front effectively to distanc
those coming before the court.

In a sense the members of the court command a code that the
peasant does not fully grasp.   They 'possess' the code by virtue
of their access to information such as government proclamations,
and they control the code by virtue of their literacy, training,
and position in the authority structure.   Bernstein, when dealin
with access to elaborated codes and the social positions that
facilitate that access, makes this point:

'...the use of an elaborated code or an orientation to its use
will depend *not* on the psychological properties of a speaker but
upon access to specialized social positions...Normally, but
not inevitably, such social positions will coincide with a stra-
tum seeking or already possessing access to the major decision-
making areas of the society.'(1965:158)

So although many elements of the restricted code still pertai
in the chief's court, the law as operative in that court is in a
process of acquiring characteristics of a type of code that in
many respects resembles the one Bernstein labels 'elaborated'.
This type of code, Bernstein states, 'will arise wherever the
culture or subculture emphasizes the "I" over the "we"'(1972:
476).   The code-user is therefore encouraged

'...to focus upon the other person as an experience different
from his own.   An elaborated code is *person* rather than status
oriented.'(1964:63)

Writing about the changing nature of customary family law in
Lesotho, Poulter states:

'There will, no doubt, be an increasing number of Africans wh

desire to regulate their family relations and succession under
the common law or statute, and there is nothing to prevent their
exercising this option. The extended family is, of course, a
traditional institution of which many Africans are justly proud.
The preservation of the solidarity of the family is likely to
come under increasing pressure as individuals become wage earners
and move to an urban environment. They will be less likely to
wish to maintain their traditional responsibilities, nor will
they in all cases be content to see their property devolve
according to customary law upon death. These influences are
going to strike at the very heart of the system. The greater
freedom of women is also going to affect the family structure.
Thus in the long run we may find an adaptation of the customary
law so that it concentrates its attention increasingly on the
individual and thus moves closely into line with the common law
and the relevant statutes.'(Palmer and Poulter 1972:172)

For the peasant, the operation of law in the chief's court is
becoming less comprehensible as it acquires more elements characteristic of an elaborated code. This trend is even more marked
in the Local Court, which bears far more clearly the stamp of
that code.

The Law-Code of the Local Court

The Local Court is the lowest level of the official judicial
hierarchy in Lesotho and, as such, is staffed by government
appointees. The court personnel in no way reflected the status
relations of the village or ward, for the president and his two
clerks were outsiders in the village; their qualifications for
holding office were education and training. Moreover, the decisions of this court were at times extremely critical of members
of the traditional power structure of the ward (6). The court
itself, far from being at the hub of village life, was situated
on the outskirts of the village, within a fenced enclosure that
contained also the staff's living quarters.

Proceedings in this court were characterized by a far greater
degree of formality than those in the chief's court. A court
messenger maintained the dignity and decorum of the court, statements were recorded and signed and, in contrast to the chief's

---

(6) There were, however, persistent rumours about pressure being
brought to bear upon Local Courts in Lesotho. Rumours of
bias were especially prevalent after the emergency was
declared in 1970.

court, regular hours were kept and cases were in general efficiently scheduled and handled. Cases were screened by the
clerks before being accepted, it being their task to ensure that
the court was not inundated with vague complaints and grievances,
with cases beyond its jurisdiction or with cases so badly formulated that the court was unable to deal with them. Even with
these safeguards, a number of such cases slipped through. It was
clear that these litigants had sought no advice from either their
chief's court or someone skilled in the law before attempting
litigation, and that their failure to do so had cost them both in
time and money.

The formal tone and complex procedure of the court seemed to
handicap some litigants. In civil cases no lawyers are permitted
to represent clients and, although their employment is allowed by
the *Central and Local Courts Proclamation* (7) and is entrenched
in the Constitution (8) for criminal cases, in no case that I
recorded or witnessed over a period of three years was any party
ever represented by a lawyer in the Local Court in the village of
study. Parties could be represented in civil cases by relatives
or other non-legal representatives having their authorization
(Palmer and Poulter 1972:497). In effect, mostly women sought
representation in this form. Some litigants, for example, were
represented by men with knowledge of the administration; in fact,
they were making use of men with special skills who, if not lawyers, were yet experienced in litigation. Certain chieftainesses
made use of representatives who were in reality troubleshooters;
their expertise in the court was evident and they were well
versed in the skills that success in the Local Court demanded.
Thus, although lawyers are not permitted in this court for civil
cases, it is possible for certain litigants to assure, through
the system of representation, that their cases are handled by men
familiar with the forms and procedures of the Local Court law-
code.

The possession of certain skills, notably literacy, gave a
distinct advantage in this court. On occasion men appeared in
court with a copy of the Laws of Lerotholi or with prepared notes
to which they made frequent reference. Lack of skill was most
clearly revealed in the handling of witnesses. Poulter draws
attention to this:

---

(7)   By Regulation 10 of 1965, section 14.

(8)   Section 12(2) (d).

'A somewhat anomalous position has resulted in civil cases because whereas there has been a shift from the "inquisitorial" to the "accusatorial" system, legal representation has not been introduced and thus the onus lies on the parties to carry on any cross-examination. Formerly they could look to the judge to ask the necessary penetrating questions to ascertain the truth or falsehood of testimony, and many litigants still lose cases today through a failure to appreciate the fundamental change that has occurred.'(Palmer and Poulter 1972:497-8)

I have seen litigants manifestly at a loss when putting questions in this court and many witnesses needed probing questions to elicit relevant evidence. As one witness said, 'That is all I know; questions will remind me'. Cross-questioning, to many litigants, was merely a meaningless exercise and their cross-examination often failed to test the veracity of statements. This lack of proficiency was highlighted by the talent of an experienced litigant who could turn examination to his own advantage.

The skills that give an edge in this court are those that depend on command of a code that emphasizes such areas as verbal explicitness, training, and a degree of specialized knowledge. These are qualities of an elaborated code, which

'...will arise wherever the intent of the other person cannot be taken for granted. Inasmuch as the intent of the other person cannot be taken for granted, then speakers are forced to elaborate their meanings and make them both explicit and specific. Meanings which are discrete and local to the speaker must be cut so that they are intelligible to the listener.'(Bernstein 1972: 476) (9)

Quite apart from the formality and complexity of court procedure serving to handicap the ordinary litigant, he is faced with the additional problems of changes that have affected the law as it is administered by the Local Court. Contracts are a case in point, and they are a predictable trouble area in a society in transition. Formerly verbal contracts were

---

(9) Paine points out that, even among users of an elaborated code, intent must be known to some extent, and metacommunication must exist in some measure, or it could not be considered a code (1973:13). The different emphasis I am after here is that in the Local Court, the onus is on a litigant to spell out explicitly his intent.

elaborately safe-guarded by the form of the witnessing that
attended them, and their observance in small communities was
underwritten by their public nature. Now explicit written docu-
mentation is generally desirable. This disjunction lends itself
to exploitation of those who still rely on verbal commitments
made in good faith.

The value accorded documentary evidence in this court compli-
cates procedures that were relatively simple under the traditional law-code. Dealing with the issue of compensation,
Poulter says,

'In line with the traditional overlap of civil and criminal
sanctions, the Rules permit a court to direct that any fine or
part thereof shall be paid to the person injured or aggrieved by
the act or omission in respect of which the fine has been
imposed...' (Palmer and Poulter 1972:500)

He adds in a footnote, 'However, we are informed that very
little use is in fact made of this practice'. In the Local
Court of study an assault, for example, would be dealt with
first as a criminal case, it being left up to the injured party
to bring a further suit for compensation. One such plaintiff,
suing the man who had been found guilty in a previous criminal
case in the Local Court of assaulting him, had his claim for com
pensation jeopardized by the fact that his doctor's certificate
had been lost in the course of litigation. The defendant was
able to question the severity of the plaintiff's injuries. Only
after he had obtained a second certificate, and brought a second
suit for compensation, was the plaintiff able to obtain satisfaction.

In terms of the customary restricted law-code, a litigant
could expect compensation as a matter of course once the *lekhotl*
had established the extent to which he had been wronged. With
the present chief's court unable to impose fines or award compen
sation, a wronged party is forced to turn to the Local Court to
seek redress. To the confusion and dissatisfaction of some, how
ever, that court will not award compensation in terms of
restricted-code expectations.

Although the formality of the court, its complexity of procedure, and the changing nature of the law all contribute toward
restricting a litigant's access to the law-code operative here,
it would be misleading to stress this too strongly. Proficiency
in the code is attainable through various channels such as

literacy, experience, and certain acquirable skills. In other respects too, the code remains within a fairly familiar framework for customary law is still applied in the Local Court and also the president's role is still in part determined by restricted-code expectations.

Poulter questions

'...whether the regular courts still try to achieve the traditional result of a solution acceptable to the parties or whether they stick closely to the letter of the law.'(Palmer and Poulter 1972:501)

In the cases I recorded in the Local Court, the president placed no emphasis whatsoever on reconciliation. He did at times assume a role similar to that of the judge in the chief's court by, for example, putting questions to establish the social background of a litigant. While this court could not be regarded as a socializing agent in the way that the men's *lekhotla* was, the president often took care to explain the law to litigants, particularly when they, by the presentation of their case, showed their unfamiliarity with more recent developments.

Although the court did not, to my knowledge, refer disputes back to the family for arbitration, it often asked whether a particular case had been heard and discussed in family council, and seemed to attach importance to the fact that certain cases had reached it only after an attempt had been made to settle them at that level. Similar significance was given to hearings at the headman's or chief's level.

While it is true then that some elements of the restricted law-code persist in the Local Court, they are in the course, it would seem, of being encapsulated by the more particular forms of an elaborated code. It was obvious that the president did not know personally many of the litigants before him, nor could he place them in their social matrices. Although he asked questions to establish kinship links and relations between parties, litigants were not viewed as total social personalities as in the men's *lekhotla*. Far more than in the chief's court, they appeared as individuals before the law. In this court then the individual is not a 'cultural agent' in the sense he appears to have been in the men's *lekhotla*.

'An elaborated code, in principle, presupposes a sharp boundary or gap between self and others which is crossed through the creation of speech which specifically fits a differentiated "other." In this sense, an elaborated code is oriented towards a person rather than a social category or status.'(Bernstein 1972:477)

With consensus and shared assumptions about role expectations not playing a crucial part in the Local Court, it follows that the form of the role relations does not necessarily receive explicit support from the code, and that there need not be a close congruence between role expectations and norms applied. Even more than in the chief's court, then, the range of discretion inherent in the role involves the litigant in 'a measure of social isolation'.

'He may be differentiated from his social group as a figure is differentiated from its ground.'(Bernstein 1964:64)

A more or less point-by-point comparison of the law-codes operative in the *lekhotla*, the chief's court and the Local Court has the danger of suggesting that the two types of code are mutu-ally exclusive or dichotomous or, equally undesirable, that the one evolves out of the other. Paine chooses to see restricted and elaborated codes as 'points on a continuum of codification' (1973:13) or, further, as encapsulated one within the other. It is the second assumption that has the greater relevance for my conclusion, since I view the two codes, as operative in the village of study, as inter-penetrating each other as a result of encapsulation.

Disjunctions and the Peasant

The disjunction that exists between the peasant's comprehension of law and the law-codes of the village courts is symptomatic of a more general dislocation in communication between the peasant and the centralized agencies of government that increasingly determine his life.

The principal chief should serve in Lesotho as a primary channel of articulation between the local community and the wider society. Ideally, his administration should serve to mediate between the national structure and his people and, in turn, to facilitate communication between the encapsulated community and central government.

From the point of view of the peasant, the chief and his administration have become increasingly identified with central government, its demands and directives. The chief draws his salary from the government, a factor which circumscribes his role, binding him more to the interests of the outside structure. Yet the peasant in this more complex society is still dependent for the regulation of many of his affairs upon an administration that often constitutes a complex and unsympathetic agency. Its ineffectiveness as a channel of communication between government and people is revealed by a consideration of the *pitso*, the communal gathering through which Basotho chiefs traditionally communicate with their people. Today attendance at *lipitso* has fallen off, for the chief has few sanctions to compel his subjects to attend. Even the monthly meetings held in the village of study to bring the ward's headmen, sub-chiefs and chiefs up to date on latest directives and laws were ill attended, and consequently this information was not efficiently relayed. The problem was compounded by the fact that, during the emergency, *lipitso* were often attended by armed police. Thus there was firmly established in many people's minds a correlation between *lipitso* and government pressure, and many refused to attend for fear. This communication problem becomes serious when one considers that, for the majority, the *pitso* is still one of the main sources of new information.

The chief's position midway, as it were, between government and people, lends itself to an interpretation in terms of patronage. From the point of view of the government, the chief and his administration have assumed a convenient position through which to disseminate and gather information. Viewed in this light, the chief can be seen structurally as a middleman. From the point of view of the peasant, on the other hand, there persists an expectation that the chief's role be that of patron, a source of dispensations, favours and protection. Neither of these conceptions of the chief's role has precise validity, however. The fact that the chief's administration can hardly be considered a channel of articulation through which communication proceeds with little distortion, clearly obscures the chief's role as middleman. There are still patronage elements adhering to the chief's role, but change has eroded their pattern. The chief today has limited patronage resources and the latitude of his role has been progressively circumscribed. Yet some peasants feel that if they could have access directly to him, he would still intervene on their behalf as father-patron. It is one of the functions of the broker upon whom this paper is based that he can gain the ear of the chief for a peasant.

PART II

The Broker as Stranger

Litaba (10), the broker, has skills and contacts which serve
effectively to mark him out as different from most of his fellc
villagers. It is fortuitous that Litaba arrived in this community about twenty years ago as 'the stranger who came to stay'
and it is not in this sense that I refer to his 'strangeness'.
By the time of his arrival he already had experience in law,
politics and administration beyond the province of an ordinary
Mosotho.

The broker's position can be summed up in terms of a string
of 'and yets'. He is a commoner, and yet privy to the chieftai
ship. He is a villager, and yet at home in circles that are
closed to the village. He has no official position in village
courts, and yet is an expert in their operations. His structur
position can then be defined in terms of a wide repertoire of
roles which his skills allow him to support.

Paine directs attention to the usefulness of regarding the
broker as a kind of stranger who has the capacity to objectify
(1973:35). It is one of the major elements of the broker's rol
to give 'legal advice'. Those who approach him for advice are
not seeking reassurance or comfort; they have a specific proble
at law of which they want an objective assessment. Litaba give
advice dispassionately, as he must to maintain this brokerage
role. His reputation as a broker depends on the efficacy of th
advice he dispenses. Litaba's capacity to objectify arises frc
extensive experience of the law-codes and their administration,
as well as from his precise knowledge of the social relations
themselves that give rise to trouble cases and litigation. He
can pigeonhole litigation in terms of the types of cases he has
seen and dealt with before, and because of his experience he ca
assess impartially the chances of a client for successful litigation.

Simmel has defined objectivity as the outcome of both engage
ment and disengagement:

'...objectivity does not simply involve passivity and detachmer
it is a particular structure composed of distance and nearness,
indifference and involvement.... Objectivity is by no means

(10) All names in this paper have been changed.

non-participation (which is altogether outside both subjective and objective interaction), but a positive and specific kind of participation.'(1950:404)

Litaba himself uses the English word *peasant* about many of his fellow villagers. He has the ability to distance them in terms of the skills and experience they do not share with him, even while participating in village activities as farmer, neighbour, friend, and so on. Villagers, by contrast, find Litaba hard to classify, and this contributes to his being viewed with a measure of ambivalence. Litaba's role — generally a leadership one — in local-level politics is equally a product of active involvement on the one hand and pragmatic control of the situation on the other.

Advice and the Law-Codes

In the first part of this paper it was shown that litigants have varying degrees of familiarity with the law-codes operative in the village courts. It is common for litigants to seek advice in this sphere, and Litaba is one of the brokers in the village who dispense it. He is in effect bridging a gap or disjunction between the peasant and the law and, in particular, he is able to instruct in areas where the law has changed.

Case 1 (11)

A yound man, Tau, was killed in an inter-village faction fight about pasturage. His three assailants were brought to trial and sentenced to varying prison terms. While they were in gaol, Tau's older brother Khotso, came to Litaba with the following problem.

"My brother has been killed,' he stated, 'but I am puzzled. His killers were sentenced by the court, it is true, but no-one said anything about compensation. It has always been that ten head of cattle are paid for a man's head. His killers have been charged now, and I know that a man cannot be charged twice for the same offence. Now what can you advise me to do? What legal steps can I take to be paid out for the head of my brother?'

---

(11) I was often in Litaba's company when he was approached for advice and when he and his client discussed the issue at hand. I was consequently able to write up interviews with Litaba's assistance. Other cases were related to me by Litaba.

"Go and accuse them in the Local court," was Litaba's reply.

"Should I wait until they are released from goal?" asked Khotso.

"If you wait for them to be released," explained Litaba, "you will fail. They were not given the same sentences and they will come out separately. You will find it difficult a expensive to have them all summonsed to appear in court agai They might go to Jo'burg to work. Charge them now while the are safe in gaol. Then they will be brought here to the Loc Court in the government pick-up and the police will have the responsibility of bringing them here."

Khotso did as he was advised and the three men were force to pay ten head of cattle altogether.

Concerning the use of codes here: Litaba has instructed a man, accustomed to thinking in terms of restricted-code expecta tions of compensation, what his rights at law are in terms of the changed and elaborated code, and so enabled him to initiate proceedings within that code to gain the traditional compensati

In conversation with Litaba about the difficulties facing pe sants whose mode of thinking was still influenced by restricted code expectations, he drew my attention specifically to paterni suits. The customary procedure in this type of case, as Litaba outlined, was to wait until the child was born, after which it was examined by experts to determine whether certain of its fea tures (the nape of the neck and the hands, for example) resembl those of the alleged father. He told me of a case that had appeared in the Local Court in which the mother of the girl tri to introduce three such experts as her main witnesses. The president had refused to allow their testimony, giving as his reason that such evidence was no longer admissible in Local Courts.

In a paternity suit that I recorded in the Local Court, in which Litaba was called upon for advice by the mother of the girl, it is noteworthy that no attempt was made to lead evidenc in these traditional terms. Litaba's advice to his client stressed rather documentary proof in the form of letters estab-lishing a liaison between the boy and the girl, times of opport nity, and witnesses to assignations.

Not only can Litaba distinguish for his client between the
restricted and the elaborated code, but he can also instruct in
how best to handle the mechanics of the codes. I have seen
Litaba engaged for hours in the business of drawing up an appeal
for a litigant. Litaba would review the whole case in detail
with the appellant. He drew up appeals in point form, picking
out as grounds such matters as inconsistencies in evidence, procedural errors, and faults he considered the president to have
made in his reasoning. This task involves both a high degree of
exactitude and explicitness and a proficient appreciation of the
procedure and nature of the law-code. While Litaba might be
passing on to his client a grasp of the mechanics of appealing,
the skills involved in the formulation of an appeal must, I would
contend, remain an esoteric aptitude. It is a task which ideally
calls for a lawyer's competence in a society where access to
legal counsel is generally restricted to a privileged few.

Litaba is known to be highly proficient in the strategies of
litigation and he is often approached for advice by litigants on
how to manage their cases in court. Not unexpectedly, he concentrates on the handling of witnesses. He has informed me that
he likes to rehearse a case and to coach the litigant in which
questions to ask to pinpoint issues and extract relevant information. The following case, related to me by Litaba, demonstrates
how he spells out the crucial points of a case for a client.

Case 2

Some years ago a man, Lehloa, had a case brought against
him by a headman, Lejaha, for not carrying out Lejaha's orders
and for failing to attend a *pitso* he had called. Lehloa went
to Litaba for advice. He explained that he was not Lejaha's
subject, but fell under another headman's jurisdiction. He
had come to Litaba because he did not know how to defend
himself against Lejaha's charge or whom to call as witnesses
to help him.

Litaba made him write down five questions to put to Lejaha
in court:
1. Am I your subject?
2. Did you allocate me a site?
3. Did I pay tax in your village?
4. If I did not apply to you for a site, and if I did not
    pay tax in your village, why didn't you bring a case
    against me then?

5. If you did not allocate me a site and if you did not
    receive my tax, how can you call me your subject?

Litaba added that Lehloa should call the headman under
whose jurisdiction he was actually living as his witness, an
establish that this was the man who had allocated him a site
and under whom he paid tax.

Lehloa was able to defend himself successfully against th
charge.

In addition to 'knowing' the codes, Litaba has a fund of wha
may be termed 'court lore'. He has a degree of mastery of the
codes that enables him not only to handle adequately a situatio
in terms of the code, but consciously to define a situation
within the codes, and thereby to use them to his own advantage.

The fact that a case may start at the headman's court level,
proceeding thence to the chief's court and up to the Local Cour
provides a tactical situation with strategic possibilities. As
Litaba explained, if one party, prior to litigation, recognized
that the dispute was such as could not be resolved by the lower
unofficial courts, or wanted a definitive judgement backed by t
sanctions of the Local Court, that party could use a certain
strategy. It would then be unwise to reveal one's hand in eith
the headman's or the chief's court by calling witnesses and
making a full statement. Far better to lose both cases and
appeal upwards, without giving the other party any insight into
the strengths or weaknesses of one's position until the case ca
before the Local Court.

At least theoretically, the use of law-codes is subject to
learning only. In restricted codes, the code is part of the
social order into which one is socialized. With elaborated
codes, the code is theoretically open to those with sufficient
training and skills (cf. Paine 1973:16 ff.). In fact, of cours
people attain competence in code usage in varying degree.

While I have focused exclusively upon restricted and elabora
ted codes in the operation of law they are, of course, not confined to that sphere, but should also be seen within the wider
framework of communication. One recognizes then that each indi
vidual makes use of several restricted codes and has access to
more than one mode of the elaborated code. Even in terms of
these 'codes within codes', the broker has a wide repertoire.
He is, for instance, asked on occasion to mediate in neighbouri

family disputes. His function here is as much to re-establish
communication within that family's restricted code, as it is to
bring to bear his knowledge of a customary law-code as applied
to family life.

The Broker and Encoding

A disputant in Lesotho is faced with a number of alternative
channels for the settlement of disputes. He can elect to remain
within a familiar customary restricted code, and take his grievance before a family moot; or he can seek adjudication from his
headman, sub-chief or chief; finally he can institute formal proceedings in the Local Court. At each of these levels, a slightly
different mode of the law-code would apply. Writing specifically
on different kinds of law obtaining in different courts, Poulter
says,

'...it may be said that the choice of court the parties make may
determine the law to be applied...Any person may bring an action
before any court in Lesotho. However, since Basotho courts are
basically only empowered to administer customary law and not the
common law, the effect of commencing proceedings in such a court
is to elect to have the matter determined by customary law.'
(Palmer and Poulter 1972:128)

While Poulter is dealing exclusively with the system of official
courts, his observation has pertinence also to the distinction I
have drawn between restricted and elaborated law-codes in the
courts of the village. The disputant must decide which court
(and hence which code) suits his case best. Since the varying
codes operative in the courts will clearly lend themselves to
shifts in norm emphasis as well, he has the further task of form-
ulating his case in terms of certain norms. A dispute must be
encoded then in terms of the options and aims of the disputants.

In varying degree, the cases above showed the encoding process
to be implicit in Litaba's role. In each case, he was formulat-
ing or encoding a case in terms of the elaborated law-code. In
the case that follows, Litaba is encoding in terms of the law-
code he perceives as most fitting for his client's problem; in
other words, he is selecting both the court and the norms in
terms of which she should formulate her case, as well as the role
she should adopt in presenting it.

Case 3

'Maserame came to Litaba for help because her husband had
married a second wife who did not hoe the lands, nor cook, a
her husband was stealing food from 'Maserame's cooking-pots
go and eat with his new favourite. She had considered takir
matters into her own hands and giving him *phehla* (12), but
phehla turned a man into a 'tame' fool, and she did not want
a foolish husband. What should she do?

Litaba said, "Take him before his kinsmen. Do not mentic
that you are jealous of his new wife. Stress rather the fol
lowing: that you are their daughter-in-law and that they as
a group are responsible for your well-being; that your husband, their brother, is neglecting you, and that you do not
know why; that he is not helping you plough the fields
although he has a span of oxen that you helped to buy, and
that he is using only to plough his second wife's field. Sa
that your husband has the audacity to steal food from you to
share with his new wife. Tell the family that you have come
before them for help as a woman who has worked hard for her
husband and children and who now finds herself in a position
where she can no longer tolerate life, through no fault of
her own.'

In discussing with Litaba the advice he gave this woman, he
outlined what her options were. If she had elected to take the
case to the Local Court, she would have alienated her husband
even further and would have found it difficult to get his famil
to give evidence against him. By keeping the case private and
appealing to the family, she would have more chance for a sympa
thetic hearing.

The Broker as 'Briefcase'

Litaba is sometimes approached by clients simply because he
has knowledge about past events that now concern their affairs.
As an old man, he has long been at the centres of decision-maki
and litigation in the communities in which he has lived, and hi
curiosity and intellectual interest in trouble cases have giver
him a dossier-like range of knowledge. Litaba himself labels
this role of his 'the briefcase'.

---

(12) *Phehla* is 'medicine' given secretly to husbands by their
wives in the belief that it will render them more manageable or 'tame'.

Case 4

   Mpho, related to Litaba, came to him for assistance. He
had been helped by Litaba in a previous dispute with the
chieftainship about a poplar wood that had been in Mpho's
family's possession for years. He now wanted Litaba to
intercede for him with the chief in a renewed dispute about
the wood, for Litaba knew its history. He knew, he said,
that if Litaba took the matter directly to the chief, he
would not lose possession of the wood.

When Mpho left after the interview, Litaba explained to me
his command of the details that made him invaluable to Mpho.
His explanation follows in full, for it shows the minutiae of
information he has at his disposal.

   'The chieftainship has tried before to take that wood.
Some of those trees were taken from roots and seeds from my
father's wood. Those were the poplars. I know where all the
trees came from, and how and where they were planted. The
older brother of Mpho's father, Tsikoane, was working at the
government tree nursery and got pines from there for the wood.
When Mpho's father was instructed by the chieftainess to go
down there to be between two headmen who were in dispute over
the area, he went there to live as her "eye". She said the
place was good: "It will be my garden," she said, and told
Mpho's father to plant vegetables there for her. "You will
also have your own yard there," she told him. He did this
willingly, to carry out her orders. She asked him to plant
trees there too, to stop erosion of a donga. Poplars and
wattles were planted in the donga.'

Litaba's involvement and interest in decision-making have
given him not only a grasp of the particulars of trouble cases,
but also a sound insight into the historical antecedents of many
of the power relations of the ward. Consequently he numbers
chiefs and other administrators among his clients.

Case 5

   In 1970 a young headman, Mohlomi, came to Litaba for
advice because he was under pressure from a neighbouring headman, Joang, who was claiming one of Mohlomi's villages as his
own. Mohlomi had recently returned after an extended period
of work outside Lesotho to take up his headmanship; he did not
know intimately the history of his area and consequently he

was not sure what his best defence would be against his
neighbour. Although he himself did not know Litaba well, he
said that his uncle, who had recently died, had told him to
go to Litaba if he ever needed advice. Litaba had been one
of his late father's contemporaries. Today, he said, he
needed his father's friends.

Litaba advised Mohlomi to leave the initiative of taking
steps about the village up to his neighbour. If Joang did
force a confrontation, Mohlomi should simply assert that the
village had always been under his family's jurisdiction, and
that Joang himself knew that. He was further to say that if
there had been any doubt about whose village it was, their
forefathers would surely have quarrelled about it.

Litaba went on to inform Mohlomi in detail about the history
of settlement in his area and how to validate beyond doubt his
historical claim to the disputed village.

Litaba himself recognizes that he is in possession of specialized information that is not generally known, for it is no longer
consciously transmitted. He explains that today there is no adequate socialization and training for those who hold chiefly
office. If my definition of restricted codes may be widened at
this point to include this type of traditional knowledge, then
Litaba's role here can be seen as that of purveyor of a code that
is essentially part of an oral tradition, one that is in the
process of being lost.

Privatization

*At village level, the people cannot see where power lies.
Clearly it is not with them. Even those who have some idea what
might be done have no idea how the political structure might be
wielded or by-passed. It is impossible for them to organize
things through existing channels and very difficult to conceive
of other channels.* (Wallman 1969:37-8)

It has been suggested that, while codes are theoretically open
to all, there are degrees of code mastery. Taking this notion
one step further, there is the possibility that access to or use
of a code may be purposeively obstructed or obscured. To describe this process, Paine selects the term 'privatization of
meaning' (1973:16 ff.) and sees in it a potential strategy for
both the striving for and maintaining of power.

'...a definition of power should refer to the capability of a
person to control (increase or decrease) the degree of ambiguity
in his message to others: intentional ambiguity, that is.'
(1973:19)

The suggestion of strategic withholding of access to a code
has particular relevance for my earlier discussion of the chief's
court. An area in which this was most marked was one directly
related to the continuing power of traditional authorities, as
for example cases in which elected land advisory boards complained that their headmen were not co-operating with them. In
a case in which a land advisory board member was involved with a
village faction protesting against what they saw as the illegal
and arbitrary actions of their headman, the member alleged to me
that the court was deliberately putting them off by repeatedly
postponing their further action with flimsy excuses. One of
these was that the court had mislaid their copy of the Act in
terms of which one of the grievances (failure to attend a vigil)
could be assessed (a refusal to *decode*). The impasse between
traditional authorities and elected land boards was complicated
by the fact that the chief himself did not have a land advisory
board elected for the primary purpose of hearing complaints about
land allocation. While blocking complaints from boards, the
chief's court did not, to my knowledge, assist any board in
seeking redress from higher authorities. The retreat of the
chief's court into a kind of privatization when concerned with
these cases may have been the outcome of two factors: the first,
their unwillingness to sanction a fellow administrator at
loggerheads with the recent phenomenon of an elected board and
the second, that there had not yet evolved a firm comprehension
of just what degree of authority and power such a board should
hold in the administration.

There is evidence for the assertion that the chief's court,
for reasons compounded by the need to assert their claim to
authority, strove to maintain the fiction that they alone constituted 'the proper channels' to the encapsulating structure,
and that they used their nodal position to reinforce and perpetuate the illusion of their own indispensibility. The congestion
of 'the proper channels' could be cut through by the broker on
behalf of a client.

The concept of privatization applies equally to the operation
of law-codes in the Local Court, but here the process is not so
much purposive as inadvertent, similar to the type of privatization that Paine defines as 'an unavoidable consequence of status-

determined sociolinguistic barriers' (1973:26) (13). This point has been sufficiently dealt with in previous sections. Suffice it to add that the broker is not subject to these restrictions of meaning.

Privatization cloaks many facets of the broker's role. For example, in Case 4 above, Litaba's explanation validating Mpho's ownership of the wood was given to me, and not to Mpho. Nor did Litaba set down in writing his evidence on the wood for Mpho to use in future disputes. The immediate effect of this is that Litaba retains Mpho as a potential client. But a more subtle kind of privatization is also at work here. In a case like this the utility of the message depends as much on the credibility of the mediator as on the content of the message. What Mpho needed was not only Litaba's specialist knowledge of his affairs, but also the weight that attends a man who has conducted this type of transaction successfully in the past and whose intercession consequently has validity. Privatization here is the outcome both of esoteric knowledge and that the knowledge is purveyed and enclosed within a specific 'bearer' role.

The Broker and the Courts

...the availability and efficacy of a code for a particular person depends, after all, as much upon his acceptance by others who already enjoy the code, as upon his ability to learn it: this holds for the E[laborated] codes as well as R[estricted] codes. (Paine 1973:18-19)

In the political mythology of the ward of study, the courts were seen as firmly embedded in and reflecting the power relations and political tensions of the ward. For example, people were quick to accuse certain functionaries of the chief as having political bias, or to maintain that a whole court, at a given time, was 'loaded' politically. There was a distinct belief that the code of law operative in certain courts or controlled by certain functionaries was distorted by political allegiances. The acute awareness that a court could be used by those controlling it to dispense political favour, was spurred by the tensions preceding and following the abortive 1970 general election.

----

(13) The taking of bribes to influence decisions would also constitute a blocking of access, and a local-level court is often subject to allegations of interest. It is extremely difficult to discriminate between rumour and fact in these instances.

It has been a theme of this paper that Litaba maintained easy access to the law-codes. This was particularly so of the chief's court in which he enjoyed a privileged position. He often took part in the discussion preceding the giving of a decision, and was sometimes co-opted into holding a court himself. In Paine's terms, his brokerage role was greatly facilitated by his acceptance on the part of those who controlled the code. It is noteworthy that Litaba's free access to the court did not in any way make him less critical of its actions. Such criticism demonstrated, by implication, that Litaba's control of law-codes was of a high order, and it was consequently part and parcel of his broker image. But his criticism turned from this professional near-carping into something far more pointed when his access to or stature in the court was threatened. One court representative put Litaba's acceptance on the part of the court into question. Initially friction developed over so mundane a thing as Litaba's special right to be provided with a chair by the court. Litaba won this round by borrowing a chair on the way to court and carrying it ostentatiously to his usual place. Much of his antagonism can be subsumed under the fact that the chief's administration was becoming notorious for laxness and tardiness, and Litaba felt that this representative was contributing greatly to the situation. Litaba remained one of his chief critics and, when he was eventually replaced, his departure signalled a reestablishment of Litaba's influence in the politics of the court'. Later Litaba was instrumental, through petitions to the chief, in successfully objecting to the appointment of yet another court representative.

Pervading the entire study of this village was a bitter dispute between the chief and his mother about control of an administrative area and the chief's court that served it. Litaba supported the chief, his main line being that, although the chieftainess had served as regent for many years and had proved her ability, it was unprecedented that the power in the ward should be split between two rulers. The situation was aggravated by the fact that, prior to the 1970 general election, this division of power was identified by some with the major schism in national politics.

Litaba became involved as leader of a faction aimed at dislodging the chieftainess and closing her court. Part of the validating framework for this factional activity was couched in terms of alleged injustices on the part of that court. It was held, for example, that the court was staffed exclusively with supporters of the chieftainess, and that it was biased against

those who supported the chief and against members of certain
political parties. Litaba did not enjoy the full acceptance of
this court, and was extremely critical of it. As a groundswell
of opinion developed against the chieftainess and her functionaries, the every action of her court was minutely scrutinized.
Eventually factional activity directed against the chieftainess
and her administration became a popular cause and she was remove
from office and her court closed. Control of the court was seet
as giving the chieftainess a platform for power by control of tl
code. This control of the code was thus cut in a movement to
pare her power.

Motivation behind the antagonism to the chieftainess's contii
ued authority was complex, but I suggest that Litaba's role in i
was partly dictated by the limited influence he had in her cour
His involvement in the faction which worked against the court ca
be interpreted at one level as directing an attempt to manage
control of the administration and selective application of law-
codes in the village.

The courts were viewed in this village then as symbolic of
power relations and, in the contest for power, courts were used
as one of the counters. Control of a court in turn assured control of the code administered in that court, and the code operative could consequently be used as a vehicle for the dispensing
of political patronage. The broker cannot afford to be excluded
from the contest whose outcome determines his access to the
codes which are part of his stock in trade.

The Broker and Transactions

A reputation for success is a broker's chief stock in trade.
Every time he gives advice Litaba is, in effect, laying his
reputation on the line. He therefore takes precautions to mini-
mize his risk. Before taking on a case, Litaba gathers as much
information as he can to establish whether or not his prospective client has a chance of success. This preliminary investigation may be likened to a bargaining process: he must be convinced that it is worth his while to take on the case. Brokerage suffers by association with failure. If, in his opinion, th
petitioner's case has little chance of success, Litaba does not
hesitate to tell him so. Even this, of course, is a form of
advice. Litaba hedges round his role with other safeguards. He
does not draw obvious attention to his services. Notably, he
does not associate himself publicly with his client by, for
instance, representing him in court himself.

Litaba does not charge money for his services (14).   Thus a
number of options remain open to him.   Firstly, it gives him
wide discretion in selecting his clientele; he is not obliged
to accept a client simply because he has the required fee.
Secondly, a cash payment would transform the broker's skills
into an easily-negotiable commodity.   The broker's talents are
not for sale, but are dispensed on his own terms.   An immediate
cash payment would serve to conclude the transaction, rather
than create an obligation.   Thirdly, he does not become the
creature of his client: there can be little direct come-back if
his advice does not accomplish its object.   All this serves to
give him an edge in retaining control of the transaction.

Paine makes a pertinent point here about a broker's selection
of clientele:

'Among the necessary attributes of power (at least that broad
category of it which is clientele-based) are possession of a
repertoire of codes *and* command over the instructions on how to
decode; thereby one may be able to include or exclude persons at
will from one's clientele.' (1973:18)

A brief look once more at the case of Mpho and his wood provides an illustration of how Litaba manages the selection of his
clientele.   It also raises the seminal question of reciprocity in
brokerage by indicating in some measure the value Litaba placed
on a client's counter-prestations.

Case 4 (cont.)

Litaba refused to intercede for Mpho with the chief.
These were the reasons he gave for 'closing the door to the
chief' to him:

---

(14) When asked why he does not charge for advice, Litaba replies
that it is his duty to help his fellows who do not have his
knowledge and who are poor.   He also maintains that he does
not help those who are 'in the wrong' in a case because he
will not support those who break the law.   Without placing
his explanation in question, it is possible to suggest that,
by viewing his activities in the context of transactions,
one can assess more nearly the more subtle accounting of
brokerage.   The fact that Litaba has on occasion sold *muti*
or 'medicine' for court cases adds a significant dimension
to this question.

After he had helped Mpho in the first case about that woo▮
Mpho had not shown himself sufficiently grateful. He had co▮
tradicted Litaba in public on an important issue and had bee▮
rude to Litaba's wife in front of a group of women. Litaba
felt he had not been sufficiently respectful, so his reply t▮
Mpho was, 'I helped you before and you were ungrateful. Whe▮
it suits you, you claim that we are related. But after I
have helped you, you disclaim all ties with me. I will do
nothing for you.'

Litaba does, therefore, expect a calling in of accounts in a wa▮
similar, I would suggest, to the process Paine refers to as
directed (generalized) reciprocity' (1971:17). Litaba seems t▮
have expected respect and a kind of followership from Mpho. Hi▮
expectations are not always as overtly signalled:

Case 5 (cont.)

When he was giving Mohlomi advice on how to protect a village under his jurisdiction from his neighbour, the course of
conversation turned naturally to affairs concerning tribal
politics. An important issue at that time was the nomination
of a senior adviser to the chief's wife, who was acting on
behalf of her husband while he was on extended leave. Litaba
considered the proposed nominee to be unsuitable. He and
Mohlomi found that they were in agreement about the candi-
date's shortcomings, but Mohlomi told Litaba that, as an inex▮
perienced newcomer to the administration, he had thus far
hesitated to make public his views on the matter. By the tim▮
the two men parted, Litaba was assured that Mohlomi would sup▮
port his faction's move against the appointment.

I can only speculate about how Litaba directs counter-
prestations from obligated clients. I do not have detailed
information, specifically case by case, on how this process
works, nor can I state that Litaba exacted an accounting from
every client. The values placed on prestations in a transaction
are, of course, determined by a consideration of each particular
instance. In the absence of such detailed situational data, I
can offer no more than broad generalizations. Litaba was committed as a politician at local level. The holding of leadership roles, I would contend, was facilitated for Litaba by the
fact that he had created a pool of followership that could be
activated as support. I would further suggest that support on,
say, a political issue would serve to reinforce rather than
cancel Litaba's hold over a client as support called upon would

in effect be reaffirming Litaba's ranking in the political peck-
ing order. A client's support on a political issue would not be
unique: he would remain one of a pool or floating bloc. In contrast, Litaba's advice to any particular client would probably
be serving an immediate and urgent need with a consequent
enhancement of its value in the transaction. Thus support would
not necessarily wipe out dependence upon and obligation to the
broker, but might well serve to perpetuate it. Confirming the
broker in leadership positions would contribute to his accumulation and maintenance of power, thus assuring his bargaining pos-
tion in future transactions. Brokerage is a cumulative process.

Patronage: the Chief and the Broker

Giving advice to chiefs puts Litaba in a position to tap the
prime sources of patronage in the ward. In gaining a chief as a
client, he is also gaining a patron, in that a chief is a client
with tangible favours to dispense. Apart from being in a
stronger position to intercede for clients with the chief, there
are other pay-offs in terms of prestige in numbering chiefs in
one's clientele.

Although the chief's capacity for dispensing patronage has
been severely curtailed, he is still indispensable to the peasant
in that so many of the peasant's demands must be articulated
through his administration.

'If I refuse the Chief's work, next time when I need a permit to
sell stock or a letter to go to the hospital, he will be too
busy. When someone "eats" my land, he will forget to send a man
to inspect the case. If I refuse the Chief he can send another
or another – always there is someone who will do his work because
we are not together. It is true that if we, *sechaba* [the
people], did come together and spoke with one voice the Chief
would hear, but anyway it is not allowed. If you are eight men
you look like enemies because you are together. And if you go
together to complain in Matsieng or Maseru, when you arrive they
will say "You are not to speak. You must have a permit from the
Chief." And if the Chiefs don't want it, what can we do?'
(Wallman 1969:34)

A chief's administration can then convert requests such as
Wallman lists into favours, instead of rights, for the peasants.
In the village of study, some peasants believed that if they
could cut through the bureaucracy of the chief's administration
and gain a sympathetic hearing from the chief himself, they might

elicit from him a reassertion of his role as patron. Litaba, as
'door to the chief', can bring someone in line for direct patron
age. In one case that I recorded from Litaba, a man who had bee
refused a site by his headman prevailed upon Litaba to intercede
directly on his behalf with the principal chief and, after pressure from the chief, the headman was compelled to allocate the
site. When the man asked Litaba what his position would be unde
a headman whose hand he had forced, Litaba told him, 'From now
on, your door will face directly to the chief'.

   Litaba also serves the subsidiary role of making the estrange
chieftainship, cut off from grass-roots opinion, aware of under-
currents among *sechaba* (the people). In this role the broker
serves as an articulatory channel of communication. His role
here is not limited to that of spokesman, however, for it is
often he who seizes upon an issue, canvasses and synthesizes
opinion and then makes direct representation to the chief in the
name of *sechaba*. At times Litaba appeared to be acting as a
gadfly, prompting the chief to take action. This prompting was
necessitated by the chief's tardiness in taking steps in certain
imperative matters that required his endorsement.

Case 6

   In 1970 the Local Court was transferred to a nearby
administrative centre. Litaba first heard about the proposed
move from the Local Court president. He went at once to see
the chief who told him that he had already received notification of it. The removal of the Local Court from the village
was seen by many as a reflection on the status of the chief
himself and this feeling was exacerbated by rumours that a
similar removal had successfully been petitioned against in a
neighbouring ward. The matter was taken up as an issue at a
pitso of the administrators of the ward, but Litaba felt that
they lacked a necessary concern and he himself drew up a peti
tion pinpointing reasons protesting against the removal of th
court.

We see Litaba here in the maintenance of his brokerage relation
with the chief: not only is he providing a service for the
chief, but he is also creating a demand for that service by noting an issue and bringing it to the chief's notice. He is
engaged in the business of making himself indispensable.

   It would be misleading to classify the chief as a patron

simply by virtue of his position or status. As Paine rightly points out (1971:10 ff.), a patron-client relationship 'must be investigated as one of management of roles'. The chief as patron in Lesotho is a situationally defined role. The granting of patronage is an obvious political resource as is, to refer to Wallman's statement, the withholding of it, and in this type of transaction, it is generally the patron who determines the values to be placed on the prestations.

The type of patronage that comes into being as a result of a transaction between the chief and the broker is of a somewhat different order. In this case the role of patron is specifically activated or elecited by Litaba as a broker. Rather than the chieftainship simply bestowing patronage on Litaba as a favour, Litaba sometimes seems to have manoeuvred in such a way as to assure himself of patronage. A mutual dependency then at times appears to invert the patron-client roles between Litaba and the chieftainship. This assumption is defined in terms of a particular situation only; the chief and Litaba are, of course, engaged in an ongoing series of transactions in which ultimately, because of his status and control of resources, the chief has more to bestow.

CONCLUSION

The broker's code repertoire has direct bearing on his facility in assuming various brokerage roles. As Bernstein suggests, *'the ability to switch codes controls the ability to switch roles'* (1965:157), and the broker's career should be viewed primarily in terms of his accumulation of skills that allow him to support a number of key roles. The continued utility of these roles is not automatically conferred by the assumption of some kind of brokerage status, but is dependent upon successful maintenance by the broker. In this process, Litaba engages in creating a demand for his services by recognizing and seizing upon issues and by preserving a measure of covertness about the 'how' of what he achieves for a client. Because brokerage is a creative process, there is a sense in which the broker must keep running in order to stand still. Litaba is consciously engaged in the collecting of information, gossip and rumour; he is always seeking to make connections closed to the other man. Brokerage demands a consciously directed engagement in affairs, along with a detached computation of the odds.

This paper has concentrated on showing how Litaba's adroitness in the law-codes of the village enables him to support the

role of legal broker. Even in this role, we see Litaba in a
number of guises: for example, his encoding or decoding for a
client is a very different process from that of opening the door
to the chief for a petitioner. His role as legal broker is
buttressed by his closeness to the chief and involvement in
local-level politics. These in turn facilitate his transactions
at law, as he can make connections with those at the centres of
decision-making who administer the codes.

Inseparable from a consideration of Litaba's brokerage roles
is the notion of the accumulation of power. Litaba could not be
a broker if he had not built up a reputation founded on a progressive series of successful transactions. A transactional
element is involved in his purveying of legal expertise. Just as
important, however, is the fact that Litaba holds leadership
positions in local-level politics and is actively engaged in the
dispensing of advice and the influencing of policy-making at
tribal level. Each of these kinds of activity has implications
for the others, and their interaction reinforces Litaba's position as a broker.

ACKNOWLEDGEMENTS

I am indebted to the following institutions: the Institute
of Social and Economic Research (Rhodes University) and Rhodes
University for financial assistance towards fieldwork expenses;
the Human Sciences Research Council for contributing towards the
costs of attending the 1974 A.S.A. conference.

REFERENCES CITED

Bernstein, B. (1964). Elaborated and restricted codes: their

social origins and some consequences. *In* J.J. Gumperz and

D. Hymes (eds.), *The ethnography of communication*, Special

publication of the *American Anthropologist* 66 (6):55-69.

Bernstein, B. (1965). A socio-linguistic approach to social

learning. *In* J. Gould (ed.), *Penguin survey of the social

sciences:*144-68, Penguin Books.

Bernstein, B. (1972). A sociolinguistic approach to socialization; with some reference to educability. *In* J.J. Gumperz and D. Hymes (eds.), *Directions in sociolinguistics; the ethnography of communication:*465-97, Holt, Rinehart and Winston, New York.

Gluckman, M. (1955). *The judicial process among the Barotse of Northern Rhodesia,* Manchester University Press.

Hailey, W.M. *1st baron Hailey.* (1953). *Native administration in the British African territories, Part V: The High Commission Territories: Basutoland, the Bechuanaland Protectorate and Swaziland:*1-147, H.M.S.O., London.

Jones, G.I. (1951). *Basutoland medicine murder: a report on the recent outbreak of "diretlo" murders in Basutoland,* H.M.S.O., London. (Cmd no. 8209).

Paine, R. (1971) (ed.) *Patrons and brokers in the East Arctic,* St John's, Institute of Social and Economic Research, Memorial University of Newfoundland (Newfoundland Social and Economic Papers, 2).

Paine, R. (1973). Transactions as communicative events (paper prepared for the decennial meeting of the Association of Social Anthropologists).

Palmer, V.V. and Poulter, S.M. (1972). *The legal system of Lesotho.* The Michie Company, Charlottesville, Virginia.

Simmel, G.   (1950).   *The sociology of Georg Simmel* (translated, edited and with an introduction by Kurt Wolff), Glencoe, Ill The Free Press (paperback edition 1964).

Wallman, S.   (1969).   *Take out hunger: two case studies of rur development in Basutoland,* Athlone Press, London, for the University of London (London School of Economics Monographs on Social Anthropology no. 39).

NOTES ON CONTRIBUTORS

COMAROFF, JOHN L. Lecturer in Social Anthropology, University of Manchester. Born Cape Town 1945; educated in South Africa and England. B.A. (Cape Town) 1966, Ph.D. (L.S.E.) 1973. Lecturer in Social Anthropology, University College, Swansea, 1971-2.
Editor of *The Diary of Sol T. Plaatje: an African at Mafeking* and author of papers on Tswana politics, law and marriage.
Fieldwork in South Africa and Botswana.

FALLERS, LLOYD A. Born 1925, died 1974. Ph.D. Chicago 1953. Lecturer at Princeton University, 1953-4. Director, East African Institute of Social Research, Makerere, Uganda, 1955-7. Associate Professor, University of California, Berkeley, 1957-60. Professor of Anthropology, University of Chicago, 1960-74.
Publications include *Bantu Bureaucracy* (1956), *The King's Men* (editor) (1964), *Law without Precedent* (1969), *Inequality: Social Stratification Reconsidered* (1974), *Social Anthropology of the Nation State* (1974).
Fieldwork in Busoga, Buganda and Turkey.

GULLIVER, PHILIP H. Professor of Anthropology, York University, Toronto since 1972. Formerly Professor of African Anthropology, School of Oriental and African Studies, London.
Author of *The Family Herds* (1955), *Social Control in an African Society* (1963), *Tradition and Transition in East Africa* (editor) (1970), *The Family Estate in Africa* (co-editor) (1964), and numerous papers in professional journals and edited collections. Field Research in Kenya, Uganda, Tanzania.

230

HAMNETT, IAN. Senior Lecturer in Sociology, University of
  Bristol. Born 1929. Educated Oxford and Edinburgh.
  Advocate of the Scottish Bar, 1957. Ph.D. (Edinburgh)
  (Social Anthropology) (1970).
  Lecturer in Social Anthropology, Centre of African
  Studies, Edinburgh, 1965-7.
  Author of *Chieftainship and Legitimacy* (1975) and various
  journal articles.
  Field research in Lesotho and Swaziland.

MOORE, SALLY FALK. Professor of Anthropology, University of
  Southern California. LL.B. (Columbia Law School) 1945, Ph.D
  (Anthropology) (Columbia), 1957.
  Served on staff of the prosecution at Nuremberg Trials.
  Publications include *Power and Property in Inca Peru*,
  Symbol and Politics in Communal Ideology (co-editor), and
  numerous journal articles and symposium contributions. Her
  paper in this column is based on field work in Tanzania among
  the Chagga of Kilimanjaro.

PERRY, JOHN A.G. Lecturer in Anthropology, Rhodes University,
  South Africa. Born 1942. Educated at Rhodes University and
  University of Natal.
  Recorder and compiler (with C. Perry) of S.J. Jingoes's
  autobiographical narrative, *A Chief is a Chief by the People*
  (1975).
  Principal fieldwork in Lesotho.

ROBERTS, SIMON. Lecturer in Law, London School of Economics.
  Born 1941. Educated London School of Economics (LL.B.,
  Ph.D.).
  Lecturer in Law at Institute of Public Administration,
  Blantyre, Malawi, 1963-4. Adviser on Customary Law to the
  Government of Botswana 1968-71.
  Publications include *Tswana Family Law* (1972), *Law and the
  Family in Africa* (editor) (forthcoming, 1976) and various
  articles. Co-editor of *Journal of African Law* and member of
  Editorial Committee of *Modern Law Review*.
  Principal field research in Botswana.

SNYDER, FRANCIS G. Associate Professor, Osgoode Hall Law School
  York University, Toronto. Born 1942. Educated Yale, Paris
  and Harvard.
  Chercheur, Laboratoire d'Anthropologie Juridique, Paris,
  1968-70. Research Fellow, Yale Law School 1970-1.
  Author of *One-Party Government in Mali* (1965) and numerous
  articles in professional journals. Field work in West Africa

SUBJECT INDEX